BULLET MAGNET

BULLET MAGNET

The true story of the most
highly decorated serving soldier
in the British Army

MICK FLYNN CGC MC

with Will Pearson

Weidenfeld & Nicolson

LONDON

First published in Great Britain in 2010
by Weidenfeld & Nicolson

An Hachette UK company

1 3 5 7 9 10 8 6 4 2

A CIP catalogue record for this book
is available from the British Library.

HB ISBN 978 0 297 85991 8
TPB ISBN 978 0 297 85992 5

Typeset by Input Data Services Ltd,
Bridgwater, Somerset

Printed and bound in the UK by
CPI Mackays, Chatham ME5 8TD

The Orion Publishing Group's policy is to use papers
that are natural, renewable and recyclable products and made
from wood grown in sustainable forests. The logging and
manufacturing processes are expected to conform to the
environmental regulations of the country of origin.

Weidenfeld & Nicolson

The Orion Publishing Group Ltd
Orion House
5 Upper Saint Martin's Lane
London WC2H 9EA

www.orionbooks.co.uk

Contents

LIST OF ILLUSTRATIONS

Bosnia 2003 – on patrol near Banja Luka

Me in turret of Scimitar, with Tpr Morgan prior to late-night vehicular escapade

Banja Luka Metal Factory, 2003–4 (Ministry of Defence)

Arms find from a small village outside Banja Luka

Afghanistan 2006–Lt Ralph Johnson sleeping

Camp Bastion, Afghanistan: L/Cpl Andrew Radford CGC, L/Cpl 'Pez', Lt Tom Long

Musa Qal'ah overwatch position: LCoH Jock Anderson

LCoH Steve McWhirter calling in air strike

Air strike hits 1km wide of target

Form-up point prior to clearing Taliban positions at Musa Qal'ah ambush site

3 Para infantry and D Squadron Scimitars moving forward to forming up point

Ambush site, Musa Qal'ah – Lt Johnson's destroyed Spartan

After the ambush – my Scimitar abandoned in a ditch

Taliban IED firing position

3 Para and D Squadron searching ambush site for missing personnel

Buckingham Palace with Shelley and Gabrielle after I received the CGC from Prince Charles

Except where otherwise credited, all pictures come from the author's own collection, or those of the author's close friends and colleagues.

MAPS

ST JAMES'S PALACE

To anyone serving in the Household Cavalry Regiment - or, for that matter, the British Army - the name of Mike Flynn is legendary. He stands for what my Regiment, the Blues and Royals, is all about; a man of great humanity and humour, but also a superlative fighting soldier. These memoirs reflect these timeless qualities with resonance and immediacy. It is as if Mike Flynn is there talking to you - and, as every young Household Cavalryman will tell you, when Mike Flynn speaks it is worth listening.

I believe that this book will take its place amongst the defining literature of this era of British military endeavour. It reflects all that is best about our superb Army and a great fighting regiment.

PROLOGUE

Northern Helmand Province, Afghanistan
30–31 July 2006

We were in the 'Wind of 120 Days'. Between June and September, a stiff, stinging breeze scours Helmand province, driving fine sand and dust into the eyes, turning noses and throats to rough sandpaper. We'd been in Afghanistan since early June, and there hadn't been a single drop of rain. Our tracks threw up huge plumes of dust that not only kept swallowing the column, but also gave the enemy plenty of notice we were coming.

Our orders were to be at Musa Qal'ah District Centre by first light on the following day.

The Musa Qal'ah DC was a fortified compound made of thick-walled mud-brick reinforced with sandbags, ramparts and lookout towers. A modern version of the movie *Zulu* was playing out there. But instead of *impis* attacking with spears and flintlock muskets, hundreds of Taliban fighters armed with rocket-propelled grenades (RPGs), heavy machine guns, hand grenades, recoilless rifles, 107mm rockets, mortars and AK47s had the garrison cut off, pinned down and under constant fire. Besieged with a small unit of Danish light cavalry and like them down to the last of their ammunition, water and food were two dozen men of the Parachute Regiment's Pathfinder (PF) Platoon. Trained to near-Special Forces levels, the PF has some of the

1

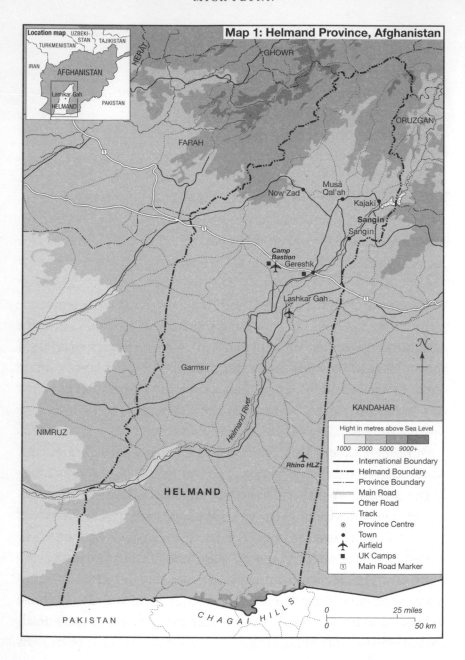

best fighting soldiers in the British Army. If those guys were in trouble, it was bad trouble.

Our job was to stop the enemy overrunning the DC and slaughtering the garrison down to the last man: use our armour and extra firepower to beat back the Taliban, secure the area and make sure the planned relief mission went in.

We had 24 hours to get there.

No pressure.

We rolled through the gates of Camp Bastion, the main British forces base in Afghanistan, shortly after dawn on 31 July. As the most experienced – and the oldest – NCO in the column, I commanded the lead vehicle in a reinforced troop of six Scimitars, four Spartan support wagons and three 105mm guns. The Scimitar is a small armoured fighting vehicle with a crew of three: the driver sits low down in the front left of the hull; the commander sits up on the left side of the turret; and the gunner sits next to him on the right. Not much bigger than a Range Rover, the Scimitar is armed with a 30mm Rarden cannon and a co-axial 7.62mm General Purpose Machine Gun (GPMG). For its relatively small size, it packs a mighty amount of punch.

On a good day, the whole trip from Bastion to Musa Qal'ah should have taken no more than six hours. But this wasn't going to be a good day. For the first few kilometres we struck fast and hard along Highway 1, the main east – west route that cuts across the heart of Helmand province. Then, given the high risk of ambushes and improvised explosive devices (IEDs), we swung off-road onto the barren open ground to the north and picked up a parallel track.

By six-thirty, the temperature was already nudging 38°C. The heat from the Scimitar's engine and electrical equipment added to the sense of being shut inside a small furnace. Like everyone else, I was already soaked with sweat and chugging water. Later on in the day, the mercury can top 50°C: hot enough to fry an egg on the Scimitar's decks, or sear the flesh if you accidentally touch the aluminium hull of your vehicle. With the heat, the flies started getting busy, the snakes, scorpions and camel spiders woke to a new day, and who could say what the human pests might have in store for us?

Making reasonable speed over the khaki-coloured moonscape, we reached the town of Gereshk, about 30 kilometres east of Bastion, well before noon. At Gereshk we ran into trouble: local Intelligence reported the Taliban had laid new minefields around the town, but as yet there were no clear lanes marked through them. Faced with that risk in unknown territory, we had no option but to dismount and sweep ahead for mines on foot, with the vehicles trundling slowly along behind.

When we were clear of the mined areas we pushed on north-west, stopping for a brew and some food when the heat was at its blistering worst before hooking back round to the north-east. We skirted the Sangin river valley towards the town of the same name. As we rolled north the land started getting hillier, the going got tougher and we began to suffer breakdowns. Mechanical, not nervous – that's old equipment for you. Attaching the broken-down vehicles and then towing them up hill and down dale slowed us to a grinding, frustrating crawl.

At dusk, two of the Spartan support vehicles broke down completely. But the news wasn't all bad: we were now no more than 10 kilometres from Musa Qal'ah. And we still had a good twelve hours before we needed to be at the DC. While the Royal Electrical and Mechanical Engineers (REME) guys in the Light Aid Detachment (LAD) vehicle tried to fix the duff Spartans, I joined the officers and senior NCOs in a quick conflab. I already knew most of the men in the circle; some of them I'd worked with for a long time. They included the column's OC, Major Alex Dick; Captain Alex Eida; Lts Tom Long and Ralph Johnson; and Steve 'Squirty' McWhirter.

'I'll stay here with the broken Spartans and the Squadron Head-quarters,' Major Dick said. 'The rest of you press on to the DC. As soon as we've fixed them, we'll come up to join you.'

'We have to get some armour up there in time for the RV,' Captain

Eida put in. A forward observation officer (FOO) with 7th Parachute Regiment, Royal Horse Artillery, Captain Eida was one of the few men in the column not in the Household Cavalry. When and if we got there, his job was to direct artillery and other ordnance onto the enemy at Musa Qal'ah.

'We need to support the drop with whatever we've got,' I agreed. 'Let's go.' We mounted up on the working wagons and set off.

It was all very well wanting to drive on to the objective, but now we faced a new problem: light, or to be more accurate, the lack of it. There was no moonlight, and no starlight. Thick clouds blanketed the whole sky. Generally, the Scimitar's sights provide excellent night vision, but if there's no light at all then the intensification system struggles to do better than the naked eye. The same was true of the individual night vision goggles (NVGs) we all carried. In the absolute darkness, both systems were no better than your Mark 1 eyeball.

Determined to keep making ground, we trundled up the western edge of the Sangin valley at a snail's pace. As the most experienced Corporal of Horse, I was still leading from the front. My driver James Leech was straining every nerve to steer a safe route across the increasingly treacherous ground. Driving in daylight would have been tricky; driving on a moonless night was in a league of its own. Leechy was on the small side, but stocky and strong with it. Straight out of the box marked 'Scimitar drivers'. He had what sounded to me like a strong Mancunian accent, but if you said he was from Manchester, Leechy went mad. 'I'm not a fucking Manc,' he'd snap furiously.

'You are a Manc, Leechy,' I'd insist. That was usually enough to wind him up good and proper.

'I'm not from Manchester, I'm from Salford. Is Salford fucking Manchester?'

'Yes, Leechy, it is. It's a suburb of Manchester.'

That really got him. Pretty soon, the other lads joined in. In the end Leechy got so hacked off he had a T-shirt made especially with the words: 'I AM NOT FROM MANCHESTER' printed across it in big letters. Nothing wrong with Manchester. Can't think what the problem was. People started calling him 'not-from'.

Peering out into the blackness, I kept up a constant to-and-fro with Leechy on the intercom (i/c), trying to help him stay on a firm track. Eyeballs out on stalks, we saw huge boulders loom up suddenly out of the night like Arctic icebergs. Leechy dragged the Scimitar round to avoid bone-crunching troughs, murderous ravines and wagon-killing wadis. What I most feared was going over a sheer drop. The ground was so rough it was like being in a small boat in high seas. Strapped inside the turret, we were constantly being thrown against our harness straps. The terrain grew ever more difficult as we tried to push on, and the pitch darkness meant that we kept losing the safe route.

Then there was a massive jolt. Leechy slammed on the brakes. I peered out into the darkness through the NVGs. It was like staring through grey-green soup. I couldn't see what we'd hit or what lay ahead of us. 'Feels like we've come off the track,' I said. 'I'll go and see if I can find it again.' Leech and my gunner, Paul Minter, grunted acknowledgement.

Paul Minter was the nephew of the famous lightweight boxing champion Alan Minter. From a hard London East End family, he was built like three brick shithouses stacked on top of one another: I'd want him on my side in any fight. A massive West Ham fan, he wasn't entirely a stranger to trouble. Along with his fighting spirit, Minty was a good gunner.

I climbed out of the hatch, jumped to the ground, crouched and felt around for some nice reassuring ruts with my hands. No ruts. I snapped a Cyalume glow-stick and shoved it in the back of my helmet. The dim light it pushed out was invisible to potential enemies, but Leechy could see it through the wagon's night sight and his NVGs. 'Simple plan,' I told him. 'I'll walk ahead and feel for the track. You keep following my glow-stick. The rest of the column will follow on behind you. OK?'

'No problem.'

I walked round in front of the wagon, stared out into the darkness, gathered up my courage and took a couple of steps forward. A few metres further on, I stopped. I couldn't see a safe track for toffee, but I sensed some kind of drop-off in the darkness directly ahead. If it was a small wadi we should be able to drive through it. If it was something other than a shallow wadi – like a 100-metre sheer cliff – then we'd either have to turn back and go around, or make camp where we were and wait for daylight.

I had a bad feeling – the kind it's best not to ignore. I took another step into the unknown, still without being able to see the edge, and then stopped again. Even when they're operating perfectly, it's hard to estimate distance or depth-of-field accurately with NVGs. I flipped them up and tried to see what lay in our path without them. No improvement. It was madness trying to move like this in the middle of a moonless night. I had to remind myself the lives of the guys up at Musa Qal'ah might depend on it.

I got down on my hands and knees and started to crawl forward. I thought I'd be safe if I moved ahead on hands and knees. My fingers went sprawling into empty space. The rest of me followed. I seemed to fall for a long time. I tried to flip round in midair, but just as I did that I hit something solid.

Rock.

It knocked the breath from my lungs. I lay there for a few seconds, winded. Looking up, I realized I'd fallen 4 metres or so over the edge of a cliff. By some miracle, I'd landed on a narrow shelf below the lip. The ledge ended a foot or so away from my right arm. Beyond it, I knew without seeing, there was more empty space. A lot more. I felt around. My body armour had taken most of the impact, but my back was now perfectly indented with the shape of the dorsal protection plate. It hurt like hell. Nothing else hurt, and nothing seemed to be broken. My helmet and NVGs were still attached, my rifle was still on its sling and my webbing kit was intact. It could have been a lot worse.

My brain started working again. 'Fuck – the rest of the column! If I don't stop them, they'll drive over the edge! They'll roll over into the ravine and I'll be wearing a Scimitar on my head!' I heard the roar of an engine from overhead and hauled myself upright. 'Stop! Stop!' I yelled as loudly as I could into the darkness above. It was useless: with their headsets on and the noise from the vehicle's engine, Minter and Leech would never hear me. It was like trying to catch their attention from the bottom of a well. I started scrabbling up the shale wall, giving it everything I had to get back up and warn them, fingers, knees and boots trying to catch a hold on the splintering face.

I had to stop them.

My head broke clear of the cliff edge. I looked back. Not 3 metres away, the Scimitar was rolling slowly towards me. I waved an arm and shouted, 'Stop! Stop!' at the top of my voice. No one could hear. I watched the massive bulk of the Scimitar grind closer and closer to the edge of the cliff.

CHAPTER ONE

I was born in Neath in 1960. We moved to Cardiff when I was three. We lived in a rented house in Windsor Road, Adamsdown, an old working-class area close to the city centre. Another family lived upstairs. We had the ground floor and the garden.

As I remember, Windsor Road was very long, it took my little legs forever to walk to the end of it. My mother, Myrna, was born in Port Talbot. Like many women then, Mam stayed at home and looked after the family. This was a full-time job, with as much unpaid overtime as she could handle. That's devotion for you. I have five sisters: Christine, who is three years younger than me, Tricia, Catherine, Bernadette and last but not least, Beverley, the baby of the family, who came along later.

My father, Vince, came from the rural west of Eire: it doesn't get much more Irish, Catholic and conservative than that. I went to visit the area he came from, on the edge of Ballina, County Mayo, a few times when I was a kid. Dad's large, rambling family had a farm there, but in those days they struggled to make any money. There was no running water in the cottage where we stayed – we had to walk down the lane to collect it from a spring. I thought that was great fun, but it was pretty basic; some of the people we knew had layers of old news-papers plastered on their walls to keep out the draughts.

Ballina's changed now, it's much bigger and brighter. But it wasn't a good place to be unemployed – if there ever is one. When the farm stopped making any money at all and began to lose it, my dad hopped on the ferry to England, hoping to make a better life for himself. He ended up labouring on the roads: laying drainage pipes to begin with, and then later on cable ducts for broadband and TV. He was your average working-class man, by which I mean everything good – fiercely independent, honest as the day is long and no nonsense. Even when he was sick he hardly ever took a day off work – if he did, then he got no money for the time missed. When we were young my dad was firm but fair. He set clear boundaries for us kids to live by.

It was just as well he did: when I was still just a nipper, the authorities started knocking down large tracts of Cardiff, sweeping away the old, grimy streets to make way for what would eventually become the shiny new docklands development. We moved out to Trowbridge Green, Rumney, on the north-eastern edge of the city, where it was a lot rougher; Mam, Dad, me, Christine and Patricia. The other girls were still a twinkle in my dad's eye. Our house was like most of the others: a small, grey-faced, three-bedroom end terrace, with a little scrap of garden at the back. Being the only boy, once I'd reached the age of ten I got a bedroom to myself, which was luxury in our house. God knows how my sisters managed in one room when they came along. I think my Mam bought a couple of double beds. My window looked south, towards the Severn estuary. On misty nights I'd hear the ships sounding their foghorns in the Bristol Channel and I'd want to be on one. I wasn't unhappy – more like restless: a part of me wanted to be free.

The people I grew up with in Trowbridge were working or lower-middle class, with a strong Welsh identity. It was a tough place to grow up – if you didn't stand up for yourself they'd pick on you. My dad was no slouch in a fight; the first time I ran into trouble as a small kid he showed me how to use my fists and gave me a few lessons in boxing and street fighting. Vince was stocky and strong, with big hands and arms from working the roads all his life.

'Keep your fists up. Move; don't stand still or you'll get hit. Jab, jab,

jab with your left – and then smack 'em in the face with your right. Feint if you get the chance, like this.' He dropped his right shoulder, went as if to throw a straight right, then snaked out a hard left. 'If you're up against a street fighter, try and get your back to something so no one can come up on you from behind, get them in close so they can't kick you, get in between a couple of parked cars if you can. Watch out for the head butt, and use it yourself if you get the chance.'

He showed me how to stick the nut on the best way, to damage the other guy, and not myself. My dad had been forced to fight hard in his day. In South Wales, Irish incomers were seen as a threat to the locals, taking their jobs away and working for less money. I didn't get hugs from my dad, I got lessons in self-defence. That was Vince's way of showing me love.

I went to St Illtyd's Catholic High School, which sounds as if it's posh. In reality, it was a standard state-funded comprehensive for people who believed the Pope was infallible – or said they did. I wore a different-coloured school uniform, which for some of the locals meant I belonged to a different tribe, along with the Donovans, the Kavanaghs and all the other local Irish Catholic families. There were times when the moves Dad had taught me came in very handy. On the estate you either fought or they made your life hell. I fought.

Despite my dad's best efforts, on the stretch of turf where we lived the only crowd was the wrong crowd, unless you wanted to live like a social outcast. I fell in with a loose gang of about ten lads, with a hard core of four or five looking to make the wrong sort of name for themselves. The rest of us floated in and out as and when. We'd meet up and get into various kinds of trouble.

I'd been taught wrong from right, but that didn't stop me joining in with some of the bad stuff when I got a bit older. It started in a small way: breaking into an ice-cream van when I was fourteen to see if the takings were still in the cash box – they weren't – and moved up the scale. One night I found myself inside a dental clinic, ransacking the cupboards and drawers, trying to find where the dentist kept his stock of gold teeth. Mr Cosgrove fitted people with gold teeth, so the gleaming, golden gnashers had to be in there somewhere. It stood to reason.

I yanked open a metal drawer. There were lots of sets of teeth inside. They gleamed a horrible white in the dark. They were probably dental moulds, but to me they looked like the real thing. Cold terror struck through me. As certain as my next breath, I felt that all those sets of teeth were going to jump out and start biting me. I wanted to run from the surgery as fast as I could. But greed, just as strong, held me fast to the spot. I stood staring down at the drawer. If only I could find all those lovely, shiny, gold teeth! Just think how I'd be in the money.

On the estate, money – especially illegally acquired money – bought you respect. It's a funny way of earning it. And dangerous: pretty soon, I'd come to the attention of the police, like some of the others in the gang already had. My dad gave me a leathering when he found out about my night-time escapades, but that still didn't stop me knocking about with the rest of the lads.

I was going in a bad direction, and at the age of fifteen I began to realize that. And anyway, the failed ice-cream van heist and the daft idea about the dentist's hoard of gold both told me the same thing: I wasn't ever going to be an international criminal mastermind.

A few months later I was mitching off school with Jimmy Donovan and Kenny Cassimas. I'd started concentrating much harder on my school work, but still took the occasional day off for old times' sake – especially when we had Maths. We snuck out through the art room – it was the best escape route, only 100 metres down a steep slope and into the bushes at the bottom. Then it was school ties off, hop onto a number 62 bus and away. We'd got about halfway down the hill running hell for leather on this particular occasion when I heard a sharp cry: Jimmy had caught his foot in a bramble root. He went flying past us, tumbling head over heels, cartwheeling out of control. He somersaulted all the way to the bottom of the slope and landed in a crumpled heap. He lay there in a daze, moaning and groaning. Kenny and I were in stitches. We laughed all the louder when we saw that his school uniform was covered in green and brown skid marks: Jimmy's mum was going to kill him. If any of the teachers saw the show from the classrooms above, they never let on. My bet was they'd seen us and they were still laughing when the bell rang for home time. The three of us flagged down a 62 and headed for the centre of Cardiff, chuckling when Jimmy's great escape came back to mind.

It started to rain, and we were trying to think of somewhere we could go that was dry and warm. Jimmy Donovan had always wanted to join up. I had no intention whatsoever of joining the British Army. Apart from anything else I reckoned my dad, who clung to his Catholic roots like ivy to a stone wall, would have killed me. So we only ended up in the Cardiff Army Careers Office because Jimmy suggested it. The boy was keen. Mustard. Kenny wasn't quite as Colman's but he was interested. I thought the pair of them were raving lunatics. But they were right: it was dry and warm in there.

The recruiting sergeant welcomed us with open arms. Business was slack that day, and we had the place to ourselves. The sergeant was good at his job, easing us in with a couple of jokes. He saw what was what, took my more gung-ho mates through to sit the test and then came back. I was just sitting there, minding my own business. The sergeant fixed me with a skinny eye. 'What are you doing here, then?'

'Nothing,' I said, 'I just came along with my mates.'

He nodded. 'They're doing the test – would you like to take it?'

I shook my head. 'To be honest, I'm not bothered.'

'Take it anyway,' he urged, 'it's better than sitting there twiddling your thumbs.' I quite like twiddling my thumbs – it beats working – but I stood up. He took me through to join the others. It was mainly English and Maths, with some general knowledge questions thrown in for good measure. Then there was a separate aptitude test, to find out which bit of the Army you'd suit best.

Kenny failed. He was very upset. I told him he should have done more school work – that made him feel a whole lot better. Jimmy and I passed. The recruiting sergeant took me to one side: 'Going by your scores, Flynn, you've got the makings of a good NCO. How about we send you to the Junior Leaders at the Armour Centre in Bovington?' I stared at him. For all I understood, he might as well have been speaking double Dutch. The sergeant recognized total ignorance when he saw it. 'The Junior Leaders at Bovington is the fast-track way of becoming an NCO in the Royal Armoured Corps,' he chanted, as if he was reading it from a book. I still looked blank. With a visible effort he mustered his patience. 'Royal Armoured Corps? Tanks and armoured fighting vehicles? Large metal things that go bang when they fire their guns?'

'Yes,' I said, 'I know what a tank is, thanks. What's an NCO?'

He pointed to the stripes on his arm. 'Non-commissioned officer – like me. Corporals, sergeants and suchlike, they're called NCOs, see?' I kept playing dumb, he'd needled me.

'So you're an officer,' I asked, 'but at the same time you're not an officer? Why not?' I could see him beginning to bristle.

'Because I don't hold the Queen's Commission.'

'Why not?'

'Because. I'm. A. Non-commissioned. Officer!' The last word came out as a half-swallowed bark.

'I see,' I said. 'So like a corporal or a sergeant, then? An officer, but not one?'

A malevolent gleam appeared in the sergeant's eye. 'Are you taking the mickey, Flynn?'

'No, Sergeant.'

'Good,' he said. 'Well, what about it, then?'

'What's the money like?'

'I can't pretend it's brilliant when you first join. But it gets better as you move up through the ranks. And remember – you get your food and accommodation for free. Not to mention excellent training; as much sport as you can handle; and you get to fire a big gun.' I thought

14

about it. The words I liked most in everything he'd told me so far were: 'money,' 'sport' and 'gun'.

'I'll think it over', I told him, 'and let you know.'

I thought about it all afternoon. Which was a long time for me, at that age. I was doing OK at school now, but I couldn't see all that much future in the local employment market. On the other side of the coin I was knocking around with the gang – not the old gang, a new one: Pat, Jackie, Andrea and Kerry. Yes, I'd discovered girls. Still, if I stayed in Trowbridge, there was a danger I'd slip back down the criminal chute and end up in Cardiff prison. Which didn't look like a very nice place. I knew that, because for the early part of my life I'd been able to see most of it from outside my front door. Either that, or I'd wind up in some dead-end job, stacking shelves in a local supermarket.

That evening, after supper, I told my mam I wanted to join the Army. She's strong, Mam, but the news threw her. She grabbed me and pulled me into a corner of the kitchen. In a stage whisper, she mouthed: 'We can't tell your dad!'

'I know,' I said. 'He'll kill me if he finds out. But I need one of you to sign the form. Will you sign it for me?'

'Are you sure, Michael? You never wanted to join the British Army before.'

'I'm sure, Mam. They're offering me a good job – Junior Leaders. It means you get promoted faster.'

'What if they send you somewhere dangerous?' I knew she was thinking about Northern Ireland. The Army had been fighting there for seven years, and there was no sign of the conflict stopping any time soon. My dad would wring my neck if the Army sent me over the water and he found out I was fighting Catholics; then he'd bury what was left of me in a nice, deep ditch. After all, he was a professional at digging ditches. In a way it was the worst thing I could do to my father – I'd be cutting my ties, all right, maybe for all time. But I'd be free.

There was a massive dose of standard teenage rebellion in all of this. Now I was fifteen and starting to feel my water, Dad and I no longer saw eye to eye on anything. The biggest cause of trouble between us was girlfriends, as in Pat, Jackie, Andrea and Kerry. Dad was such a staunch Fenian that if I met a girl and wanted to take her home, then she and I both had to pretend she was a Catholic. Or better still, a Catholic who wanted to be a nun. Given that the last thing any of the girls I knew wanted was to take the vow, this made things difficult; so difficult that in the end I gave up trying to bring my girlfriends home. I'd persuade them we had to go to their place instead. If they noticed my lack of hospitality I'd tell them, 'You wouldn't like my house,' when what I really meant was, 'You wouldn't like my dad. Especially when he finds out you don't know one end of a Hail Mary from the other.'

My father was stuck in time and place, trying to impose the old, 1950s rural Catholic Irish ways he'd grown up with onto a new generation: me. He went to Mass every Sunday, regular as clockwork. He'd get hopping mad when I refused to go with him. If I went out in the evening he'd tell me I had to be back home by a certain time, which might have been all right if the times hadn't kept on getting earlier as I grew older.

So knowing he'd hate me joining it was part of the Army's attraction. My mother made it plain she didn't like the idea of my joining up one little bit. But she liked the head-to-head between her husband and son even less. A few days later, when my dad was out working, she signed the parental consent form.

Once I'd made the decision and the form had gone in, I was impatient to leave home. But in the end, I had to wait five months until I reached the school leaving age of sixteen. In the meantime, I decided the best course of action was to lie low and do what my father said. Which made things between us a lot easier. So did the fact that, because I'd told him I'd be learning how to fix engines, my dad thought I was doing an apprenticeship. By the time I was sixteen we were getting on reasonably well. When the day came round for me to go, Mam and

Dad came to the stop with me. Mam wished me love and Dad wished me well. I climbed on the number 62 bus. Only this time, I wasn't a truant, nor a trainee crook. I was a tank boy in training.

CHAPTER TWO

Bovington camp and the Junior Leaders' Regiment was a bit of a shock to the system – especially the ferocious discipline. There always seemed to be someone yelling at you, and the reason they were yelling frequently struck me as small-minded, unnecessary or plain stupid. It was the standard treatment most armies employ when it comes to moulding new recruits: they want to knock the civilian out of you, and the soldier in. My dad was strict, but he was my dad; plus, he'd put in the time and the effort to earn my respect. Most of the guys in my face now were only four or five years older than I was. To me, they were hiding behind the power of their stripes. Where I came from, if someone got in your face and started yelling like that, you stuck the nut on them first and asked questions later.

They had some strange ideas in those days, which were almost guaranteed to cause problems. One was the queueing up for the milk machine. They worked us really hard at Bovington, so we needed a bit of building up. Only there was never quite enough milk to go round. One day, I was waiting in the milk line as usual when a tall, skinny bloke pushed in at the front of the queue. Neither of the trainees in front of me said anything. I overtook them and walked up to him: 'Hang on a minute, mate,' I said, 'there's a queue here.'

He looked at me scornfully: 'I'm in pass-out term – *mate*. That means I get to go before you – so piss off.'

'Pass-out term' was the year ahead of our own; they liked to believe this made them superior and gave them special rights. I couldn't quite see how it made any difference to the milk queue. And I didn't like the guy's attitude. I stepped round, grabbed him by the shirt front and said, 'Listen, *mate* – there's other people in this queue before you. Get to the back.' I must have been having a bit of a bad day. 'I'm in pass-out term,' he insisted. He was talking, not listening.

'You will fucking pass out if you don't get to the back of the queue.' He tried to stare me down. When I didn't blink he said, 'Let's go outside.'

'Fuck going outside,' I snarled.

I yanked on his shirt front, nutted him and then slammed him backwards into the milk machine. It smashed, spewing milk everywhere. 'Pass-out term' was on his arse in a big, white spreading puddle of spilled milk. He looked dazed: that would be the head butt. Another bloke from pass-out term was standing there. He came up to me and said: 'I see you're good with your head. But there are other ways of using it. You know?' He was telling me to take it easy, but I wasn't in the mood to listen. I was about to tell him to fuck off as well, when he held out his hand. Thirty seconds later, the orderly corporal came running up. He grabbed hold of me and marched me off to the jail. Not many people got milk that day. And I got seven days ROPs (restriction of privileges). No use crying.

I managed to get through the rest of my fourteen months' training at Bovington without getting mixed up in any more trouble. I passed out as a trooper in December 1977 and joined B Squadron, The Blues and Royals Regiment in Detmold. Back in the deep dark days of the Cold War, Germany was seen as the front line in case of hostilities with the Soviet Bloc. But instead of the Communists, once again I found myself fighting my own battles.

I was minding my own business having a drink in 'the Piggery', otherwise known as the NAAFI bar, one evening. The 'crows', as the older hands called new members of the regiment, used to sit and drink in rows at the tables in this great big long bar. There'd be a row of A

Squadron, B Squadron and so on. We hardly ever mixed: the Army can be very tribal, not just between regiments but within them. Despite the rigid separation, you did occasionally bump into someone from another squadron. On this particular evening, I found myself talking to a bloke in A Squadron. A Very Tall Bloke. 'Anthony Thornett,' he said, sticking out a bony hand. Tony was a little bit older than me, and by nature very cheerful: he always had a smile on his face. One of the things I liked about him, apart from his easy-going nature, was that although he had one official girlfriend, he also had a whole string of part-timers. I could relate to that – or at least aspire to it.

I'd just sat back down with a fresh round of drinks when the duty corporal, Paul Buxton, came up to the table. Bucko was a mean man. Baiting crows was his favourite sport. 'Time you were out of here, Flynn,' he said.

I glanced at my wrist-watch. 'Out of here? Why? It's only ten o'clock.'

'You've had too much to drink. Go to bed.' I'd had five beers, true. And true, I was still only seventeen. But I certainly wasn't drunk and I wasn't causing any trouble, just swilling and chilling. And they'd told me it was a man's life in the Army. 'No,' I said evenly, 'I'm not going to bed. I'm having a drink with my mates.' I could feel myself starting to get riled. Who the fuck did he think he was, telling me to go to bed like that? My dad?

'You are fucking going, Flynn,' he said, taking a step closer. 'Out you go.' I had a glass in my hand. I should have put it down. Instead, I stood up, grabbed Buxton by the throat and put him up against the nearest wall. I held the glass up in front of his face. 'You try and fucking put me to bed,' I said quietly, staring into his eyes. At this, about ten other people in the Piggery came up and pulled me away. They wrestled the glass out of my hand, frog-marched me to the door and threw me out.

I went to my room and lay down on the bed, furious, planning all the things I was going to do to Bucko when I next got the chance Finally, I dropped off to sleep. A short time later, the door burst open. Three or four of Bucko's mates charged in. They were drunk and the smell of alcohol filled the tiny room. They rushed me, lashing out with their fists and boots. I sprang out of bed and fought back. The drink slowed them, and I managed to get in a few good whacks before I got a kicking.

After my visitors had left, I lay back down on the bed feeling even more sore and sorry for myself. A few minutes later, an older trooper everyone called Joker came in. He didn't knock and I hadn't asked him, but in he waltzed and sat down on the end of the bed. 'Are you all right, Taffy?' I lay there in silence, nursing my bruises and my hurt pride. Joker moved up the bed and leaned towards me, smiling, and before I knew it he was stroking my hair. I pulled myself up painfully and shoved his hand away. 'I'm all right – don't bloody touch me! Fuck off and don't come back!' He left. It wasn't the best night I'd ever spent. And along with the treatment from Buxton it put a serious question mark in my mind over Army life.

Still, a few weeks later, things improved. The squadron went to BATUS, otherwise known as British Army Training Unit Suffield, the huge armoured warfare training facility run jointly with the Canadian Armed Forces in Alberta. The range they have over there is enormous. In fact, it's the same size as Luxembourg. There was great excitement as tank regiments deployed to BATUS for six weeks' training. The live-firing Medicine Man exercises were about as close as you can get to war without actually being in one. Everybody joins in: infantry, artillery, armour, air defence, close air support, engineers, logistic units, you name it. When the whole thing gets rolling at full tilt, it's like being caught up in a rehearsal for Armageddon.

At Detmold, the Army had trained me to drive the Chieftain main battle tank. Charging about the Canadian wilderness in a 55-tonne metal monster firing live 120mm shells and a co-axial GPMG chain gun was my idea of paid fun. But not as much as the larks to be had in Great Falls, Montana, a few hours further south across the United States border.

On completion of the first Medicine Man exercise, a coachload of us went down to Great Falls on a weekend jolly. Great Falls, which sits astride the Missouri River, was brill. They had moose there, or at any rate they had a statue of a moose in the middle of town. And they had spit-and-sawdust bars with pool tables and country music. 'I like America,' I told the boys after we'd been in Great Falls for a couple of days. 'In fact, I like it so much I'm going to stay here a bit longer.' I might just have been a little bit headstrong back then.

In the fond belief I was joking, they laughed at me. 'Don't be daft, Mike. We have to be back up at BATUS tomorrow. And when we get back, they're sending us to train for Northern Ireland.' I'd forgotten about that. I quite fancied the idea of fighting, even if it meant fighting on my father's home turf.

Still, I bloody-mindedly shook my head. 'I don't care. I like it here a lot, and I'm staying.' That evening I got chatting to a couple of the local ranchers. They told me Seattle was the place to be: it was full of game girls and there was a much better chance of finding a job there. Next morning, the rest of the boys went back north on the bus to rejoin the unit. I hit the highway and thumbed it 100 miles or so further south, to a small town called Livingston. If I'd taken to Great Falls, I liked Livingston, Montana, even better. It was a real cowboy town, in the wide open range land not that far north of Yellowstone National Park. Livingston was even more traditionally Western than Great Falls. They still had spittoons in the bars: and they needed them. Just about every man in the place went around chewing – and spitting – tobacco. Framed by mountains and surrounded by rolling prairie, Livingston wasn't crowded and cramped like the place where I lived: its open, free-and-easy Wild West atmosphere made me feel happy. It reminded me of Westerns I'd watched on telly with my dad when I was little, only with country music instead of *The Big Country* soundtrack.

With the rest of the lads gone I stayed in town for a couple of days, learning to play poker and drinking beer in the local bars. On the third morning I hit the road again. The first person to pick me up was a local farmer. We got talking as he headed west, and I asked if he had any work. 'Well,' he told me in a drawl that was so slow it took him about a week to get the words out, 'I'm getting roads put in on my farm, right now: the company that's doing it hails from Chicago. I know they're looking for hands. I can talk to the guy in charge of the gang if you want?'

I did want.

We reached his farm. It was roughly the size of Wales. Sure enough, there was a gang of about two dozen men laying Tarmac across bits of the landscape. I started chatting with them and we got along OK. An hour later the boss turned up. It was my kind of job interview: no forms, no referees and no bullshit, just me driving a scraper slowly down a dirt track for about ten minutes. Not that much of a problem after driving a 55-tonne Chieftain tank across the Canadian wilderness at top speed. Next thing, I had a bunk to myself in a Portakabin and was laying roads and digging ditches good style. If only he'd known, my dad would have been proud to see me established in the family business – only with rattlesnakes for company instead of earthworms and rabbits. As far as my family knew, I was on my way back to BAOR Germany. I wondered briefly if Mam and Dad would be happy when they found out I'd gone absent without leave (AWOL) from the British Army.

After a month of laying roads, the rest of the gang went back to Chicago. I'd earned a fair bit of folding money. I decided to use the cash to go and see some more of America. I thumbed it all the way across the States to the Twin Cities, Minneapolis-St Paul. I stayed in Minneapolis for a few days with one of the two girls who'd picked me up on the road, then moved on. I was wondering what to do with myself – in the long term, the short term and even in the next ten minutes. I'd just turned eighteen. I was an illegal immigrant on the run in a foreign country with no passport or documentation other than my Army ID card – and with no fixed abode or steady source of income. Tramp status beckoned. And I was hungry.

The manager of the road-laying company had given me his card and said that if I ever needed more work then I should get back in touch with him. As I headed for the bus station, I realized I'd already decided to do just that.

One extremely long but memorable Greyhound journey later, I arrived in Chicago. I found a phone booth and rang the number on the manager's card, and to my surprise and relief he immediately offered me more work. I joined up with the same gang again and we set about giving the city what builds cities: Tarmac, concrete and nice, long stretches of paved road.

One Saturday afternoon when we were free, some of the guys invited me along to one of the city's 24-hour discos. I'd never been in a 24-hour disco before; in fact, I didn't even know they existed. I came from Cardiff.

The disco was a riot, throbbing with loud music and filled with people, all packed into a massive building on three floors. The joint was about five times the size of the Cardiff Top Rank dance hall. With five times the girls. Great! It had a sound system that punched the ears and brain like the road drill I'd been using that same morning, only now I no longer had a set of ear plugs. All the men were walking round dressed like John Travolta in the film *Grease*, and all the women looked to me like sexier versions of Olivia Newton-John. In other words, extremely horny.

I caught the eye of a girl sitting with a couple of her mates at the next table. She didn't resist when I sat down and we got talking. When she said her name was 'Candy' I just managed to stop myself from making any dimwitted comments about how sweet she was. She had a strong Chicago accent. 'What part of Texas are you from?' I asked her, joking.

She slapped me on the arm – it was meant to be playful, but I'm sure it raised a bruise – she was well put together and no mouse. 'Stoopid,' she said. 'I'm from the Windy City, right here – Chicago.' I bought us another drink.

'Are you from England?'

'No, I'm from Wales.'

'Where's that at? Is it a town, or something?'

'It's a country,' I told her. 'It's near England, but Welsh.' Candy had never even heard of Wales; she thought this was very funny. I liked the way she looked when she laughed: she was young, she was pretty, she was fun and she had her own place in Near West Side. My kind of town; my kind of girl.

After two or three more drinks and a slow dance, we were in love. A few days after that we were living together. Candy even took me to meet her folks, now we were really full on. 'Right,' I thought in an 18-year-old-first-love kind of way. 'This is IT: this is the woman I want to be with for the rest of my life.' And it was serious – we're talking marriage. That meant I had to become a legal citizen of the United States. But before that could happen, I needed to be legal in the UK. A slight hitch in the grand plan.

There was only one thing for it: I had to go back to Britain, hand myself in to the Army, do my time, get them to kick me out and then fly back to the love of my life and eternal happiness. That was the plan. What could possibly go wrong?

CHAPTER THREE

I arrived back at Heathrow, took the bus to Paddington station and caught the next train down to Cardiff. I had a couple of cans of cider to ease the journey, fell asleep on the other side of Bristol and ended up in Swansea. Jet lag. Or cider lag. Or both. When I finally made it back to Cardiff later that night, I booked myself into the Centre Hotel, overlooking Cardiff Rugby Club. After the fleshpots of Chicago, Cardiff looked smaller, and greyer, and even more done-in than I remembered. But then I was looking at the world through love-tinted, Candy-striped Uncle Sam spectacles. It was a rainy Wednesday night and the whole place felt dead on its feet. Feeling a bit lost and lonely I found a telephone, called up my old pal Jackie and invited her round for a few drinks and a night of hot pash. There's loyalty for you.

The next morning I went up to see my mam and dad, explained that I'd been on the run and told them I was going to hand myself in to the police. But that evening I went out on the lash with a few of my old school friends. There was an Eisteddfod on in Cardiff at the time, so we decided to pay it a visit. We were very pleased to find the Eisteddfod included our own special kind of culture: a beer tent. I got so drunk I fell asleep under a table. I woke up at three o'clock in the morning, freezing cold. My mates had disappeared. There was a jumper lying nearby: assuming it belonged to one of my mates I got up and put it on. It was a bit small for me, but at least it helped keep me warm. Still pie-eyed, I staggered outside and ran straight into a couple of policemen.

After a spot of the old 'Ello, ello, what have we got here then?' routine they arrested me for being drunk and disorderly and in possession of a woollen garment two sizes too small for me, took me down the police station and bundled me into a cell. I woke up next morning with a brain like a dried walnut and a throbbing hangover, wondering where the hell I was and what the hell had happened to my mates. I dimly remembered getting arrested, and the horrible surroundings suggested I was in a police station. Small mercies. At least now I was in the right place to hand myself in.

A sergeant let me out and said I could go, as long as I promised not to be a naughty boy again. I said: 'I'm on the run from the Army and I want to give myself up.' The sergeant did a double-take. When I'd repeated the story a couple more times and he'd caught up, he took down my details and went off to check on my story. There was a long pause, while I sat in the waiting area reading an old newspaper. Eventually the sergeant came back. 'We have no paperwork that says you're AWOL from the British Army, Mr Flynn. Which being the case, you're free to go.'

That struck me as odd. Maybe the Army hadn't noticed I'd run away? Or maybe – I thought about the milk machine fight, sticking Buxton up against the wall and a couple of other minor incidents that no doubt featured lovingly in my personnel records – they were secretly glad I'd done a runner and didn't want me back?

Whatever, I was free to go. I thought about that. I could walk out of there, grab a cab to the airport, get on a plane and be back in Chicago the next night. No one the wiser. I wanted to go, oh how very much I wanted to go back to my true love's arms – but not if it meant trying to survive in the States on an illegal footing. How would I be able to get married, or drive a car, or do any of the other important things in life? I told the desk man, 'If you ring up the Blues and Royals – that's my unit in Germany – they'll confirm I'm AWOL.'

He looked at me blankly. 'Germany?'

'All right,' I said, 'just ring up the Household Cavalry barracks in Knightsbridge and give them my name. Tell them I'm absent without leave. They'll call up my home unit in Germany and confirm it.' At the end of another long pause, the Sarge went away and made the call. About an hour later, he came back out. 'Trooper Flynn?' he said sternly. 'Get back in that cell.'

A few days later I was back in Germany, standing in front of Regimental Corporal Major (RCM) 'Smacky' McDougall, flanked by two Blues and Royal corporals. We called McDougall 'Smacky' because he had a face like a battered old plimsoll. A well-hard Glaswegian, Smacky marched me in to see the colonel of the regiment. The CO's real name was Lt Col Hugh Smith, but everyone called him the Hook. Which might have been because he had a hook where his right hand had been before he'd lost it. The Hook had a very unsettling habit of rubbing his hook violently up and down on the sleeve of his good arm when he was feeling annoyed. He gave it a tremendous rubbing now. Judging by the hook action, I expected him to kick me out of the regiment right there and then – after I'd enjoyed a luxurious five-star vacation at the regimental jail in Detmold.

I was ready to go: once I'd been through however many weeks of hell they decided I deserved to spend inside its grim walls, the plan was they'd show me the gate, boot me out and tell me never to darken the army's doors again. But plans are one thing, life is another.

The Colonel was busy with his paperwork. The silence was enough to make you deaf. I stood there at attention for what felt like a month of Sundays. At last the Hook looked up and caught my eye. 'Where have you been for the past three months, Trooper Flynn?' he asked mildly.

'America, Colonel. Mostly Chicago.'

The Hook rubbed his sleeve, held his hook up to inspect the shine and then made a few more marks with the pen on the sheet of paper in front of him. At the end of another month of Sundays he looked up again. 'I see. And how did you manage to support yourself while you were on the run? Did you find work?'

I explained about the construction company, how I'd made money, found a woman and somewhere to live. When I came to the end of my little yarn he caught my eye again: 'I know what you're up to, Flynn. And I know what you want. But you're not going to get it – not on my watch.' The ground slipped a bit under my feet.

'How do you mean, Colonel?' Smacky swivelled, leaned, stuck a bulging red face into mine and shouted: 'KEEP SILENT! ONLY SPEAK TO AN OFFICER WHEN HE ASKS YOU TO SPEAK. DO YOU UNDERSTAND?' at the top of his voice. I gulped and nodded. Smacky looked as if he was about to have a heart attack.

In the same quiet voice the Colonel said, 'You're a young lad, Trooper Flynn. And yet you managed not just to survive in the United States but to find yourself a job and somewhere to live.' I thought, 'And a girl: don't forget the girl.' The Hook had more to say. 'That shows initiative. It also tells me you're the type of soldier I want in my regiment, even despite your unauthorized absence. So here's what I'm going to do: I'm going to give you twenty-eight days in jail. When you come out, you're going to rejoin the squadron and start training for Northern Ireland.' I opened my mouth to protest, remembered Smacky and thought better of it. 'You're going to do the tour of Northern Ireland with us, Flynn,' the Hook told me, after he'd given his curved bit another good going over. 'It will be finished before you know it, and you'll be a better man for the experience. By the time you're due to leave the Army you'll be twenty-one, and if we do it this way then you won't have to go into civilian life with a dishonourable discharge spoiling your future prospects. You can go back to the United States as a legal citizen. Now, how does that strike you?'

The Hook was giving me a chance. The question was, did I want to take it? The answer, now I was back in Germany, was 'Yes'. The magic of Chicago hadn't faded – I was still hell-bent on going back to Candy and the fleshpots. But Colonel Smith was right: it was much better for me to wipe the slate clean and start over. I'd enjoyed my taste of freedom – enough to know I wanted more. But unless I jumped over the desk and set about him there and then, they weren't going to boot me out. I would just have to write my fond goodbyes to Candy.

'Twenty-eight days imprisonment. Do you accept my award?'

'Yes, Colonel.' I wondered what would happen if I said 'No'.

'Very well. March out.'

'Salute!' Smacky yelled. I saluted.

'About turn!' I turned about. 'Quick march!' he bellowed and I started marching. Just as I was about to hit it, the door flew open. The provost staff corporal had been listening, and he'd snatched it back in the nick of time. 'KEEP YOUR BLEEDING ARMS STRAIGHT WHEN YOU MARCH!' yodelled Smacky in my left ear, shattering the fond daydream I was just slipping into – starring my American sweetheart.

It was so, so good to be back.

From the Colonel's office I went straight to the regimental jail. Army jails in 1978 weren't very nice places. I doubt they're any better now. Unless you were having the provost sergeant's baby, you got hell. I didn't even know the provost sergeant, so I got the full treatment – much of it from Provost Staff Corporal Freeman, who was known to all and sundry as 'Concrete'. Freeman thought he'd earned the nickname for being hard, but not everyone thought he was the sharpest knife in the box. Concrete and his team of helpers beasted me – drove me physically and mentally as hard as they could. The regime was horrible, and horribly relentless. We had to get up at the crack of dawn. As soon as the harsh neon strip light came on you had to jump out of your pit and get to work on your 'bed block' – that is, make your bedding up into perfectly square blocks with perfectly square corners. I got so that my bed block was a razor sharp rectangle, perfect in all its parts. Even so, most mornings Concrete or one of his henchmen swept it onto the floor and shouted, 'That's a fucking *rubbish* bed block, Trooper Flynn! Pick that fucking mess up off the floor and do it again!'

Twats.

Then it was the fastest shave in the West, with one of the staff shouting 'Get a fucking move on!' all the time as you scraped away. After that we got marched down to the canteen in quick time for a five-minute breakfast. After breakfast came drill, followed by cleaning duties. When everything was so clean you could eat your dinner off it, they gave us more drill; then it was back to cleaning again in case it had got dirty while you were out in the rain doing drill; then it was physical training; then it was outside for more square-bashing; then it was PT; then it was drill again; and so on and on until you collapsed exhausted back into bed at nine o'clock – if you were lucky and hadn't earned an extra punishment duty for some imaginary offence.

All the harsh treatment and exercise made me stronger and fitter. Not to mention frustrated and angry as the days went by. But there was no outlet for the volcano that was building up inside me. Until, that is, an officer came to my cell one day and asked me if I wanted to join B Squadron's boxing team. There was a tournament coming up. They'd heard I liked a bit of fisticuffs and they were looking for volunteers. I jumped at the chance – not least because it meant I got out of jail four days early. I rejoined the squadron and started training for the upcoming tour of Northern Ireland during the day, and the upcoming boxing tournament in the evening. I was fit as fuck and raring for some action. Maybe I'd get a chance to take revenge on one of the duty officers who'd taken such pleasure in making my life so very horrible inside.

The squadron had a boxing coach, I never really got to know him all that well, but his name was Captain Brown. I spent two weeks training with him and the rest of the team. Brown watched me sparring a bit in the training ring on day one, then he stopped the bout and drew me to one side. 'You're telegraphing your punches, Flynn. You always do the same thing: drop a shoulder and feint with that arm, then punch with the other hand. Any half-decent opponent's going to pick that up right away and you'll get outboxed.' I was doing what my dad had taught me, but that was just about all. Captain Brown taught me to mix up my moves, stop being so predictable.

The day of the tournament came round. My first opponent was Lt Rollo. He's now Lt Gen Rollo, but in those days he was just another part of the regimental machinery. I'd met him in the course of my sentence, he'd given me plenty of grief and as far as I was concerned he was a member of the enemy camp. The bouts lasted three rounds of three minutes each. The bell rang for round one. I thought, 'Right, he'll be expecting me to wade in with fists flying, then pick me off with his moves. If I keep my head and box, I can beat him.' Which is exactly what I didn't do: I was so keyed-up and angry I waded in with fists flying. Rollo got it straight on the button. Through luck or good judgement, I knocked him out inside the first thirty seconds. One of the enemy was lying face down on the floor, exactly where I thought he belonged. And I was through to the next round.

My next opponent was another officer, Captain Barclay. I refuse to believe his family had anything to do with the banking business. Barclay had been in my face a few times. In the regiment he was known as the Hanging Judge: when he was dishing out punishment, he always put on an old-fashioned, full-bottomed wig. He thought that was funny – while the rest of us didn't. He'd given me plenty of extra duties during my time in jail, not very much of which I thought I'd deserved. I liked Captain Barclay even less than I did Lt Rollo, and I was looking forward to giving him the same treatment.

My initial success had made me confident. A bit too confident. 'You're bloody going to get some too, mate,' I thought, as I watched my new opponent doing his fancy warm-up routine. The bell rang for the start of the first round. I stepped out to meet the Hanging Judge. Next thing I knew I was flat on my arse. There were stars exploding inside my head and I couldn't work out what the hell had happened. I heard a voice coming from far away, counting out numbers. 'Must be at least "eight" by now,' I thought – it felt as if I'd been down on the canvas for a couple of days. But then I heard: 'Two, three, four …' Fuck, he'd hit me square on the jaw, put me down and now the ref was counting me out. I had to get back up and return fire. I climbed groggily to my feet and shook my head. Captain Barclay was smirking at me. It was clear he thought he had me bang to rights: it was just a question of finishing the job.

I was furious, but mostly with myself: Barclay was a real boxer and he'd taught me a valuable lesson. Don't get too cocky and too sure of yourself – it lays you open to unpleasant shocks. We set to again: he had a clever way of feinting with his left, and as I knew from hard experience, a nasty, pile-driving straight right. And he was quick on his feet. For two rounds, he ducked and weaved and avoided my best attempts to deck him. No two ways about it: he was the hardest opponent I'd ever fought. But towards the end of the third and final round I caught him with a left uppercut, followed that with a thumping right cross and he crashed to the canvas. He climbed to his feet on the count of seven, but I got the decision on points. Who knows? Perhaps Mr Barclay learned something useful from the contest, too.

CHAPTER FOUR

I'd done my basic training at Bovington and then trained as an armoured cavalryman, but Sennelager made all that seem like preparation for Toy Town. We were tank soldiers, but now they were training us to fight as infantry in the most difficult of all the jobs you can get in any army: urban warfare. For that they'd built what they called the 'Tin City', at Sennelager just outside Paderborn. The Tin City was a wood and corrugated iron mock-up of some typical bits of urban Northern Ireland, where we got to play Cowboys and Indians with real guns and blank ammunition. Great fun.

Less fun was the fact that the Troubles in Northern Ireland were nearing their peak: in the ten years or so since they'd started, dozens of people, civilians, Irish Republican Army (IRA) and British Army alike had been killed and injured. So the training for tours of duty in the province was intensive and highly specialized: soldiers from other regiments played the part of the local 'civpop' (civilian population), behaving in a suitably aggressive and hostile way: shooting, bombing, rioting, chucking stuff, spitting and swearing and generally getting in your face. We practised patrolling the Tin City in a 'brick', or four-man unit of infantry, and then as part of a 'multiple' or larger force made up of two or more bricks.

The first thing they issued me with was a whacking great elephant gun: the 7.62mm self-loading rifle, or SLR. The SLR was a monster, but in the best way: very powerful, very reliable and in the right hands extremely accurate. It stopped large objects dead in their tracks – especially people. It was an excellent weapon and some of us still miss it.

Steve Ribton, a young guy from Andover, shared a room with me. We got on well. Steve had joined up at the same time as me, but instead of Bovington he'd done standard new-entry training at Pirbright. He had an unusually long and bony head, which had earned him the nickname 'Screaming Skull'. Steve didn't take crap from anyone, but he was solid and calm. It took quite a lot to wind him up to the point where he'd start a fight. I didn't have that problem.

We learned a whole set of new skills at Sennelager: how to conduct foot patrols in a hostile urban setting; how to deal with nail bombs, petrol bombs and IEDs; setting up and managing effective and safe VCPs (vehicle check points); riot control; house searches; making arrests; lots and lots of target shooting and weapon handling; helicopter-borne infantry operations – the full Monty. I took to the training like a duck to water. For some reason, I just plain flat-out enjoyed being a regular infantryman.

One evening, a few of us in B Squadron went down to a local bar called the Treffpunkt in Detmold for a refreshing few litres of Herforder Pils. It wasn't a very big place. In fact, it was so small we couldn't help noticing there were several members of A Squadron in the bar. One of the A Squadron guys was a monster: about six feet five inches tall and a good eighteen stone, with a huge barrel chest and a shaven head; he looked as if he wrestled crocodiles in his spare time, for fun. I'd noticed him before, gobbing off and throwing his weight around in the pay queue. And taken an instant dislike.

Watching him, I still didn't like what I saw: he was nudging Steve aside to get served first at the bar. Maybe the Hulk was just clumsy? Or maybe he was a bully. I started to lose it. I gave the Hulk the eye – and he gave it right back. I got that feeling you get when you know you're going to have a fight, a kind of tingling anticipation mixed with an edge of fear. It was the Cardiff coming out in me, the rogue side. If

I was looking to excuse my aggression, which I'm not, I'd say that most of us weren't spending enough time in the company of women. There was way too much testosterone washing around in the bloodstream.

The Human Shed kept clocking me back. He was so big I knew my only chance was to get my retaliation in first. Holding eye contact, I walked towards him. The moment he was within range I threw my best punch at his head without warning. My fist connected with his chin and he staggered back. He shook his head and wobbled a bit, but then the Shed's head came up and he gave me a look that would strip paint. 'Shit,' I thought. 'I haven't put him down.' Then he was on me. He grabbed me by the shirt front and I reeled backwards. It was like being run down by a train. My back hit a chair and we catapulted into the table behind. The furniture splintered and we went down in a cartwheeling heap, fists flailing.

In seconds, we'd turned this little German bar in this small German town into a scene from the bog-standard Western: the bit when mass fighting breaks out and the saloon gets trashed. The Hulk and I careened round the place trying to knock lumps out of each other, smashing glasses, turning furniture to matchwood and spilling beer. The little old lady who ran the bar and her equally small and aged husband did their best to get between us, but the red mist had come down. We were ready to kill. There was a toilet in the corner: its door usually opened into the bar. We crashed into it at full tilt, knocking it clean off its hinges. The door slammed flat on the bog floor and we went down with it. Still fighting. Classy.

When they saw the door go, the other lads decided enough was enough. A pair of strong hands grabbed hold of me and dragged me off my opponent. I spun round ready to take on the new threat and saw that the person who had hold of me was Steve. Another couple of guys got hold of the Hulk, pulled him to his feet and held him back. We glared at one another, gasping for breath. My nose was bleeding and some of my clothes were ripped: one of my ribs hurt like hell and there were bruises coming up in places where I hadn't even realized he'd hit me. The Hulk had a black eye that was swelling up nicely, and a nasty-looking lump on his chin where I'd first whacked him. 'You two stupid bastards can shake hands,' Steve said. 'Go on – get on with it.' The Hulk's hand came out. I took it.

'Right,' Steve announced, 'get your money out, the pair of you: first you're going to pay for this damage. Then we're all going to sit down and have us a friendly drink.' So that's what we did: coughed up and said sorry to the bar's owners. Now we'd stopped fighting and I looked at him properly, I realized the Hulk was the biggest bloke I'd ever met. I must have been out of my mind to take him on.

'My name's Mike Flynn. I'm from Cardiff. Who are you?'

'Rupert McKinney,' said the Human Shed thickly over his war wounds, with a crooked smile. In the way of these things, the more we talked, the better we got on. We'd cleared the air, established mutual respect and recognized that neither of us was going to be regimental top dog. We ordered several glasses of strong lager, helped clear up a bit, sat down and got collectively hammered.

As I listened to him talk, I realized that McKinney was quite a clever guy: he thought about things, not least when it came to fighting. Maybe that was why I hadn't been able to finish him off. Or could it have been his sheer size? Twenty-many years later, Rupert McKinney and I are still friends.

On the night before we were due to leave for our first tour of Northern Ireland, we all went to the Piggery for a few pints. I'd been playing rugby that day, and after the game we carried on the motion in the NAAFI bar. I was pretty tired and all I wanted to do was relax and enjoy a bit of a drink while there was still a chance. Like everyone else. Everyone else, that is, except Trooper Eddie Maggs. Maggs had always been a bit of loner: often brooding and tucked up in himself, he'd suddenly launch into an aggressive outburst for little or no apparent reason.

After a few rounds, things got a bit lively in the Piggery. Some of the boys had their kecks down, doing highly original and amusing things – like the Dance of the Flaming Arseholes. It's important to understand how this time-honoured and venerable Army ritual is performed. A pint glass of beer stands at a measured distance from, the line of squaddies who are eager to win it. The first man drops his trousers and kecks and pushes one end of a set length of toilet paper up his bum. The other end dangles just above the floor.

With a flourish and a few well-chosen remarks, the master of ceremonies sets fire to the free end of the bog roll. Then with butt cheeks tightly clenched and, in most cases, hands clasped firmly around the balls, the eager squaddie waddles over to the glass of beer, manoeuvres the flaming end of the bog roll carefully into position, squats down and quenches the flame in the amber liquid. Unless, that is, the flames reach his rear end first, in which case he sets off round the bar at top speed, yelling and flapping and trying to put them out. While this is going on, everyone sings a background chorus of that age-old soldier's song: 'Get 'em down, you Zulu warriors! Get 'em down, you Zulu chief, chief, chief!' at top volume. Royal Engineers, naval types and, of course, boy scouts will know other versions of this song. For rugby players, the dance is often best performed *on* the bar after scoring your first try. Insiders agree that the 'Chief! Chief! Chief!' bit is greatly improved by banging a beer tray on your (or somebody else's) head, in strict time.

In the Army, the winner is the duck impressionist who takes the *longest* time to get his arse over the glass and extinguish the flaming paper. Balls of steel or – better still – asbestos are a big help. The Dance of the Flaming Arseholes is especially good as a safety valve when a big, scary tour is coming up and everyone is half looking forward to going, half apprehensive. The old-style, hard, shiny bog roll the Army issued in those days was the best for the job, because it took longer to burn. The modern, tissue-paper stuff burns much too quickly, you've got to leg it double-quick, which means the whole thing is over too soon. That's progress for you.

The one golden rule of Army drinking contests it's essential to remember is this: eating is cheating.

By half past ten, everyone in the Piggery was pie-eyed, including Eddie Maggs. Maggs was loud and brash, especially with a drink inside him. He looked pissed off. I asked: 'What's the matter, Eddie?'

Eddie looked up. 'Fuck off. When I get to Northern Ireland, I'm going to shoot me some Irish twats.' At the time, I didn't pay him much attention.

CHAPTER FIVE

As a unit, B Squadron deployed to Glassmullan barracks, while A and C Squadrons went to Woodburn barracks, also in Andersonstown, Belfast. Glassmullan camp wasn't all that big: about the size of your average school playground, it was an outpost in bandit country. The accommodation was basic: eight rooms set to either side of a corridor that ran down the middle of a long metal shed known as a Corimec: four men to a room, single beds, no bunks. Corimecs are quick to erect and pretty quick to strike down, useful for an army like our own that keeps getting asked to fire fight around the globe. They can be single or multi-storey. The single-storey ones we had in Glassmullan had had the shiny corners knocked off them at the hands of many different units.

To stop IRA gunmen lining up on us, Glassmullan camp had high outer walls made of wriggly tin. There was a narrow gap between that corrugated iron outer skin and the breeze-block walls of the barracks proper. If you were feeling brave enough and were willing to ignore standing orders, you could jog around the cramped camp in the gap, always hoping the IRA didn't do a random drive-by shooting and get lucky as you ran past on the other side. There was a loading bay just inside the main gate – a large sandbox in a wooden frame where we unloaded our weapons when we came back in from patrol, and loaded them on the way out.

'Andytown' lay between the Andersonstown Road and the Falls

Road, smack in the middle of Belfast's Catholic heartland. With my background and upbringing I should have been feeling right at home, but I couldn't have felt more unwelcome: I was in the British Army uniform that at least 99 per cent of the locals hated. You knew they hated you because they hinted at their feelings on a daily basis, in the form of nail bombs, mortars, petrol bombs, stones, bottles, shootings, half-bricks, V-signs and lots of inventive verbal abuse. Luckily, most of the hard objects they threw or fired at us missed. But it was a rare day in Andytown when IRA footsoldiers didn't carry out some kind of attack on the British Army. It was mostly routine stuff: sniping from nearby houses, drive-by shootings at the gatehouse, lobbing a couple of mortar bombs. But sometimes the players organized what they called a 'spectacular', or a big, well-planned, concerted attack.

My father didn't know I was in Northern Ireland – he thought I was still out training on the ranges in Germany. My mam and my sisters had done a great job of keeping it under wraps, but I knew the day was coming when I'd have to tell the truth. In the meantime, when the army gave me leave, I'd usually avoid home and avoid the issue, and stay with a mate.

Our first fortnight in Andytown was relatively peaceful. But for A and C Squadrons over at Woodburn barracks, the night of 29 February 1979 came with some very unwelcome trouble. The squadron OC, Major Barnes, had organized a disco in the barracks. Good idea in some ways – keep the lads happy, boost morale. But the evening's festivities were scheduled to include both drink and women. The hierarchy was all for the lads enjoying themselves, but they thought allowing women on base and mixing them with alcohol was a recipe for trouble. This time Major Barnes thought it would be OK.

Tim Mardon, A Squadron's senior Lance Corporal of Horse, was the guard commander that evening. Since I wasn't actually in Woodburn barracks on the night in question, my account is based on Tim Mardon's.

Mardon asked Major Barnes if the members of the duty guard might be allowed to pop into the disco during the course of the evening, have a lemonade or two and not miss out altogether on the fun. Major Barnes said they could, but only for an hour each and no more than one at a time. The eight-strong guard on duty that night included LCoH Jim Pitt, Lance Corporal (LCpl) Geoff Towse, Trooper Archie Andrews and Trooper Maggs.

Mardon sorted out a roster so that individual guard members could take an hour off in turn. Pitt went first, then Andrews. They had a bit of a sherbert, tried to chat up a bird, then came back on duty again when their hour was up. Maggs went next. When Maggs didn't report back to the guardroom at the end of his allotted hour, Tim sent Andrews and Pitt to look for him. Maggs was still in the disco, propping up a large glass of vodka. A glance told the other two that Maggs was drunk. They brought him back to the guardroom.

Mardon confronted Maggs. 'I rearrange the stag so you can have an hour off, and this is how you repay me – by getting fucking pissed! Give me your weapon.' Reluctantly, Maggs handed over his SLR, and Mardon locked it safely away. 'You're a twat, Maggs,' he told Eddie. 'Go and get your head down and sleep it off.' There was no actual jail in Woodburn barracks, but there was accommodation for the duty guard. Andrews and Pitt took Maggs to one of the rooms and locked him in.

Mardon had an Irish girlfriend, Sheila, who'd come to the disco to see him. When his own free hour came round, Mardon told Towse and Pitt: 'I'm not actually going to be in the disco – I'm going to take Sheila to my bunk and talk about the weather. I'll be back in an hour. If there's any drama, you know where to find me.'

Towse manned the guardroom desk; Pitt took up duty at the main gate. Somehow – no one ever seems to have found out exactly how – Maggs got out of his room. He came up to Towse: 'I need a brew, Geoff – can I go to the cookhouse and get one?'

'You're not allowed to leave here, Eddie – but I'll ask Jim.' Towse called Lance Corporal of Horse Pitt: 'Can Maggs go to the cookhouse and get himself some tea?'

'Fuck all to do with me, Geoff – you're on the desk.'

'Fuck it,' Towse told Maggs. 'Go and get a brew, but come straight back here with it and don't be long.'

Maggs did not go to the cookhouse for a cup of tea. Instead, he went to Rupert McKinney's room. McKinney was asleep in bed minding his own business. Maggs banged on the door until he woke up. When McKinney opened it, Maggs said: 'Hey, Rupert, I need your gun.' McKinney thought the request was a bit strange, but Maggs's own SLR might have had a malfunction and he knew Maggs was on duty. He handed Maggs his rifle and went back to bed. Maggs filched some magazines from the flak jackets hanging on the pegs in the corridor. He loaded the rifle, made it ready, left the accommodation block and headed for the patrol gate. A small side gate, the patrol gate was fastened with a Chubb padlock. Maggs tried to shoot it off. He managed to hit it a couple of times, but the padlock stayed stubbornly intact.

By chance, a patrol was just returning to barracks. Hearing the shots, they assumed they were under fire from outside the camp perimeter and called in a contact report. And all hell let loose: half the camp grabbed their weapons and started spilling out to deal with the emergency. Mardon shot back to the desk like a jack-rabbit. 'Where's the shooting coming from?'

'Don't know.'

'Maggs. Where the fuck's Maggs?'

'He went for a brew about fifteen minutes ago. I told him to come straight back.'

'Fuck!' Mardon said, and started running.

Unable to get out through the patrol gate, Maggs went round to the rear sangar (fortified sentry post), a 3.5-metre high watchtower. Entrance to the sangar was via a ladder and a trap door. Maggs himself was supposed to be on duty in the watchtower, but since he was pissed, another trooper had taken his place. Hunkering down against the rear wall, Maggs pointed his SLR at the sentry. 'You've got the keys to the gate,' he shouted. 'Throw them down. I want to go out.'

'No can do, Eddie. Why don't you put the gun down?'

Maggs raised the rifle instead, and opened fire. Bullets whacked into the sandbags, the sentry ducked down. Homing in on the gunfire, Tim Mardon, Stu Sibley, Staff Corporal John Tucker and Lance Corporal David Mellor came steaming up. Someone climbed behind the wheel of a Humber Pig parked nearby, switched the headlights on and trained them on Maggs. The whole scene was floodlit now, as if it was in a theatre.

Maggs started yelling: 'I want to talk to Tim! I want to talk to Tim!' Taking the request as a good sign – and hoping Maggs would give himself up – Mardon started walking towards him. But as soon as he moved, Maggs opened up at him. Dodging behind the Pig, Mardon shouted: 'You fucking maniac, Maggs! Put the fucking gun down!'

Good thing about an army base is that there's always some bugger who can really shoot. Stu Sibley had just returned to the regiment after a stint intelligence-gathering. He was a crack shot. Turning to Tucker and Mellor, Sibley told them: 'I'll get round the back of Maggs and see if I can disarm him. You two stay here and don't move.' He started to move round onto the rampart next to the sangar, hoping to creep up on Maggs from behind. But instead of staying put where they were, Tucker and Mellor started edging towards Maggs. They meant to get as close as they could and then rush him.

Maggs saw them coming. He shot Tucker dead with a single bullet, then switched aim and fired at Mellor. The high-velocity round ripped Mellor's guts wide open. Clutching his stomach, he fell to the ground.

Sibley had a 9mm Browning pistol. As Maggs fired at Tucker and Mellor the sangar sentry opened fire, hitting Maggs but not killing him. Sibley stepped forward, raised the Browning, took careful aim and squeezed the trigger. Maggs took a bullet to the head and fell dead.

Sibley called for medics and an ambulance. Maggs and Tucker were beyond help, but after two weeks in intensive care, Mellor made it back to the land of the living.

Major Barnes was moved to another post.

CHAPTER SIX

That's how I met two of my best mates. Two of the troopers who'd been drinking with Eddie Maggs immediately before the shooting were transferred from A Squadron to B. It looked as if they had been tarred with guilt by association. One of them was the same Tony Thornett I'd met at Detmold, he of the many girlfriends. The other was Anthony Dykes.

Small and lean, with light brown hair and the drooping Zapata-style moustache so many people wore back then, Dykes found a bunk in the room across the corridor from mine. He was older than me – twenty-five – which seems like a lot when you're only eighteen. 'Dykesy', as everyone knew him, was a decent bloke: easy-going and easy to talk to, like Tony Thornett. Unlike Thornett, though, he was married. Living across the corridor from him, I gradually got to know Dykes better. You could always rely on him for sound advice, and he'd never make you feel stupid or small about asking the question. Dykesy, me and Tony Thornett were a team.

Once he'd moved across to B Squadron, Dykes didn't have a regular place in any of our bricks: he was what we called 'floating'. But he often operated in the other four-man brick that went out in tandem with ours. With the punishing schedule of duties and patrols it was great to have the extra help. A few weeks later, on 5 April 1979, we took over as the Andersonstown police station 'security force'. Two bricks were going. I was in one, Dykesy the other.

46

I'd come off guard early that morning and started getting all my admin squared away for my two-day stint at Andersonstown nick. We were looking forward to leaving Glassmullan and going: it would be a change of scene, if nothing else. The police station down there was smaller. It was a bit like Colditz, only without the glamour: breeze-block and wriggly tin walls, with a massive 10-metre-high steel-mesh anti-mortar fencing. The cage rose vertically all around the perimeter, then the last 3 metres of fence angled sharply inwards. Let's just say it wasn't a friendly looking place. But then the IRA was going through a phase of firing home-made mortars at us from the back of flat-bed trucks, parked a few streets away. The fencing was meant to catch the bombs – before they hit anyone inside.

It was time to leave but I was still in the shower, getting cleaned up. Never slow on the uptake, Dykesy came up and said through the curtain: 'You really want to let me drive the puddle-jumper today, Mike. You just haven't realized it yet.'

'Get off,' I said. 'The puddle-jumper's mine – and I'm driving it.' The 'puddle-jumper' (short-wheelbase Land Rover) wasn't really mine, it was the army's, but there were only two of us qualified to drive it in our section – Dykesy and me. I liked driving the puddle-jumpers – they were powerful and the tyres made a great sound when they whizzed on the road.

'Go on, Mike,' Dykesy argued. 'You're not even out of the shower yet, and it's nearly time to go: someone had better get it ready.'

I grabbed a towel. He was right – it did need 'first parading' – checking over for oil, water and the rest of the routine stuff. 'Go on then, you jammy bastard,' I told him. 'The keys are on my bedside locker.' Dykesy wandered off to get them.

On such tiny moments our whole lives can turn.

We were ready. We had these so-called flak jackets, which didn't offer any protection: even low-velocity rounds passed straight through them. When I asked one of the corporals what was the point of wearing them, he said: 'They keep your bits in when you've been shot. So the medics can patch you back up.' Thanks, pal. We also had these rubber shoulder protectors, which were supposed to absorb the SLR's recoil. The recoil was pretty meaty, but if you held the rifle correctly in the first place – pulled it hard back into your shoulder and leaned into the weapon – you didn't really need the pad. We liked the protectors though, we thought they made us look well hard.

We were in a convoy of two: Dykesy was driving the puddle-jumper directly ahead. I climbed into the back of a Humber Pig with Steve Ribton. As we settled down inside, Steve said, 'It's been really boring since we got mortared down at the shopping centre. I wish something would happen.' I knew what the Skull meant – we kept hearing about firefights in other parts of Northern Ireland, but neither of us had ever actually been in one. The order mortar shell fired at us didn't really count. As a soldier, you fear battle. At the same time you want it to happen. But there's an old saying: 'Be careful what you wish for.'

We were bumping along, eyes peeled for snipers and bombers, as usual. The Humber Pig was a 1-tonne light armoured truck with a long, ugly snout and the driving characteristics of the animal in question. When you could get it to go forwards in a straight line it was used for patrolling and ferrying soldiers around. For operations in Northern Ireland it had twin wire-mesh gates fitted on the back end. They came out to the sides like wings, so that infantry could advance behind them in relative safety. That's why the Humbers were also called 'Flying Pigs'. As long as you were inside the Pig, its hull offered some protection from the stones, half-bricks, bottles, nail bombs and other things the locals threw at us when the mood took them.

Word came through there was a bomb threat on the Andersonstown Road. That meant all traffic had to be diverted onto the Falls Road. Including our two vehicles. It also meant we had to fight our way through a god-almighty traffic jam, moving at a snail's pace. It turned out there was more than a bomb threat. There was some kind of real trouble at the bus station beyond the roundabout we were now approaching. The radio crackled into life again: a gang of lads had torched a couple of buses. That was a bad sign: the IRA often got teenagers to create a diversion before a 'spectacular'.

If Andersonstown police station doesn't figure in *The Guinness Book of Records* as the world's most bombed and shot-at law-enforcement facility, then it probably should. It has long since been demolished, but at the time the cop-shop sat on a triangle of land between the Falls Road and Glen Road. Once they'd met, at the east-pointing apex of the triangle, the two roads became the Falls Road. The Milltown cemetery lay a short distance south.

Despite all the excellent training we'd done for Northern Ireland at Sennelager, the Army was still doing some things that were bone stupid. In the case of the Blues and Royals, the most stupid thing we were doing was relieving the guard at RUC police stations at the same time every day. In the face of a terrorist threat, any predictable routine can be fatal.

Sad to say, many of our officers clung tight to the comfort of Army routine and bullshit. As a result, the IRA knew full well we'd be at the gates of Andersonstown nick at 1100 sharp every morning. Not only that, but the guys who'd been on watch in the sangars quit them *before* the relief guard arrived, climbing into the vehicles at the same time as we got out of them. That meant there was no one looking. And no one except the gate guard on the end of a weapon. Anyone would think we were on ceremonial duty at Horse Guards Parade, not in the middle of a deadly conflict In some ways, we were our own worst enemy.

The further Steve and I followed Dykesy down Glen Road, the slower we went, because of the traffic Finally, we came within sight of the Andersonstown RUC station's main gate. Through the Pig's wire-mesh-covered windscreen, I could see the bus station about 100 metres further down the road. Sure enough, a single-decker vehicle was blazing from end to end, belching fire and grey smoke high up into the morning air.

A civilian housing estate mixed with a few shops occupied the land opposite the RUC station's main gate. The houses were jerry-built, three-bedroom, two-storey places with little patches of garden at the rear. They reminded me of our own family home back in Cardiff. Most of Belfast, especially the mean-looking council estates we patrolled near-daily, reminded me of Cardiff. There were knots of teenagers hanging on the street corners: if I'd been dressed in civvies I could easily have passed for one of them.

The traffic ground to a complete halt, then started again, then stuttered along a bit further. At the time, I thought nothing of it. But the slow speed was bad – very bad. Under normal circumstances we'd have come flying along, the sentries would have been waiting ready to open the gates and we'd have swung inside without giving any potential attackers time to line up their gun sights. Now, we were crawling. We finally reached the main gates. Dykesy turned the Land Rover's nose in towards them.

Gunfire ripped the morning air. My first thought was 'Contact!' My second was 'Yes!' Steve had got his wish: we were in a full-blooded gunfight. It was my first time under fire. For the first few seconds I didn't even think about the danger. Then I heard ricochets slapping into the Pig's hull. I was sitting directly behind the driver. Past him I could see the Land Rover ahead of us had crashed into the left-hand gate pillar. Slewed round, it was blocking the entrance and Dykesy lay slumped against the steering wheel. I'd never seen a dead person before, but the stillness of his body told me the worst.

We roared in through the entrance, shoved the Pig's metal fenders up against the back end of the wrecked puddle-jumper and bulldozed it out of the way. Inside the Pig we had what we called a Clarabel. The Clarabel was a device that showed the direction of rounds fired at the vehicle. It had a big circular dial like a clock face, with little lights around the outside that lit up to show the direction of incoming fire. In training, it had worked really well. What they hadn't told us in training was that the Clarabel also picked up and indicated ricochets. I looked at the dial: every single light was illuminated. There was a hurricane of lead coming at us, bullets were ricocheting everywhere, and as far as we could tell from our magic device they were raining in from every direction. I thought we were surrounded. For a moment, I sat frozen.

The Pig started to shudder, rocking under the impact of high-velocity rounds. I sat frozen for a moment. Then I thought about it. The IRA favoured Armalites. 'The Pig's armoured, but a high-velocity round from close range is still going to whack through and hit us.' Even with the doors shut there was a strong chance we'd be killed. There was no point sitting inside a tin can waiting to be shot. Better to get out and carry the attack. Or at least try. 'Let's get out,' I said, and Steve reached for the handle. We threw the Pig's back doors wide open. As soon as we did that I heard the high-pitched buzz of bullets passing close by. 'Fuck,' I shouted. 'Maybe that wasn't such a great idea!'

Fear flooded through me. Then the training took over. Hit the deck. Find the source of fire. Fire back. Be the robot; do what you've been trained to do. We tumbled out, ran forward a pace or two and dropped flat. I made myself scan round the whole time, trying to work out who was firing at us and where they were hidden.

Tony Thornett's head exploded next to me. Bits of skull and brain flew across the pavement. 'Fucking Jesus!' I thought. 'Gotta move, Gotta move!' There were people screaming and shouting everywhere, shots going off but I was locked in my own bubble. I glanced at Tony Thornett again. He was making a gurgling sound, the air rattling in his throat as his body tried to keep breathing. Was that Tony? That wasn't Tony any more: he'd gone. 'Medic!' someone shouted. There was no medic, we were on our own. I looked up and saw my brick commander, Dave Rushton, leaning over Dykesy at the wheel of the Land Rover, trying to give him first aid.

Fear gave way to self-preservation, and immediately after that, to anger. Pure and cold-blooded. It was the first time I'd felt it: the kind of controlled rage that means you're ready to kill, but your mind is clear and cool as glass. You're still thinking fast, keeping your training and your wits about you. A little arrogance can also be useful in the mix: you have to believe you're better than the enemy, get some contempt for them going. If you believe you can win, it increases your chance of winning.

The gunfire was ferocious. Bullets fizzed and snapped past my head. More rounds thwacked into the Pig. The noise was deafening: the crack-thump of Armalite fire, the rounds crunching into the breeze-block wall next to us; a staccato rattle as a spray of bullets stitched across the Land Rover's metal skin; the deeper bark of SLRs as some of our guys fired back. I still couldn't see the gunmen – where the fuck were they firing from? Gun smoke and smoke from the burning buses was drifting down the street, and the haze and the noise and confusion made it very hard to know what was happening.

Steve was lying tucked just inside the main gate. I was hugging the deck just outside to the right. We got up and started moving forward. To my left I could see some of our guys lifting Dykesy out of the Land Rover. I turned my head to the right. Thornett lay motionless a few steps away. I found it hard not to stare at the grey stuff and blood leaking from his shattered skull. Where was the duty gate guard?

A gun system opened up on us from the right. It's true what they say about time: when bullets start to fly, it slows down to a crawl and everything seems to take ages to happen. The weapon made a deep, ripping sound, like a huge piece of Velcro: a machine gun. Looking past Tony Thornett, I saw the hijacked buses burning outside the bus station, spreading more and more smoke up the road. A white van was parked up in front of them. Its side door was standing open. An object inside it spat ripples of orange flame: a US-made M60 machine gun. Steve and I were already down as flat as we could get: I could feel the small stones and gravel in the road on my skin.

I lay there just thinking the same thing over and over: 'Fucking hell, fucking hell, this is murder.' There were rounds flying everywhere, the hornet buzz of bullets as they flew past. Despite all the soldiers who'd already been killed in the Troubles, they still didn't want us wearing steel helmets. If we looked warlike, it might upset the locals. I had my soft regimental beret on: that wasn't going to stop an Armalite bullet. It certainly hadn't done anything to save Tony. My thoughts came in stupid fragments: 'You should wear helmets for war.' 'But we aren't at war with the Irish, are we?' And then: 'I'm only eighteen – this is shit.'

It was.

Then it struck me: the way Tony was lying meant the gunmen had to be firing from across the street. I looked up. The curtains at the upper storey of the house directly opposite were jumping and twitching. So that's where the fuckers were hiding. There was the 'crack!' of a high-velocity rifle from up there, followed by a telltale orange flash and then a thump. The Skull and I started firing back. The people in the vehicles stuck in the traffic jam were diving for cover, white-faced and terrified; I could see them disappearing under their dashboards and behind their seats. My heart was beating like a trip-hammer, smashing against the inside of my ribs.

I looked across the street again. An alleyway cut north into the heart of the housing estate opposite the main gate. It divided a pair of semi-detached houses from what looked like a boarded-up business next to them. The house on the right had a protruding front window with a vertical red-and-white barber's pole in it. The ground floor of the left-hand house had been converted into a florist's shop. Adjoining gables pierced with a single window connected the properties on the first floor. There was a 'closed' sign on the door of the barber's shop. Odd that it should be closed for business on a weekday morning.

One of the guys who was helping to move Dykesy took a round. It travelled right down inside his flak jacket. The bullet only skimmed the flesh of his back, but with the sharp stinging burn of it he thought he'd been seriously injured. He started shouting, 'I've been hit, I've been hit!' He fell to the ground, writhing and clutching at his back. 'Fuck!' I thought, 'What do I do?' I was a tankie. I might have done my time in the Tin City, but they definitely hadn't told me how to behave when I was pinned down in the street under fire from several directions at once, with my mates lying dead and injured all around.

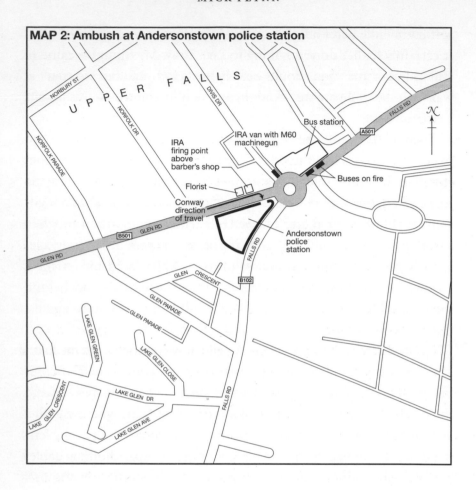

MAP 2: Ambush at Andersonstown police station

My brain jumped back into gear. I glanced at Steve and nodded at the barber's shop. 'They're in there. Let's get forward.'

The moment we stood up, the players on the machine gun down the road let rip with a new burst. The big rounds cracked and snapped through the air. We put our heads down and ran full tilt. By some miracle they didn't hit us. There was a small brick wall fronting the shop: we reached it and crouched down. The machine gun was still firing straight up the street at us. I swivelled and knelt up on one knee to return fire. The end of my SLR was wavering, the van and the gun system looped in the sights. No need to cock the weapon – we patrolled with one up the spout and the safety catch on. As soon as we'd come under fire I'd flicked the safety off. I steadied the rifle and squeezed the trigger. The weapon bucked against my shoulder. As soon as I opened fire the van's door slammed shut. It screeched off towards the Upper Falls.

I saw a gate ahead of me. The first thing I thought was, 'Bomb; booby trap.' We'd been told in training that the IRA liked to do that: set an ambush and then lure you onto a pre-positioned bomb as they ran away. The gate had to be a favourite for booby traps – attach a trip wire to it and we'd be goners the instant we opened it. But I had a mission now – it was cold and clear in my head: I was going to get round the back of the shop, cut off the escape route for the gunmen inside. And then, with a little help from my friend the Skull, I was going to kill them.

First, I had to get over that obstacle without being blown to shreds. The gate was a metre high. I stood up, took a flying leap and cleared it by at least a foot. I was wearing all my kit, my ammo pouches, hefting a loaded SLR – to this day I still don't know how I managed to jump that gate. Except that by now I was running on the strongest of all drugs, pure adrenalin.

Steve had automatically gone left to the front of the house. I raced down the alley along the side of the shop. At the corner I looked across the back garden. A man was trying to climb a wall about 20 metres away. He wore dark, scraggy clothes and his hair was round his shoulders. The skanky fuck was clutching an Armalite in his left hand.

Raising the SLR, I took aim and opened fire. I put down four rounds at him. He slithered over the other side of the wall. I didn't think I'd got him – if you hit someone with a round from the SLR they tend to stay down. I started running after him, going hell for leather through the garden. I could hear a car revving up on the far side: that made me run even faster. There was a screech of burning rubber and that was it – when I peered cautiously over the wall they'd got away. Hit and run, that was all the IRA were good for. I stood there for a moment, staring after them, shaking with frustration, anger and shock.

I made my way in through the back door of the barber's shop. I knew Steve had gone in the front. Our job now was to clear and secure the house. There was a woman in the kitchen. About fifty-eight years old, she was tied to a chair. Her husband was tied to a second chair.

The gunmen had commandeered the house and tied the pair of them up to stop them raising the alarm. Fat chance of that happening, especially in the woman's case: the rope around the harridan's wrists was hanging loose and she was laughing at me. She had her head back and her teeth bared and she was laughing her head off. 'Stupid bastards,' she said.

I felt the quick bite of a new anger: my mates had died out there in the street, and here she was sitting in her kitchen, laughing at us. I took my hand off the rifle: what about an almighty backhander to wipe the grin off her face? At that moment, Steve appeared in the other doorway. 'What's going on?' he said. 'What the fuck are you doing?'

I nodded at the woman. 'She's laughing at us.'

'No she's not, she's sound. Leave her alone – let's clear upstairs.'

Dave Rushton and a team of RUC police officers came rushing up. 'The back garden,' I said. 'I saw one of the fuckers jumping a wall round the back.'

We raced round and banged on the next-door house. A woman answered, her thin face pinched further with fear. Steve said, 'Did you see anything?'

She shook her head. But then, as we turned to go she called out, 'A man ran through my house and into the garden. He had a gun, but I didn't see where he went after that.'

We ran into the garden, but we knew we were going through the motions. The gunmen had long gone. But we still had to check. As we trooped our way back through the house the woman touched my arm: 'You look a bit shaky. Would you like a cup of tea?' I was trembling, in shock, but I hadn't realized it.

'No thanks,' I said, 'I'm fine.' We stopped and she poured out the tea anyway. When we'd slugged it down, a transport took me and Steve up to Musgrave Park British Army Hospital to get checked over. They took us into a small room, and a nurse came in and gave us another brew. Once I'd calmed down, a nasty thought came into my mind and refused to budge: if Dykesy hadn't persuaded me to let him drive the Land Rover half an hour earlier, then it would be me lying dead out there in the street now, instead of him.

It was weird seeing the nurse all starched and neat and normal like that. For her this was just another working day. Not for us.

She sat down and gave the pair of us the once over. 'Are you boys all right?'

I felt cold inside and it wasn't the weather. 'Fine,' I said. 'Thanks. Fine.'

Steve's face was as pale as a sheet; I bet mine was the same. 'I'm OK, too, thanks,' he said gruffly when the nurse asked him. We went back down to Andersonstown in a Land Rover. The RUC and the Army had put a strong presence out on the streets to show we weren't intimidated, to make the gunmen understand we weren't going to go away because we'd lost a couple of men. Four hours later, they sent me and Steve back out on patrol.

CHAPTER SEVEN

After that ambush, my whole idea of what was happening in Northern Ireland and what we were doing there changed forever. I'd lost good friends. I wasn't in some kind of alternative Trowbridge estate or having fun in the Tin City. These people could be as nice as pie to you one minute, and the next they'd be doing their utmost to kill you. The acorn had been planted in my brain that would grow into the habit of a lifetime: be watchful at all times. When you're least expecting trouble, that's when it will happen. I still carry the wariness I learned on the streets of Belfast with me to this day.

Given that the IRA was looking to kill as many members of the British Army as it could whenever it could, we were often stuck in barracks, sometimes quite small barracks, for long periods of time. There wasn't much to do – in most cases there wasn't even a proper gym. We'd run around the camp perimeter, stopping occasionally to do press-ups in an effort to stay fit. For entertainment, there was only the TV. Our favourite programme was *The Kenny Everett Show*. Not least because it had a regular slot featuring Hot Gossip, a troupe of slinky, sexy dancing girls who knew how to dress to impress.

To stop people going stir crazy, the Army did its best to organize outside activities, especially sports matches. For obvious reasons, these were mainly inter-unit or else against the RUC. In those days I played a lot of rugby, as second row or flanker After one match, an RUC man on the opposing team came up to us and asked, 'Do any of you play hockey?' The boys looked a bit blank – most of us came from the kind of background where you played hooky, but as to the game played with funny-shaped sticks and a ball: zip.

The RUC man looked us over. 'The thing is,' he said, 'the RUC ladies' team can't hardly get a match. They're really good – so good, not many of the other women's teams want to play them. They were thinking if they played a men's team, now, it might give them a bit of a run-out?' There was a short silence. Visions of long-limbed, athletic women in gymslips formed and took control of our collective imagination.

One of the lads piped up. 'I play hockey.' The man standing next to him said, 'I play, too.' Steve Ribton cottoned on straight away: 'And me – I love hockey. In fact, it's my favourite game.' The Skull wouldn't know the end of a hockey stick if it hit him on the head. But I could perfectly understand where the boys were coming from. I tried to make myself heard above the din. 'I'm in – put my name down on the list.' But already there were more than a dozen guys signed up ahead of me. Every bugger volunteered – the RUC man almost got buried in the rush. By the time I got a look-in, the only position left open was goalkeeper. Like Steve, I'd never played hockey in my entire life. But a chance to meet some fit, sporty ladies – now that was too good to pass up.

A couple of weeks later, we went off to play the match. As always, we travelled under armed escort. Army regulations banned independent travel outside the 'ring of steel' except when on official duty. The ring of steel was the fenced and patrolled security area in the heart of Belfast that enclosed the main commercial and shopping area. To get in, you had to go through a turnstile. You were searched for weapons and bombs and you had to show your ID. Once inside, life was reasonably normal. On this trip, the idea was for the coach and its driver to wait at the venue while we had a post-match drink with the ladies, and then take us back to camp under escort in the same way. The hockey pitch was next door to the White Forge Club, an RUC social club in South Belfast.

We took to the field and sized up the opposition. Now we were here, the ladies looked a lot less long-limbed and lissom than they had in our fevered imaginations. They looked businesslike. Formidable. Not to say, tough as old boots. We bullied off, which is apparently what you do to start a hockey game. Just as I'd feared, I'd put my name down so late I had to play in goal. I'd never played hockey before in my life. And now I was trying to defend it, the goal looked a whole lot bigger.

About ten seconds later, a rock-hard hockey ball came whizzing out of nowhere and hit me like a bullet on the inside of the right thigh. The ball had travelled so fast I hadn't even seen it. It stung so much it made my eyes water. I stood there moaning and groaning and rubbing the spot. The lady who'd hit it was standing in front of me with a big grin on her face. 'Are you all right?' she asked.

'Fine,' I told her through gritted teeth. 'You've only gone and broken my leg.' I picked the ball up out of the goal where it had ricocheted and chucked it back to her. She was anxious to get on with the game. I was anxious to get on with the post-match festivities.

'You know,' she said in a concerned voice, 'you really should be wearing some protection.'

'You're telling me,' I said. All I had between me and terminal injury was a set of football-style shin pads under my long woollen socks. My army boots were about as much use as a crutch in a swamp against high-speed hockey balls. Worse, I had no protection for the most important bits: my undercarriage and face.

The centre-forward person who'd already half-crippled me was still hanging about. 'I can't do anything till half-time,' she said. 'But then I'll go and see if there's anything in the pavilion for you.'

'I might be dead by then,' I said. She laughed and went back to the game.

I'd been joking, but it was no joke: by half-time I was a mass of bruises, up and down both legs, across my chest and arms, everywhere. Not only that, but the RUC ladies were 13–0 ahead: they were nasty, vicious, venomous women, and they were having the time of their lives. They kept firing these bloody bullets at me. I kept trying to stop them, or failing that, which was most of the time, at least get out of the way. At half-time, bless her, the opposing goalkeeper came up with a set of cricket pads and, wonder of wonders, a cricket box to protect my wedding tackle. But I still got battered – and the team with me. The final score when the women had done drubbing us was 28–0.

I hobbled back to the pavilion to shower and change, then joined the others in the bar. Finally, a game I could enjoy. But the RUC ladies didn't seem all that interested in socializing; quite a few of them were married to RUC officers. Still, where there's life there's hope: the White Forge Club had a disco on that night. Steve Ribton was flying wingman with me, as usual. 'Shall we take in the disco, Skull?' I suggested. 'See what's what?'

He shook his skeletal head. 'I'm stony, Mike – down to my last 50p. You?'

I shook my head sadly. 'The same – broke. Not a penny to my name.'

'We might as well go back to camp on the bus,' Steve said forlornly. 'There's not much point staying here if we can't even buy a drink.'

I looked around. There was a one-arm bandit standing to the right of the bar. It looked lonely and underused. 'Tell you what, Steve, why don't we chuck that 50 pence of yours in the fruit machine? You never know your luck.'

We walked over. It was your standard fruit machine: feed it money, pull the handle and hope you line up three of a kind. The jackpot was £100. To win it, we needed three of the '£' symbols in a row. Skull put the money in; I yanked. The fruit and the £ signs spun round on the tin wheels. The first drum clicked to a stop: it was a '£' symbol. A second '£' symbol slid into place alongside it. Steve nudged my arm. 'Hey up!' We all knew how fruit machines worked: they gave you the promise of riches, then snatched it cruelly away. Could this be the exception that proved the rule? A third '£' symbol dropped into the win bracket. There was a strange, gurgling sound, as if the machine was clearing its mechanical throat. Then it began to cough money. One pound coins spat out and rattled into the tray, filling it to the brim and then spilling over. We stepped in and caught the overflow, amazed. Steve shouted, 'Fuck me, we've won! Mike, we've won!' above the noise.

'Steve,' I yodelled back, 'we're rich! Rich! One hundred pounds! Steve, we've won a hundred pounds!'

In those days, it was a small fortune. I grabbed the Skull by the arm and we did a little jig. By now, the coin tray was full, there were £1 coins all over the floor and the whole place had ground to a stop, watching as the one-arm bandit spewed all those lovely metal drinking vouchers. We scooped up the money, stuffed it in our pockets and lugged it across to the bar. The barman beamed at us. 'I suppose you boys would be wanting a drink, would you? To celebrate your winnings?'

'Two pints of lager, please,' Steve said. 'And no crisps.'

We had a few drinks, the evening wore on and the music started up in the disco next door. 'Come on,' I told Steve, 'our luck's in tonight, we can't fail.' High on our winnings, we sauntered through and sat down. I had the strong impression that most of the women in the place were eyeing us up. Obviously the fact they knew we were loaded had nothing to do with that. I looked across the room and my gaze met a lovely pair of sparkling eyes. Luckily, they belonged to a girl. She was dancing with another girl, but still. She had a pretty face, dark, tumbling hair that fell to her shoulders in loose curls, long legs – there were two of them – her own teeth and a couple of other attractive features. All nicely packaged in a short red dress. I was attracted. No, smitten.

Whether my eyes sparkled back I can't say – they should have done, because by now I'd certainly had enough to drink. They must have done something, because the next thing I knew we were sitting at a table together, talking. My new friend had a lovely twang to her voice and she was great fun to be with.

'Julie.' She held out her hand. 'Julie Murray.'

A secretary in a psychiatric practice, she was from a third-generation Scottish immigrant family. Her dad was a staunch Protestant and to prove it the family lived in Dundonald, East Belfast. I'd immediately forgotten about Steve, but when I looked round he was doing all right for himself with Julie's mate.

We had a bit of bop and then the slow dance came on, which is generally a sign that it's time to go. It was time to go; I knew this because our corporal, Dave Rushton, came up to the table: 'Come on lads, the transport's waiting. It's time we got back.'

I said, 'Scouse, we've got a lift with these two women we've met. We'll get back to camp under our own steam. I know it's asking a lot, but can you keep it quiet?'

Instead of working the stipulated two hours on/four hours off 'stag' or guard duty, our brick had worked twelve hours on the trot, swapping spells with the other half-section so as to get a full 24 hours off. The guys we'd swapped with were now manning the sangars, doing their twelve hours: even if we got back to Glassmullan really late, they should let us in without any problem. Dave was taking a bit of a chance breaking regs, we all were, but he nodded like the good bloke he was. 'OK – but watch your backs – the Provos love half-pissed soldiers wandering around the city alone and unarmed in the middle of the night.'

We nodded. 'OK, Scouse. Don't worry – Julie here will look after us.' Julie had a car. The idea was she'd give us a lift back to the centre of Belfast and from there we could catch the Army shuttle back to barracks, no problem.

Dave went off with the other lads to board the transport. Just then, the sound system struck up with 'God Save the Queen'. We stared into the bottom of our empty glasses. I was thinking it would be great if we had a decent national anthem, something that really made you want to get up and sing. To our surprise, there was an almighty scraping of chairs. Every other bugger in the club was on their feet at full attention, gazing loyally ahead with their right hands pressed flat across the heart. Steve and I sat there, waiting. The anthem finished. A shadow fell across the table. We looked up. Four very large men were looming over us. One of them bellowed: 'Why didn't youse fuckers stand up for the Queen?' I glanced at Steve, hoping for help. Like me, he'd lost his tongue. They moved a step closer. They didn't look at all happy.

'You're a pair of disloyal little bastards, so you are. I tell you what we should do – we should take the pair of you outside and give youse a good beating. Teach you to show some respect for the Crown.' A good many seconds ticked by, while our physical well-being hung in the balance. Then, to our massive relief, the four did an about face and stalked off, shaking their heads in disgust.

'I think it's time you left,' Julie said, helpfully. That was a bit of an understatement. We got into her car and Steve disappeared into the night with her mate. Julie and I got down to business. We were in the middle of having a snog when Steve's long, bony head appeared at the driver's side window. His date had gone home, and there was safety in numbers. Julie said, 'I can't really take you back into the city, you know – if they catch me they'll know I'm a Prod.' I realized she was right. If they stopped her, the Provos would know she was a Protestant right away. Just as I could tell whether people lived in East or West Cardiff from their accents, so the Catholics and Protestants in Belfast had no problem telling one another apart. And once she'd dropped us off, she'd have to drive back through the city alone.

'It's OK,' I said, 'we've got loads of money left. We'll get a taxi.' We swapped phone numbers and Julie set off home.

By now, it was past midnight. I tend to live life on the assumption that things will go all right. Which is fine until they go wrong. Like now. We tried to get a taxi. All the taxi firms we called laughed, told us we must be kidding and put the phone down. It meant driving through the heart of Provo territory, which was something they never did. We were stuck. Finally, a solo minicab operator agreed to take us – but only from the White Forge Club to the edge of Andersonstown. He'd drop us off there and we'd have to walk the last mile or so to the camp.

Needless to say, this was a mad, bad and dangerous idea. The IRA had wormed its way into the city's taxi network. If you were Catholic the fare was minimal: for about 30p you could go as far as you liked. In one way it was a kind of social service, hearts and minds stuff, and given the city's transportation system much needed – not least because the Provos kept hijacking and burning the Corporation buses. The problem for us was that some of the drivers prowling the city were eyes and ears for the IRA. Our hair and clothing screamed, 'British squaddie'. If one of the taxi touts spotted a couple of young, short-haired lads wandering about and radioed it in, then it would be the IRA counting out a jackpot for the evening and not us.

Our minicab turned up. The driver was really nervous about picking up two soldiers. He kept peering out into the darkness, as if expecting an ambush at any second. But he drove us to the agreed spot on the edge of Andytown and stopped. I looked at Steve. It wasn't all that far to the camp now – about a mile and a half as the crow flew. But we both knew the chances of trouble were high. By now it was getting on for one in the morning.

I leaned forward to talk to the driver. 'Look, if you'll take us a bit closer, we'll give you ten pounds extra on the fare.' At the time, a tenner was a lot of money.

He shook his head: 'It's not worth it: I'm a Protestant cab driver in a Catholic area. You know how the black taxis work. If they catch me, I'm dead meat.'

Tricky. I tried my best persuasive voice. 'Go on – we'll seriously look after you.'

He thought about it for a bit. Then he said, 'Tell you what: I'll take you another mile – to the Busy Bee and that's it.'

The Busy Bee was a shopping centre half a mile from Glassmullan barracks where the IRA had mortared us one time when we were out on patrol. I said, 'Great – but by the time you turn round and loop back from the Busy Bee, you'll be going up the Springfield Road anyway. You can drop us off near the barracks and then you can make a break for it.'

He looked at me doubtfully. 'You'll get us all killed,' he said, but he gamely put the car into gear and we set off. We'd just started rolling when he looked in his mirror. 'There's a black cab following us,' he said, the words tumbling out in a rush. 'Hold on – I'm going to speed up.' He had a fairly new Ford Cortina, which could shift a bit. He put his foot down and we shot forward. 'Jesus,' he said, 'Christ.' He was watching in the rear-view mirror more than he was watching the road. 'They're coming after us,' he jabbered, 'they're coming after us!' I glanced back. Sure enough, the black taxi was racing along behind, hammering hard on our heels.

'Don't worry,' I said, 'it'll be OK.' Sometimes I wonder where I get all the optimism. The cabbie, meanwhile, had gone dead quiet. He was gripping the steering wheel as if it was his last chance of life, knuckles gleaming white with the force of his grip. We screeched around a corner. Glassmullan barracks suddenly appeared on our right, coming towards us at high speed. But our driver had forgotten about us. All he wanted to do was shake off the taxi and get clear of Provo turf. I shouted, 'Hang on, that's the camp! Slow down, we have to get out!' To my relief, he slowed. I flung him an extra fiver on top of the indicated fare; it wasn't the tenner I'd promised, I couldn't find one in the rush. But he was out of there so fast I don't think he even noticed the money.

We shot out and legged it as fast as we could towards the main gate. The black cab hurtled round the corner behind us, hit the revs and arrowed straight for us. I was praying no one would lean out of it: open up on us with an Armalite or chuck a hand grenade. We reached the gate and battered at the huge sheets of wriggly tin. Steve was shouting: 'Let us in! Let us in!' at the top of his voice.

Our driver didn't waste any time: already the Cortina was no more than a set of red tail lights speeding off into the darkness. The black taxi slowed as it drew level and the driver leaned out. He gave us the standard Bogside hard look. We were outside an army barracks shouting to be let in: you didn't have to be Einstein to work out what we did for a living. He picked up his radio mike and started talking in to it. At that moment, the wicket gate swung back a couple of inches and a suspicious-looking trooper holding an SLR ready for action glanced out. 'Ribton and Flynn,' he said. 'Might have known it would be you two. Get inside, quick.' When he saw the weapon, the black cab driver floored it and shot away.

To this day, I don't know if our own cabbie made it back to safety, but it's a pretty good bet he did. No reports of murdered minicab drivers popped up in the local paper next day.

That was the kind of thing eighteen-year-old British Army soldiers got up to at the height of the Troubles, or at least it was the kind of thing me and Steve did. The lure of Julie brought me out to Dundonald many a time, always and strictly against Army regulations. I'd be lying on the sofa with Julie, canoodling and watching *Match of the Day* – women really appreciate men making the effort to multi-task like that on a Saturday night – when I'd get this odd, stinging wave of guilt. My mates were out on patrol or doing duty back in camp, and here I was in civvies leading the life of Riley, snuggled up in the arms of my girl. It was my free time and I'd earned it, but still it felt somehow wrong, like bunking off school. Even today, when I come back from a tour of Afghanistan, a part of me feels the same unease: the other guys are still out there, carrying the fight at risk of their lives, while I'm on the sofa watching *Match of the Day*. As you go along in the Army and the whole thing of working as a unit starts to kick in, you can start to feel a strong sense of collective responsibility.

The loss of my two friends Tony Thornett and Anthony Dykes was something that didn't really make any sense to me. I knew the extremist

Republicans hated us – but enough to murder two young blokes in cold blood?

It became a lot easier to understand why some people loathed the British Army so much when we were out on patrol a couple of weeks later. It was late, and for once the midnight city was quiet and calm. We came to a row of shops topped with flats. At the back of the shops was a grotty little access road for deliveries; on the far side of that I made out a row of lock-up garages. Lock-ups were always of interest to foot patrols: bad people stored things in them – things like arms, ammunition, explosives and money. We walked across to check them out. One of the gloomy garages was standing open. As we drew near it we heard an odd rustling sound. That particular night we were patrolling as a two-brick section of eight. The corporal in overall charge was a big, beefy John Bull character named Ross West. I knew West from playing rugby. He was large, he was aggressive and he was a bully. He never gave me any grief – he knew I'd stand up to him if he tried anything on. But still I didn't like him one little bit. Unless we were on duty together I steered clear. Luckily, our brick was only rarely teamed with West's. Tonight we'd drawn the short straw. Whenever this happened our own corporal, Dave Rushton, did his best to keep West under control. But even Dave, who was no lightweight, struggled.

West was leading the section from the front. As we neared the doorway where the noise was coming from, he held up his hand. The rustling stopped. We shone our torches into the dark mouth of the lock-up. There were two young kids in there, sixteen or seventeen, obviously boyfriend and girlfriend. We'd interrupted them in the middle of doing what boyfriends and girlfriends tend to do.

'Who are you?' West demanded. 'What the fuck are you doing? Show me your ID.' He shone his torch in the lad's face. We each carried a book of snapshots that featured known IRA members, their known associates and in some cases family members. This kid's face was in the book. He was from a big, pro-IRA family whose members were suspected of aiding and abetting illegal activity.

West called Zero, Squadron Headquarters: 'This is Patrol One Zero. We have stopped and are interrogating a suspect, name so-and-so. Request P-check.' A P-check was a personal identification check. Zero checked the Vengeful database. Vengeful was the all-seeing, all-knowing intelligence system used to log and monitor IRA activity. The youth had told us the truth – the address and the other details he'd given West checked out. It was obvious he wasn't up to anything illegal. On the contrary, he was only doing what we all wished we were doing instead of clumping round the city in our DMS boots in the middle of the night on some manky patrol. Vengeful came back: 'He's a P One stop – hold him there and find out everything you can about him.' A 'P One' meant the youth was priority one, at the top of the list when it came to making checks and gathering intelligence. Bad luck for him.

West grabbed the lad by the shirt front. He leaned up close. 'What are you doing here? Are you storing weapons in this lock-up? Ammunition? Does she carry the stuff for you under her skirt?' He nodded and leered at the girl.

The lad's girlfriend was getting more and more upset. All of a sudden she piped up: 'I'm going.' He said, 'You're not going alone, I'm going with you.'

'Shut the fuck up!' West barked. 'You're not going anywhere: the pair of you are staying right here until I tell you otherwise.' The lad turned, took his girl by the arm and started to walk away. West stepped sideways, drew his arm back and smacked the kid flush on the side of the jaw. West was big and the kid was slightly built – he crumpled to the ground in a heap. The girl started to scream. West turned and slapped her hard across the face. She stopped screaming and started crying. It made a sharp, bitter sound that went right through me.

The suspect struggled to his feet. He was dazed but he was as game as you like, he squared up to West and started trying to have a go. Game, but extremely unwise. Another man in West's brick grabbed the lad by the throat, rammed him up against the garage wall and held him there. While he was helpless, West planted a flurry of vicious, pile-driver blows into the kid's ribs and stomach, rounding it off with a couple of smacks in the face. I'd been watching our 'six', or rear aspect – that was what you were supposed to do when the first brick was conducting an arrest. Except that they weren't, they were conducting an exercise in bullying.

By this time, I'd seen enough. There was no need for any violence – all we had to deal with was a courting couple. All right, the lad was from a suspect family, but that didn't mean he was Public Enemy Number One. This wasn't about my coming from a Catholic background or anything like that: what was happening in front of me was plain wrong on any level.

'Hey, Russ – this is wrong,' I said. 'There's no point in slapping him around. Just ask them what they're doing here and let's get on.' I was nineteen years old and a junior trooper. He was a full corporal in his mid-twenties.

'You,' he snarled, 'can keep your fucking mouth shut.'

With that, he hauled off and gave the kid another bang in the face. The guy was in bits, his nose was bleeding heavily and he looked as if he had at least one broken rib. Breathing heavily with the effort of smacking up a young kid, West grabbed the radio and transmitted: 'Suspect is resisting arrest, we're bringing him in.' For the detainee, this outcome made things even worse: given his background, in all likelihood Zero would send him to sample the tender loving mercies of the local RUC interrogation team. At that time we'd arrest people and when they heard they were being sent for interrogation they'd crap themselves on the spot.

As usual we had a floating 'satellite' or back-up Land Rover circling the area. We called the satellite in and they lifted the kid. Because of our gallant leader's aggression, the incident had escalated from a harmless snog in a lock-up to a violent, unnecessary drama.

Three days later, we went to do what we called the 'early knocks'. The first and most important early knock was at the family home of the kid we'd arrested. It was three o'clock in the morning, which definitely meets my definition of early. The idea of early knocks was to inconvenience and harass targets, catch them at it if they were wrongdoing, catch them red-handed planning mayhem or handling explosives, whatever. Imagine how much the local population loved us when we forced them out of bed at gunpoint in the small hours. Often the women would be scantily dressed. We'd examine their personal belongings, chuck their clothes and possessions about the place, even rummage through the contents of their underwear drawers in the search for weapons and ammo, or for any sign they were mixed up with the IRA. Hearts and minds; hearts and fucking minds

We reached the kid's address. The corporal in charge of the search just about bashed the door off its hinges. Then, with the family shouting abuse from the hallway, he read the search warrant out loud: 'Acting on information received, as members of Her Majesty's Forces we have authority to gain access to your premises . . .' We clattered in. They were yelling: 'You fucking Brit bastards, fuck off! Why are you doing this?'

It was a good question. One that I certainly couldn't answer.

It felt wrong: when the British Army first went into Catholic areas of Northern Ireland, they were seen as protectors – the locals made them cups of tea and handed them biscuits. In the years since then, they'd come to hate us, and all because we were going at it the wrong way.

The kid we'd arrested was upstairs in bed. He had a black eye and a broken nose and he was in a very sorry state. Nobody roughed him up any more: West wasn't with us that morning, thank God. Even so, the hatred in the stares of the people in the house was enough to freeze the blood. The boy's mother was yelling blue murder, the father was swearing and ranting, there were young children all over the place crying and wailing. The whole place was in an uproar.

The violence meted out at the lock-up was untypical in my experience of Northern Ireland. But I knew from listening to barrack-room chat that incidents like it happened only too often. The whole town knew we were 'donkey soldiers', as they called us, because of our Blues and Royals cap badges.

Not all that long a time later, on 20 July 1982, the IRA targeted our regiment with a booby-trap bomb in Hyde Park. The nail bomb was concealed in a blue Austin car. The bombers detonated it as a troop of Blues and Royals from Knightsbridge barracks made their way along Rotten Row. It killed three troopers outright. A fourth died later of his injuries. The device also killed seven horses and injured seventeen innocent bystanders. A second bomb exploded under a bandstand in Regent's Park a short time after the first. A Royal Green Jackets band was playing music from the show *Oliver* to an audience of tourists and office workers. The explosion killed several bandsmen and injured dozens of spectators. Sometimes, some units overstepped the mark in Northern Ireland. But could anything we'd done to the population justify cold-blooded carnage like that?

CHAPTER EIGHT

The Army sent me back to Detmold at the end of June 1979. The squadron had to get the Chieftain tanks ready for the Lifeguards, who were taking over duty in Germany. Pretty quickly, I discovered that everyday life on a tank squadron in Germany was really, really boring. We'd get up in the morning still half-drunk from the night before and line up on first parade; march down the vehicle park; work on the tanks all day; come back from the vehicle park; get washed; have some scoff; go down the NAAFI and have a few drinks; carry on into town and get completely pissed; have a fight; come back; go to sleep; get up; line up on first parade; go down the vehicle park; work on the tanks all day; come back from the vehicle park. Then we'd get washed; have some scoff; go down the NAAFI and have a few drinks ... At the weekend, the only difference was you got up at 1130, had brunch ...

There were three regiments of men quartered in the small town of Detmold alone. The chances of finding attractive female company were almost nil. A few people ended up going out with some serious gronks, any port in a storm. There's no telling what the local women thought of us.

We lived for an exercise – that tells you how bad things were, but even those were mostly repetitive: if it didn't break down on the way, you'd park the Chieftain out of sight on the side of the hill, wait for the 'enemy' to come down the valley on the other side, pop up over the ridge, open fire, kill all the enemy tanks and then get back down out of sight.

Why was there always so much work to do on the tanks? Because the MoD in its wisdom had negotiated a British Leyland input on the Chieftain's L60 engine. Rolls-Royce had designed and built the original unit, but BL engineered the engine so badly it was constantly leaking oil. You only had to look at the damn thing and it would start spurting diesel. We were constantly busy repairing gaskets and flanges, stripping the L60 down and reassembling it, trying to make these horribly-manufactured bits of metal stick together and work. Personally, I never wondered why the politicians had to stay on the right side of countries in the Middle East – we needed all their oil to make our tanks run.

In an effort to escape the boring routine, I took up rugby again. You still got drunk and had a fight afterwards, but at least you had a game and a bit of a runabout in the fresh air first. It was on the rugby field that I met another lifelong friend, Ray Dobie. Smallish with blond hair, Ray had been in the term below mine at Pirbright, but I'd never got to know him. He was from a similar background to mine: working-class council estate, only he'd grown up on the streets of Speke, near Liverpool.

A qualified physical training instructor, Ray reminded me really, really strongly of the bonkers Mel Gibson character in the first *Lethal Weapon* movie, mainly because of his dodgy shoulder. Ray was good at rugby, especially when it came to throwing a long pass. The only trouble was if he threw the ball too hard his right shoulder would pop out. He'd stand there with his arm hanging loose, yelling for someone – usually me – to help him put it back in. I'd grab his forearm and hold it while Ray worked the shoulder joint back into place.

It was a big relief when we all got posted back to Combermere barracks in Windsor early in 1980. At least now if we got bored we'd be on home turf. And in Windsor it was a lot harder to get bored: there were plenty of nice pubs and a steady supply of nice women to be found in them.

We formed a drinking gang centred on the White Swan that included Klaus Fisher, Steve Ribton, Gary Birch, Dave Voyce and later on Pete Fugate. We were all the same rank, and all about the same age.

Klaus Fisher was a really good soldier, excellent at any job you gave him. His real name was Jeremy Fisher, but because he was big and squarely built, and we thought he looked like a Prussian storm-trooper, we started to call him Klaus. Eventually he took to the nickname, and began to introduce himself as 'Klaus von Fisher'. It sounded impressive – better than Jeremy, anyway. Klaus kept getting promoted, but because he was a drama on the piss, he'd get busted back down again. Tall and ginger-haired, Klaus was absolutely, totally, 100 per cent dependable. Until he'd drunk half a bottle of Black Smirnoff, that is, at which point he turned into a social hand grenade. If you mixed Klaus in with just about any bunch of people and enough alcohol, pretty soon bits would start to fly in every direction.

Dave Voyce was known for having short arms and deep pockets. When it was his turn to buy a round he quite often seemed to go missing. One day, out on the gunnery range, Dave forgot he was standing directly in front of a Scimitar's gun barrel. Without thinking, he swivelled round and walked slap, bang into the muzzle. It raised a perfectly circular, 30mm lump on the left side of his forehead. Instead of going down as it healed, the lump started to grow, until Dave ended up with a kind of small, flattened horn of bone sticking out of his head, exactly like a cow's horn when it's been sheared off. Later on, Dave whacked the other side of his head on something else that was hard and unyielding, and a second baby horn grew out of his forehead on the right side. It was smaller than the first horn, but at least it evened him up a bit.

Gary Birch had a sharp face and a sharp Scouse wit that made him a frontrunner in the never-ending contest to see who could pull the most women. Once he had them laughing, females turned to putty in his hands. I used to stand off and pick up points when Gary was on top form.

Pete Fugate, who always reminded me of an old-fashioned Victorian policeman, came to Windsor from Knightsbridge barracks with a whole wodge of other blokes. Their forced transfer was part of the toxic fallout that hit the regiment when the *News of the World* published details of the alleged 'tykeing' scam. The newspaper ran a story alleging that to boost their pay, some of our soldiers were offering the youngest, best-looking lads to older gay men in the pubs and clubs of Knightsbridge and Mayfair. When they got a nibble on the hook, they'd take the punter for as much food and drink as they could, then they'd take him to a nice quiet place, withdraw the offer of young male flesh and make off with his money. As far as I'm aware, Pete Fugate had nothing to do with the tykeing, but he got moved in the general clear-out with all the others.

During one of the Saturday evening sessions later on that year, a few of us went down to the Knights Tavern opposite Windsor Castle for a change of scene. I was propping up the bar minding my own business when a tall, pretty, long-legged blonde woman in grey furry-top boots came into the pub with a friend. Our eyes met and she smiled. I looked round to see if there was a rich, handsome bloke standing behind me, but the blonde was smiling at me, so I smiled back. She really was tall, only a little shorter than me. I offered to buy her a drink and she accepted. When I asked her what her name was she told me 'Denise'. Denise and I hit it off straight away: we must have done, in no time at all we were going out together.

In 1981 Denise fell pregnant. We got married in haste as you did back then, but the baby miscarried. We'd had a proper wedding ceremony – parents, church, the works – but the marriage felt somehow wrong from the off. At twenty-one, I was still a baby, still a bit too young to know my own mind. You have to be incredibly lucky to meet the love of your life at that age and get it to stick.

Denise and I were only married for a few months. We separated eighteen months later, in the New Year of 1982. The solicitor I talked to told me it would cost £500 to get divorced right away, or £300 if we waited two years. On a trooper's pay and more or less constantly broke, I naturally leaned towards the second option. While I was still hesitating about what to do, I met a legal clerk in Windsor courthouse. She listened to my sorry tale, and then took me under her wing: 'You can divorce your wife yourself, you know.'

'Really? How?'

'Wait here. I'll just go and get you the forms.' She disappeared for a couple of minutes, came back and handed me a sheaf of paperwork. 'All you have to do is fill these forms in correctly, get your wife to sign them, lodge them with the court and it won't cost you a thing. You'll still have to wait for a couple of years, but at least you won't have to pay so much money.' I filled in the forms, Denise and I parted on good terms, we handed back the married quarter, divided up the record collection and that was that.

Or so I thought.

It was all above board and in the open, by mutual consent, and with both families kept fully informed. If not, in the case of my mother, in full agreement. I moved back into Combermere barracks in January 1982 and fell straight back into the classic routine of the single soldier: out drinking every night, constantly chasing women – a completely irresponsible way of life and looking back on it not very grown-up. I still needed to learn a basic degree of self-respect. And there's nothing like going to war to help you learn it.

CHAPTER NINE

I was lying in bed with Rachel one morning when the telephone rang outside in the corridor. Rachel was my steady girlfriend after the split with Denise. I watched in appreciation as she got up to answer it. It was Saturday, 3 April 1982, and in bed with Rachel was a very pleasant place to be – whether or not she was in her nurse's uniform.

It was Keith, a mate of mine from B Squadron on the other end of the line. There was an unusual note of excitement in Keith's voice: you can hear these things better on the telephone. 'Mick,' he said, 'you've got to get back here – the squadron's been detailed off to go to the Falklands.'

I started laughing. 'Yes, and you can fuck off if you think I'm falling for that one.'

'No, Mick, seriously,' Keith said. 'Haven't you been watching the news?'

I knew Keith knew I was with Rachel, I assumed he was winding me up. 'Pull the other one, mate – it's got bells on.' Maybe he was bored and he'd decided to try for a late April Fool's joke? At any rate, he wasn't going to fool me that easily. After a couple more tries at convincing me to report back for duty, Keith gave up and put the phone down. Rachel and I picked up where we'd left off. We didn't even make it to first base: one minute later, the phone rang again.

'Seriously, Mick, you've got to get back to Windsor right away. Put the TV on and watch the news.'

'The news is, Keith, I'm here in bed with Rachel and you're in the barracks on duty. Go away and play with your drill boots.'

It got rid of him again, but his voice had sounded flat that time, deadly serious. I reached across and switched on the set. Sure enough, there was a news flash on ITV: the Royal Marines detachment on the Falkland Islands was lying face down on a road with a bunch of raggle-taggle Argentine soldiers standing over them trying to look hard for the camera. A tiny worm of doubt started to turn in my mind. I'd never heard of the Falkland Islands, let alone been aware they were British. At first, I thought the announcer was talking about Falkirk in Scotland. But Keith was on duty that day. And the Marines lying face down in the dirt like that didn't look good: in fact, what was happening to them was extremely annoying. Suppose he wasn't having me on after all? The telephone rang for the third time. When that happened I knew this was the last big, comfy bed I'd be sleeping in for a long time.

When the news we were going to the Falklands came through, the squadron had just moved me from SHQ Troop to 4 Troop. I was standing in the NAAFI queue one lunchtime when Ray Dobie came up to me.

'You just got my job,' he said. 'And I want it back.'

I stared at him, mystified. 'What job?'

'The one you just took as Paul Stretton's gunner. That was my job until four days ago. Now you've got it.'

We sat down. Paul Stretton was 4 Troop's Corporal of Horse. I'd only recently met Stretton and I didn't really like him. He took the piss out of everyone. As a new Scorpion gunner I made my share of mistakes, which gave Stretton the opportunity to make me look foolish. His put-downs were often very funny, but that only made them more cutting. He'd had a touch of polio when he was younger, and it came back to hound him from time to time. The fact that he walked with a bit of a limp didn't stop him being an excellent gunnery instructor.

'Why did they move you?'

'I'm due to go on a course,' he said. 'It came up at the wrong time.'

We all wanted to go to war, otherwise there wasn't much point in joining the army. 'Sorry mate,' I said. 'There's fuck-all either of us can do about it.' We got talking about other things

In those days there wasn't all the lead-up time there is now before a unit deploys in theatre. In this case, there was hardly any warning at all: only eight or nine days from that Saturday morning phone call, I was boarding a ship for the Falklands. There was so much to do and so little time to do it that unless their families lived in or near Windsor, most people couldn't even go home and say a proper goodbye to their loved ones.

The next day I rang my mam and dad. My mother answered.

'I'm off to war, Mam. They're sending me to the Falklands.'

'I saw those Royal Marines on the television – what a shocking thing.'

We talked a bit about how the family were getting on. Then, after a pause, my mother said: 'Look after yourself, Michael, won't you?'

'Don't worry, Mam,' I said breezily, 'I'll be fine.'

She said, 'Here's your dad, he wants to talk to you.'

My father came on the phone. After we'd compared notes on the weather, he said: 'Do like your Mam says and take care of yourself down there.'

'I will, Dad. Drink a pint of Brains for me down the Fox.' The Fox and Hounds in St Mellons was Dad's local, Brains Brewery's Best was the house beer. It still is the best, but I'm not convinced it makes you any more intelligent.

I did honestly believe I'd come back from the South Atlantic safely. It was my first proper war, the only thing I really felt was excitement: it never occurred to me I might come to harm. There was a massive buzz around Combermere barracks: everyone was pumped up, there were people flying about all over the place on urgent missions. We were getting lectures and extra shooting practice, collecting our winter kit, packing everything up ready for the off. Within the week, we were on board the *Canberra* and steaming south.

In civilian life, the *Canberra* was a floating hotel for rich people. I'd always wanted to go on a winter cruise, but I'd never been able to afford one. Now, the Army was billeting me on a lovely big ocean liner – for free. And what a liner: she had chandeliers and marble staircases, opulent lounges and bars on almost every deck; there was a big swimming pool amidships, a theatre, a gym, it took at least a day to walk around the monster; there were loads of restaurants, cafés and bars and more than 2,000 cabins. Sadly, the ship was minging with blokes and they closed all the bars for the duration. I half-expected in-cruise entertainment, but that had been pulled along with the alcohol. The Great White Whale, as we called her, had turned into a massive troopship in the space of a few days. Engineers and welders buzzed about, beavering round the clock to install helicopter pads.

Several hundred of the *Canberra*'s civilian crew had volunteered to remain on board. Hundreds of soldiers, mainly Paras, were crammed in wherever there was room, and in some cases where it looked like there wasn't any. Space was so tight that Major Sullivan, B Squadron's OC, was refused permission to sail with us. Instead Lt Mark Coreth took command of 4 Troop, with Lt the Lord Robin Innes-Ker leading 3 Troop.

Our driver on the Scorpion was a trooper named Frankie Widowson. Frankie was a one-off: he thought sideways and out of the box about everything. With Frankie, nothing was normal, you could never have a straight-line conversation that came to a logical end. Instead, you came back to the same place where you'd started out, only slightly off to one side and trying to catch up with Frankie's unique way of reasoning. I'd get furious with him. His gear changes were so bad, the Scorpion would lurch into some obstacle Frankie had completely failed to see – and I'd end up head-butting the gun sight.

Our troop got allocated a lovely set of rooms. Superb. But then gradually, as the major units realized there were only twenty-eight of us tankies, we got bumped down the pecking order. A few days later, we found ourselves sharing quarters with the ship's Chinese laundrymen. In the laundry.

The *Canberra* sailed at 2000 hours on Good Friday, 9 April 1982. Loads of families came to see us off at Southampton docks. As we steamed south, they kept us really busy doing physical exercises, shooting practice, drills, sporting activities and all the rest. With all these crack troops on board, every bugger was trying to keep fit. You got woken at the crack of dawn by a constant thump, thump, thump from overhead, as large soldiers thudded round the upper decks. And it was the last thing you heard at night before going to sleep.

An Intelligence officer gave us a background briefing on the Falklands. He said more than 500,000 sheep lived there but only about 2,000 people. It sounded like a lot of sheep, even though I came from Wales. He also said that the weather was always unpredictable and often horrible, especially now the southern winter was coming on, and that the local economy was nothing to write home about. He said the Argentines, who called the islands 'Las Malvinas', claimed they were theirs. But the Falklanders saw themselves as Brits and were determined to stay that way. It was our job to protect the islanders and take the islands back for Britain.

Like most units on their way down to the Falklands, 4 Troop sent a letter to *The Sun* newspaper asking for female pen-pals. There must have been plenty of game girls in Britain, because pretty soon the letters started to flood in. Everybody looked forward to the intermittent mail deliveries, especially since quite a few of them contained photographs. These were mostly head-and-shoulders shots, but a fair few revealed a lot more of the women who'd sent them. In some cases, everything.

We set up two boards of photographs: a gronk board and a rude board. Gronk-board snaps were arranged in descending order, with the woman voted ugliest first. The pretty ones we guarded jealously to ourselves. Rude-board photographs were ranked according to how much they revealed.

I wanted to win both boards: I enjoy winning. There was a small amount of money riding on it, too. At first, I had no luck: some of the other guys had much uglier gronks than any of the women whose letters I opened. Then one day I ripped open an envelope from a woman in Newport. The letter began: 'I am a curvaceous blonde. I'd love to meet up with a handsome soldier.'

'Newport,' I thought, 'that's not far from Cardiff. Curvaceous sounds good. Blonde sounds good. And I'm obviously handsome. I'll get her to send in a photograph. You never know, she might be a looker. Maybe we can meet up when I get back on leave.'

Newport woman wrote again, this time enclosing a snap of herself. I stood holding it for a moment. Then I let out a whoop and ran for the board. 'Look at this crocadillapig! You lot have had it, the gronk board's mine!' The rest of the lads gathered round. There was an awed silence. Then Frankie Widowson said, 'He's right – that's the ugliest woman I've ever seen. She's got two heads.'

'She's got more bellies than the Michelin Man,' Gary Birch said. 'And she's fatter. Awesome.'

Klaus Fisher reached for the photograph. 'Give it here, Mike, I'll stick her at the top of the board.'

A couple of days later, I got lucky again. I opened a letter from a woman in Slough and out fell a batch of Polaroid photographs. They left absolutely nothing to the imagination. In fact, they revealed things about the female anatomy that were new to me. I pinned them up on the rude board. The lads gathered round to look. There was another respectful silence. 'Rudest photographs I've ever seen,' said Frankie Widowson. 'How the fuck did she manage to get her legs like that?'

I won both boards. I was well chuffed.

We made a pit-stop at Freetown, Sierra Leone for fuel and water. Lots of the locals came up alongside the ship in little wooden bumboats and canoes. They started shouting and holding stuff up for us to see, trying to sell us everything from wooden masks and carvings to jewellery, parrots and even small monkeys.

We were all pretty bored, but no one wanted to buy a parrot. The food on board was fairly decent. After a while, one of the Paras picked up a deckchair, held it carefully over one of the canoes and dropped it. The canoe rocked from side to side and started filling up with water. The bloke in it started yelling and screaming and waving his fists at the ship. Result. Suddenly, deckchairs started raining down on the bum-boats from a great height – everyone wanted to be the first to sink one. Eventually, one of the Paras hit the side of a canoe. It capsized and went under. The new game was to try and see who could sink the most. We were just getting into the swing of it when an officer came running along, flapping his arms and shouting. 'What do you men think you're doing? Stop that at once!' We stopped. But not before we'd sunk three of the enemy canoes.

At noon on 20 April, the Great White Whale anchored half-a-mile off Ascension Island. We still didn't know whether we'd actually be landing on the Falklands, or whether the political negotiations we heard about occasionally on the news might result in a peaceful settlement. We did know we'd arrived at a hot, shitty little rock humming with troops, ships, aircraft and contractors working at top speed to transform it from a sleepy mid-Atlantic staging post into a springboard for attack on the Argies.

Now we were on the Equator, the cold-weather gear we'd all been issued with came in really handy: balaclavas, mittens, sweaters and windproofs are useful in 40°C heat. The next day, we transferred from the *Canberra* to the assault ship HMS *Fearless*. It didn't have any chandeliers or marble staircases, but it did feel a lot more warlike. On 6 May, the *Fearless* headed south from Ascension Island with the rest of the fleet. It was a strange feeling, seeing all these ships steaming south in convoy. I was part of a giant British task force the likes of which hadn't been seen since the end of the Second World War, and most likely wouldn't be seen again.

A few days later, we caught our first glimpse of the Falkland Islands. The Argie occupation forces there had already been under air and sea attack from British forces. RAF Vulcan bombers had bombed the runway at Port Stanley airfield and fired anti-radiation missiles at the enemy radar.

Next thing we heard, the fleet submarine HMS *Conqueror* fired three old-fashioned torpedoes at the Argentine cruiser *General Belgrano*. Two of the tinfish hit the enemy ship and exploded, ripping holes in her hull. The *Belgrano* sank forty minutes later, taking 368 Argies with her. That's when we knew – we were getting off the boat.

The *Fearless* dropped anchor shortly after midnight on Friday, 21 May. Later that morning, the grating noise of a buzzer alarm blared over the entire ship as it closed up for action stations, and all these Navy guys started thudding around the metal decks in their steaming boots. Lt Coreth briefed us that we'd arrived at Fanning Head, a promontory in San Carlos Water on the western side of East Falkland. Our Scorpion would be going in with the rest of 4 Troop to support the Paras. The attack was due in at dawn. Most of the enemy units were dug in around the islands' capital, Port Stanley, on the eastern side of the island about 60 kilometres away: the idea was to sneak up on their blind side. Cut off their tails and see how they ran.

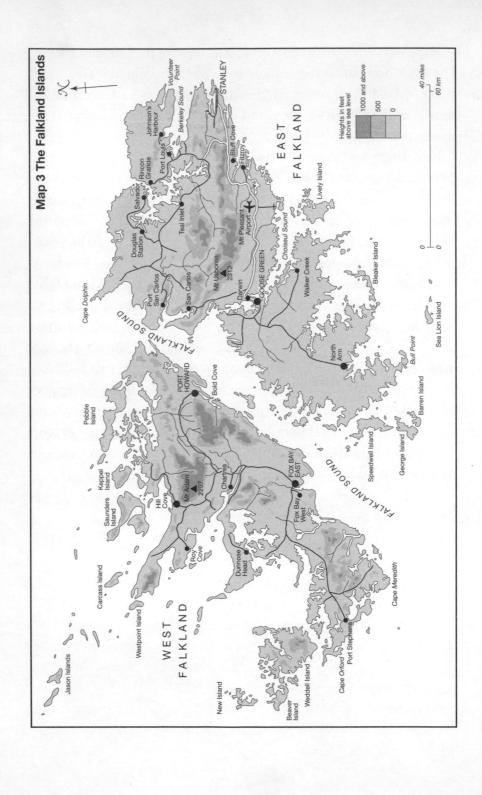

Map 3 The Falkland Islands

CHAPTER TEN

I didn't sleep much that night. I was too keyed up. When the time came to mount up on the vehicles and get in the landing craft utilities (LCUs) for landing, we all gathered round in a big bunch and shook hands. People muttered daft things like: 'See you in a bit' or 'Good luck!' It felt really stiff and awkward, but we all wanted to do it: none of us knew if or when we'd be coming back.

The *Fearless* had a rear dock that flooded, which meant that the stern doors could swing open and the landing craft could motor out. Our own Scorpion was waiting right up in the LCU's bow, with a Scimitar parked up alongside. In case of trouble on the way out, we'd use our armour and our guns to protect the Paras, who were waiting in the well of the vessel behind us. Dawn came and went, and we were still hanging about. You could feel people getting tenser and tenser: when you're due to go into action, waiting is the worst thing. Fear and loathing factor, all round. I asked Paul Stretton if he knew what the problem was. He shrugged. 'I heard the dock doors are jammed. There's no way we can get off until they fix it.'

It was dark in the assault dock – like being in a big, dimly lit metal box. We waited in silence, each with our own thoughts. I kept thinking, 'What if it's like it is in the films? Like it was at D-Day or Dunkirk? All those shells and bombs raining down, people drowning, machine guns firing straight across the beach cutting everyone to pieces?' In an effort to lighten things up, Paul Stretton started telling jokes. He was one of

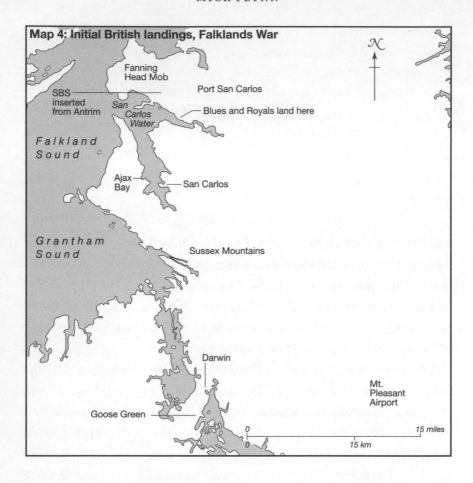

Map 4: Initial British landings, Falklands War

those people who seem to have a book of jokes in their heads, I'd always wished I could do that. But in the taut atmosphere, even Stretton's so-bad-they-were-good jokes were falling flat. Then he piped up: 'I've just remembered – it's Flynn's birthday today.' I pretended I hadn't heard him, but he called out: 'How old are you today, Mike?'

'Twenty-two,' I mumbled, 'but . . .'

'Come on, then,' Stretton said in his best Butlin's redcoat voice. 'Let's all sing Happy Birthday.' He started singing. The next thing I knew, all the Paras on the landing craft had joined in. When I heard that, a lot of my fear fell away.

Suddenly, the doors swung back. Daylight flooded in and our landing craft surged out of the dock. I looked up and saw the shingle beach directly ahead. It looked close enough to reach out and touch. The singing stopped, and we all fell quiet. I was scanning through the gun sight for enemy, my finger on the fire button, but all I could see was a barren headland: treeless brown and grey hills with the odd patch of yellowy tussock grass, hardly any houses, hardly any tracks and no cover other than the stone outcrops. It reminded me of Dartmoor.

Shells from the Royal Navy gunfire support ships whistled in over our heads. If there were any Argies out there waiting to jump us then they were wearing some heavy incoming. We powered in towards the beach. I'd been expecting a massive firefight from minute one. But there was no opposition at all. We landed on a nicely shelving bank of shingle. Neat. We'd rehearsed the assault on Ascension Island in brilliant, roasting hot weather on bone-dry rock. Now, we were landing in the teeth of a biting Antarctic wind – in mud. When the ships stopped firing, it all felt really strange, almost surreal.

'Take us up to the top of the bluff there, Frankie,' said Stretton, 'And don't hit anything on the way.' We roared up onto the higher ground behind the beach and took up an east-facing defensive position. Then 3 Para swarmed up the slope and dug in around us. We knew the enemy had strong garrisons at the settlements of Darwin and Goose Green, both less than 30 kilometres distant. If the Argies were going to put in a counterattack it would have to come from that direction. To the west we had an unbroken view of San Carlos Water, the narrow sea inlet where HMS *Fearless*, HMS *Intrepid*, the *Canberra* and a flotilla of logistics ships now lay at anchor. Several grey-painted Royal Navy escort ships were anchored to the south of them, as a screen against the expected Argie air attacks.

While we were digging in on the headland, all the available landing craft and helicopters started shuttling weapons, ammunition, supplies and troops to shore. I watched a detachment of Rapier anti-aircraft missile units come in, complete with their crews. They set them up on the high ground around us.

I heard a loud noise and looked up. A Gazelle reconnaissance heli-copter appeared about a kilometre south of our lines. I was just think-ing that it was flying a bit low and slow and too close to our front line. Suddenly I heard shooting. A four-man Argentine observation team had been guarding San Carlos settlement. Heavily outnumbered, they were retreating south in the direction of Darwin.

Bullets slammed into the Gazelle. It rolled and tried to escape. More Argie gunfire slammed into it. The pilot lost control and it crashed into the ground. The Argies kept firing at the crew, although I thought the two of them had already been killed.

Next thing, two jets roared in around the corner of the bay. They were enemy Skyhawk fighter-bombers. No doubt the enemy OP team that had shot down the Gazelle had called them in. The ships' loudspeakers were blaring, 'Air raid warning red, red, red!' It was already too late. The enemy aircraft shot in so low over the water I expected them to crash. Instead they pulled up slightly as they neared the anchorage. Black-painted bombs fell from their grey bellies. I saw one hit one of the Royal Navy escorts: amazingly, it didn't explode.

The Navy and Royal Marine gunners put up a hail of return fire. But as far as I could see it had little effect. A bomb exploded on the stern of a frigate: with enemy aircraft coming in all the time now, the ships were taking a real pasting. We had a grandstand view from our position, but there was little we could do to prevent the carnage.

Placing the Rapier anti-aircraft missile batteries up on the headland had been a mistake: the Argie pilots were making their attack runs at such low level that the Rapier units were unable to get a radar lock against the ground clutter. The Rapiers needed to be down on the beach, which was where they were later moved.

Some of the artillery lads let rip with Blowpipe shoulder-fired anti-aircraft missiles. The first Blowpipe shot out of the launcher, flew vertically up into the air and then crashed back down to earth again near the launch point.

'That's not how they're supposed to work, is it?' I asked.

'Too fucking right it isn't,' Stretton agreed. 'Much too close for comfort. Must have been a rogue round.'

The next Blowpipe missile flew straight up into the air like the first, flipped at the top of its trajectory and began arrowing straight back down. Wisely, the guy who'd fired it scarpered as fast as he could. The missile hit the ground where he'd just been standing with a loud thump. Its warhead hadn't exploded, but firing Blowpipes had just become the world's loneliest job. It turned out the units were unduly sensitive to damp. In the Falklands in winter, where it was continually dank and dripping, that really wasn't such a good thing.

Shooting down planes is much, much harder than it looks. We'd tried to hone our anti-aircraft gunnery skills on target drones, up on the Castlemartin ranges in Pembrokeshire. (Also pretty damp, as damp goes.) The drones were large model aircraft controlled by a hand-held remote. Even though they travelled very, very slowly – at about 20mph – and even when they were crossing directly in front of us at a gun-friendly height we found it very difficult to hit them with either 30mm or GPMG. The Argie planes were coming in at more than ten times that speed, at oblique angles, and very low.

I might not have taken to him at first, but as soon as we got to the Falklands I realized just how good a commander Paul Stretton really was. He was unflappable, and he always seemed to be in a good humour. I can't speak for Frankie Widowson, but I found Paul's solid reassurance really good for morale. 'We're never going to hit those fuckers,' he said, pointing at the latest pair of Skyhawks rocketing in over the sound at near-zero feet. 'But if they stray in our direction, open fire. If nothing else, it might scare the pilots.' I fired short bursts of GPMG at the scudding Skyhawks if they strayed over our way, but as far as I could tell, I never hit a thing.

But we did see one Skyhawk brought down over the anchorage that day. A Sea Wolf missile from one of our destroyers hit it. When the A-4 crashed and splashed, everyone cheered.

By the evening of day two, there were hundreds of infantry dug in around us: I'd never seen so many soldiers in one place. There was only one Argentine air raid that day; we heard they'd lost nine aircraft on day one. But next day the air strikes came back in, crippling another of the Navy escorts. I thought if things went on like they had been, then we'd have no Navy left – and the Argentines would be short an air force.

For the first three days we slept and ate on the vehicles, cramped together and freezing in the tiny space. The cold bit down into your bones. With fuel in very short supply, we had no heating. We could only run the engines for long enough to keep the batteries charged. It might have been freezing in the Scorpion, but for the infantry out in the open it was even worse: at least in our aluminium shell we had some kind of shelter from the perishing wind.

I found the whole experience incredibly exciting. Then, on the third night, we hit a low: we had a 'blue-on-blue', or friendly fire, incident. We were on standby at the rear position. It was just before dawn and the weather was worse than ever – freezing snow flurries mixed up with sleet. A patrol from 3 Para had been out probing for enemy to the east and south. The wind suddenly dropped and a thick mist came down. As he tried to come back in, the patrol commander lost his bearings. He kept reporting he was within 400 metres of our position. But when the mist broke for a moment, we could see that he wasn't. I could hear the 3 Para watchkeeper on the radio net, constantly telling the Para patrol commander officer to check his grids.

Then, four kilometres to the north, the outlying Para sentries reported two enemy patrols advancing towards our lines. They said they were sure they were Argies. To neutralize the threat, 3 Para called in a fire mission. The artillery had been waiting to fire the 105mm guns. Now they had the chance.

The first salvo screeched overhead. As soon as the shells exploded, the lost patrol commander came back up on air: 'Contact! Enemy artillery fire.' Then he fell silent. Brigade told us to move north and take on the enemy threat. Frankie gunned the engine and we roared off, the mist still swirling. I was peering through the sights, desperate to locate the enemy and take them on. I spotted troops moving to our front and right and called it in. Stretton had seen them at the same time. 'Contact!' he reported, 'enemy infantry, 600 metres front.'

'Engage!' Brigade ordered. I pressed the fire button. The high-explosive shell screeched off towards the target. As soon as it exploded, the lost patrol commander reported: 'We're being engaged by 66.' He meant the 66mm shoulder-fired rocket in use with both Argentine and British forces.

Then Stretton realized what was happening: 'Check fire! Check fire! They're not enemy forces – they're friendly. We're engaging friendly forces! Check fire!'

But just before the 'Check fire' call reached them, 7 Para's guns fired a last salvo. The shells killed two of the lost Para patrol outright, and injured several more.

The incident was hushed up so as not to undermine morale. But it taught me a lesson, one I drum into the young soldiers under my command until they're sick of hearing it. Know where you are on the ground at all times. Your life may depend on it. By all means use a GPS if it's working – but make sure you can still pinpoint your position on a map if it isn't.

We'd never practised throwing hand grenades from an armoured vehicle, but it's a useful skill to have if the enemy's threatening to overrun you. Next day, we parked up in line abreast next to a large pond, leaving plenty of space between the wagons. The idea was, we'd all take it in turn to chuck a hand grenade out of our hatches into the pond. With any luck, we'd stun or kill some fish into the bargain, and we'd have a nice, fresh fry-up for dinner instead of boring old compo rations. Pete Fugate was driving the other Scorpion immediately to the right of ours. I bet he wished he was back in the White Swan.

Pete took out a hand grenade, pulled the pin and went to launch it into the pond. I was watching closely: it was my turn next. As his arm came forward in the throw his elbow hit the driver's sight. The grenade fell from his grasp, rolled slowly along the Scorpion's front decks, dropped over the edge and plopped to the ground. Directly in front of the vehicle. Nobody else seemed to have noticed. I yelled: 'Take cover!' burrowed down into my seat, put my hands over my head and tried to make myself as small as possible. There was an almighty bang. Fragments of hot metal flew everywhere, rattling against the hull. Our first real experience of being under Falklands fire had come from our side. And we didn't even catch any fish.

A Chinook helicopter came thundering up with what looked like a giant pair of black rubber bollocks hanging off its underside – portable fuel bladders for the use of. We had to pump the petrol into the wagons by hand. At least it helped to keep you warm. More compo rations came up with the fuel and some much-needed drinking water.

The order came to break out. Brigade told 4 Troop to make for Teal Inlet, a sound about 40 kilometres east on the other side of West Falkland. Our role was to act as classic light cavalry – forge out ahead and detect the enemy; determine his strength, location and capability; act as the eyes and ears of the main force; and engage if and when necessary. Teal Inlet was only a hop, skip and a jump away from Port Stanley. But there were plenty of Argentine forces dug in on the mountains that protected the capital.

Before the Falklands War, most people reckoned that armoured vehicles like the Scorpion would be useless over marshy ground. The opposite turned out to be true: their tracks dispersing the weight amazingly well, the Scorpions and Scimitars ate up the spongy ground.

Brigade had allowed us three days to reach Teal Inlet. Barrelling on over bogs where the infantry struggled and sank in freezing cold mud over their ankles, we reached our objective late in the evening of that same day. We set up a defensive perimeter. The barometer was falling like a stone. The temperature was dropping with it and the snow showers were getting longer and stronger. Our troop commandeered an empty hut – it was more of a lowly cattle shed – but at least it gave some shelter from the biting wind.

Not far from the hut we found an abandoned shop. Inside, lurking on a shelf at the back, Dave Voyce and I discovered three dusty bottles of sherry. Spoils of war. We hadn't had an alcoholic drink for many weeks, far too long for a bunch of healthy growing lads. We shared the hooch out between the twelve members of the troop. After a couple of pulls on the old Amontillado I started feeling very mellow. We were sitting around having a laugh and a joke when Paul Stretton suddenly decided it was time Dave Voyce and I had a shave and a haircut. He had a point: my sideburns were round my chin. Dave had the bushiest bandido moustache in army history and his hair was curling down over his collar. Stretton told us to go and get cleaned up. That meant going outside in the cold to fetch some water from the wagons. Dave looked across at Stretton. 'It's lovely and warm here in the shed. Can't we do it a bit later?'

He wasn't having any. 'Go and get some fucking water. And hurry up.' Neither of us moved.

Stretton jumped to his feet. 'OK,' he said, 'grab Voyce.' We all set on Dave, me included, and held him down. Stretton started hacking at his moustache with a pair of old-fashioned clippers he'd found. Even if you kept still they tore fucking great lumps out of your head. And Dave didn't keep still; he was kicking and yelling. In the mayhem, half his moustache came off along with big patches of his hair, leaving all these bite-sized bald patches on his scalp. But Dave put up a good fight. When we let him go the other half of his moustache was still in place.

Dave glared at me. 'Traitor!' he shouted. 'Get him!' The boys pinned me down on the floor. That's mates for you. By the time they'd finished, it looked as if a pack of rats had chewed at my hair. I had one long rat-eaten sideburn running down the right side of my head and no furry bits at all on the left side. Stretton seemed to have mellowed by now, but he was determined, I'll give him that. 'You still look like tramps,' he said. 'Go and fetch some water and shave properly.'

About 20 metres from the shed we ran smack into 2 Para's regimental sergeant major. There was an officer straight out of *Blackadder* with him. The pair of them looked as if they'd just stepped off the parade ground. We stopped and saluted. The RSM stopped and stared. His gaze took in our generally filthy and dishevelled appearance. Then it travelled over Dave's half moustache, my single overgrown sideburn and the moth-eaten hair cuts. The RSM's face turned a dark shade of red. His eyeballs started bulging and his mouth opened wide, ready. He reminded me of someone I'd met before: Smacky. Then he started shouting, and once he'd started, it felt like it would never stop. He gave us the worst bollocking I've ever had in the field. And put us on report.

CHAPTER ELEVEN

Mount Kent came up in sight to the east, one of the mountains that lay between us and the enemy in Port Stanley. From our base at the shed we began probing towards it. SAS patrols had reported enemy activity. As we drew near we sighted the Argentine positions: a system of deep trenches and bunkers cut across the west-facing slopes. We manoeuvred until we were hull down in a natural depression. The fold of land we were in was like a purpose-designed bunker, with a clear field of fire to the enemy trenches. It couldn't have been a better position.

Paul and I were scanning hard for targets. He was using his binoculars, I had the gun sight. I spotted a couple of Argies digging in on a shoulder of ground about 4 kilometres away. The Scorpion's 76mm gun had an effective range of 6 kilometres, which put them well within range. 'Paul, I can see enemy troops digging in, to the north-east at about four clicks.' It was the first time I'd seen the opposition close up. At 10x magnification, even in the overcast conditions I was startled by how clearly I could see them. Grey-clad and grey-helmeted, they looked to me a bit like Second World War German soldiers. Studying the area more carefully, I saw that there were dozens of Argies spread across the face of the slope. Most were already dug in, but a few were still busy hacking new slit trenches in the bony ground.

'Seen,' Stretton said. He reported it up to Brigade. Brigade told us to engage when ready. We watched the Argies for another minute. It was obvious they had no idea we were there. 'OK,' Stretton said, 'Let's have at them.' I turned the fire control switch from machine gun to main armament. I was holding two hand wheels: the one in my right hand made the gun traverse, the second made it elevate. The enemy were too far off for direct lay – which is where you simply slap the sight directly on the target and let rip. For indirect lay, I'd have to use the Quadrant Fire Control (QFC). It sounds technical, but all that happens is the sighting system helps you elevate the gun the correct amount for a given distance. When I was happy with the elevation, I said: 'On!'

Stretton glanced at me. 'Fire!'

I pressed the fire button. 'Firing now.' The first shell winged off to the target, hit the ground about 200 metres in front of the Argies and exploded in a shower of earth and rock.

Through the binos, Paul was watching fall of shot. 'Add 400,' he said. I corrected the elevation to make the next shell land about the same distance beyond the enemy position and fired again. The round landed 200 metres plus, or beyond the target. We'd straddled the enemy postion, which is the golden result of gunnery. Now, if we halved distance we should get a hit.

Stretton said: 'Drop 200.'

'On.'

'Fire!'

'Firing now.' I pressed the fire button.

I followed the orange tracer as it floated towards the enemy, then focused in on the two Argies, who seemed oblivious to the fact that we were ranging in on them. They were standing together near the trench. To me, it looked as if they thought their own artillery was firing. The 76mm high-explosive round hit the right-hand Argie square in the chest. He turned into a red fog of blood. 'Yes!' I shouted. 'Target!' I moved the sight a fraction. His neighbour had disappeared too – the blast and hail of exploding steel must have blown him to smithereens as well.

A second before, there had been two live human beings digging in. Now, there was nothing. Already, I was scanning for the next target. I'd gone through the death thing outside Andytown barracks in Northern Ireland. Learned how to cut myself off. It felt weird to have killed the Argies, but I didn't feel guilty: I was doing the job the Army had trained me to do. It came down to us or them.

One thing was for certain – the Argies on that part of Mt Kent had no idea what had hit them. With only our turret projecting above the natural hide, except in the actual moment of firing we were very, very difficult to spot. But the moment that third round hit, the hillside came alive. The Argie troops started running round, diving in and out of trenches in total shock and panic. A few fired their weapons at random, but we were well out of small-arms range. In any case, they still weren't exactly sure where we were. Stretton reloaded and I fired another round. There were so many targets now there was hardly any need to take aim.

We put harassing fire down on the enemy in earnest, round after round landing smack in among them. It was a bit of a festival – for us. In a little while we began to hear return artillery fire whistling overhead, but it was overshooting our own position by a long way: if anything, it looked as if the Argies were firing at the Paras coming up on foot about six clicks to our west.

I was inexperienced in tank warfare then, so when Paul Stretton told Frankie to move out I was so surprised I protested: 'But this is a brilliant position! I'm getting pot shots and they can't see us! Why don't we stay here?' We were ruining the enemy's day while the Paras and Marines came forward. Why would we want to move?

Stretton ignored me. It was just as well: less than thirty seconds after we moved, an enemy shell whistled in and exploded on the exact spot we'd just quit. I took the 'fire and movement' lesson I learned at Mt Kent that day all the way to Iraq twenty-one years later: no matter how good your firing position, always move once you've fired. If they have any brains at all, the enemy will have fixed your muzzle flash and be lining up on you to return the favour.

While we'd been picking off Argentine targets on the western side of Mt Kent, the 500 men of 2 Para had fought a bitter battle to take Darwin and Goose Green. On 28 May – one week after we'd landed – they overran the enemy lines there, taking more than 1,000 Argentine troops prisoner.

Weighed down by massive Bergens, GPMGs, SLRs, MILAN anti-tank weapons and all the rest, the Paras and the Marines slogged it all the way across East Falkland to Teal Inlet. At the same time, 5 Brigade landed at San Carlos Water. The badly needed reinforcements included 1st Welsh Guards, 2nd Scots Guards and 1/7th Gurkha Rifles. Brigade decided that the Scots and Welsh Guards should move round to East Falkland by sea and put ashore at Bluff Cove and Fitzroy. The settle-ments faced one another across a bay about 30 kilometres to the south-east of Port Stanley. The idea was to get most of 5 Brigade up near the key battle zone as soon as possible, ready to punch up into the Argen-tine underbelly from the south.

We could feel the pace of the campaign starting to quicken. Stretton told us: 'The Welsh and Scots Guards are coming round by sea and landing at Fitzroy. Our job is to cover the landings.' We set our vehicles up next to the command units of the Welsh Guards and the Scots Guards in a field on top of the headland overlooking Fitzroy and Bluff Cove. We were less than 15 kilometres from Port Stanley.

The Landing Ship Logistic (LSL) *Sir Galahad* with some 350 men of 1st Welsh Guards on board arrived at Fitzroy Cove just after 0800 on 8 June. We watched as she anchored a short distance out in the bay. Everybody expected the Guards to come ashore without delay. Even I knew that leaving loads of men bottled up in a big, soft target like a transport ship was asking for trouble. But by 1300 hours, the Welsh Guards had been sitting just offshore for the best part of five hours. It would be a pretty big surprise if Argentine units in the local area hadn't seen and reported their presence.

I heard someone banging mess tins together and thought: 'Air raid!' For air attack we were supposed to blow a whistle, but no one had a whistle, so we all banged anything metallic that came to hand. There was a headlong rush for the wagons. I jumped in, made the machine gun ready and started scanning the sky for enemy aircraft. A voice kept shouting 'Air attack! Air attack!' in my headphones. I already knew that – but where were the Argie planes? I heard a sudden roar from above and glanced to my right.

A Skyhawk shot past less than 200 metres away. The plane was so low I saw the pilot's face as he turned to look at us. Fuck, that was incredible! It came from directly behind our position. The gun range opened fast: as he speared out to sea, I lined up on him and opened fire. The tracer followed the speeding plane, just like a dream. Too slow. With every nerve and fibre I willed it to hit him. It didn't. Then everybody opened up on the Argies at once – the whole sky blossomed with tracer and lead. The thud of the 30mm rang through my earphones.

There were more Skyhawks now: they seemed to be everywhere. Looping round, they raced back in on their bombing runs. Then three attacked the *Sir Galahad* at once. One bomb hit the ship, then another. There was a massive explosion. In seconds it was blazing from stem to stern.

Watching from the bluff, it was hard to believe how quickly and disastrously the fire took hold. In less than a minute, it was out of control. Filthy grey-black smoke cut with long tongues of orange flame enveloped the ship. We watched, sick to our stomachs, as the thick, rancid, choking smell of burning diesel filled the air.

Desperate to escape, the Welsh Guards and the ship's crew scrambled to launch the boats and life rafts. They were swarming down rope ladders and jumping straight into the freezing sea, anything to escape the galloping flames. The *Sir Galahad* was a floating bomb. There were tonnes of ammunition and fuel at the heart of that inferno, if all that went up then the whole ship would vaporize. Despite the risk, helicopters came down low next to the blazing ship. Some used the downwash from their rotors to push the life rafts and boats with their loads of men towards the shore. Others winched men directly off the stricken ship or pulled them out of the water. Whatever the pilots did, they were extremely brave. We had to sit there, watching helplessly as good men got blasted and burned to death.

At the ghost of a chance, I was opening fire. In the very few minutes the attack lasted, 3 and 4 Troops had fired thousands of rounds. Only one of us got lucky: Eddie Tucker, a young 3 Troop Scimitar gunner I knew well. Eddie had a clip of three APDS rounds loaded. He took a bead on a Skyhawk and aimed off ahead of it. By luck or great shooting, one of the heavy shells smashed into the Skyhawk's tailplane. The fighter-bomber crashed headlong into a fold of land a couple of clicks to the north. A fireball went up. But with the horror that had come on the *Sir Galahad,* no one had the heart to cheer.

More explosions rocked the ship as the ammunition stores cooked off. It was a race to evacuate the men who were still aboard. Many had lost their clothes in the blast and flames; dozens had suffered terrible burns. A medical unit that had already landed set up an emergency dressing station; 3 Troop used their vehicles to move some of the less badly injured up to the casualty station for triage. Once they'd been given first aid, a helicopter shuttle flew the badly injured over to the hospital ship *Uganda* in San Carlos Water. In the course of that terrible day, the *Uganda's* onboard medical teams treated 159 casualties. The dead were lined up on the beach in black body bags, ready for burial.

CHAPTER TWELVE

We held the position at Bluff Cove for three days while the remaining Welsh Guards reconstituted back into a fighting force. The whole time, the *Sir Galahad* burned below us in the bay. Once the blaze had at last died away, a Royal Navy ship came up, towed the smoking metal shell out to sea and sank it. The ship is there to this day, a war grave.

Despite what had happened, none of us believed for a minute we were going to lose the war. The attack on the enemy positions around Port Stanley now moved into top gear. Everyone wanted the job done. We were more determined than ever to get the Argies defeated so we could go back home.

Initially, 4 Troop was ordered to join the Paras in their attack on Wireless Ridge. We were the rearmost vehicle in the column that set out. We were rolling along over a stretch of heath when two Welsh Guard despatch riders broke out from behind and swung right and south of us to overtake.

We'd been warned that the area we were now going into might be mined. I don't know if anyone had warned the despatch riders. They were both on cross-country bikes and the ground in that area was firm. They were riding quite close together, with the second man just behind and slightly off to one side of the first. Then the lead rider hit an anti-tank mine. The explosion threw him and the motorbike high into the air. I watched as man and machine seemed to hang there for a moment and then fell crashing to earth. The blast blew the second despatch rider backwards off his bike. Peppered with fragments of motorbike and mine, he lay silent for a moment, then started screaming. It was broad daylight. We could see everything, but we couldn't do anything to help. We wanted to drive straight across the moor and give them first aid, but where there's one mine there are almost always many more.

'Stop!' Stretton told Frankie. We halted, along with the rest of the column. Some infantry came up behind us, including a trio of Royal Engineers. The Sappers started probing towards the stricken men. We quickly saw the ground was rotten with mines: dozens of anti-armour and anti-personnel mines, all mixed together in a lethal carpet of explosive and steel. The first despatch rider stopped screaming. A short time later, the second man fell silent in turn. By the time their would-be rescuers reached them, both men had died of their wounds.

Our orders changed and we swung north: 4 Troop's new job was to

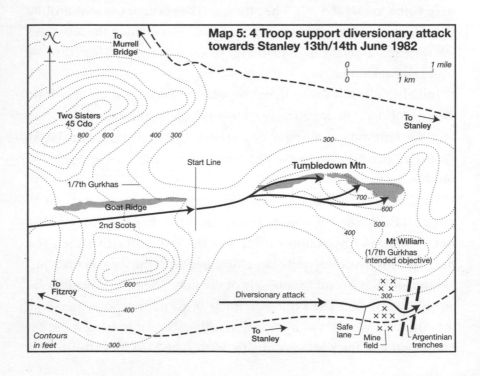

support a diversionary attack by the 2nd Scots Guards on Mt Tumble-down. The Scots Guards started the attack just east of Goat Ridge, a long, thin rib of ground between Mt Harriet and Two Sisters.

Under cover of an artillery barrage, on the night of Sunday, 13 June a spearhead platoon of Scots Guards with 4 Troop's Scimitars and Scorpions in support put in a feint assault against Argentine positions on the lower slopes.

It was pitch-dark and freezing cold. We pushed through the narrow lanes the Royal Engineers had cleared through the enemy minefields. As we advanced, the lead Scorpion directly ahead of us, Lt Coreth's, hit a mine. The explosion blew the vehicle off the ground. At first I thought they'd been engaged by an enemy Panhard tank. I started frantically scouring the landscape to all sides, trying to spot and kill the threat. Badly shaken, Lt Coreth, Trooper Jed Farmer and Lance Corporal 'Lamb Chop' Lambert abandoned the stricken wagon and jumped up on our decks. We dropped them back at a bandaging station for treatment. By a miracle, none of them had suffered anything worse than cuts and bruises. The rest of us pushed on.

Without warning, we came up on the enemy trenches. Looming suddenly up in the night, they looked liked something out of the First World War. The Scots got to within 5 metres of the first trench. It was dead quiet. Drill Sergeant Danny White stuck his head over the top. I'd met Danny, a big character in every way, in passing at Pirbright barracks. As he peered down into the enemy position, the Argentine defenders woke up. One raised his rifle and shot Danny in the head. Then everyone cut loose at the same time. Tracer flew everywhere, grenades started to explode, screams, yells and shots filled the air. The Scots charged forward, storming their way through the enemy lines with fixed bayonets, stabbing and shooting as they moved.

When and where we could, we lent suppressing fire. Sometimes I couldn't fire at the Argies even when I could see them: with much of the fighting hand-to-hand, we had to be really careful not to kill our own men. But when it worked, the armour/infantry combo was extremely effective. I began to get a sense of when to fire, when to hold back, learn how to manage my frustration when I could see but not engage a target. I had no sense of time passing, there was only the quick, relentless pulse of battle.

The assault on Mt Tumbledown now spread out and broke up into a series of vicious firefights, many of them eyeball to eyeball. In the pitch-dark, with not enough NVGs and patchy communications, individual Scots patrols fought through the Argie positions one trench after another, clawing their way up the slopes. The ferocity, skill and commitment of the defending troops came as a big shock. We found out later that the Argies on Tumbledown had been an elite unit.

As they cleared through the enemy lines, many of our own troops swapped their Army issue SLRs for the Argie version of the same weapon. Unlike the SLR, the FN had a 'full auto' setting – useful for spraying rounds into trenches at close quarters. Captured Argentine '66' fire-and-forget shoulder-launched rockets also came in handy for smashing enemy hard points. Despite the ferocious resistance, by 0800 on 14 June, 2nd Battalion, The Scots Guards had taken Tumbledown at a cost of nine men dead and forty-three injured.

To the south-east of us, 1/7th Gurkhas had taken Mt William with barely a shot fired. The Argie troops had run away to Port Stanley, leaving the Gurkhas furious at being cheated of a good scrap.

As day broke, we got a brief update. It was more good news: while the Scots Guards had been slogging up Tumbledown, 2 Para had fought a bloody battle to take Wireless Ridge; 3 Para had overrun the enemy on Mt Longdon; 45 Commando had taken control of Two Sisters; and 42 Commando had blasted and shot their way to the summit of Mt Harriet.

British forces now controlled the twin parallel fingers of high ground dominating the easterly route into Port Stanley. In the light of the new day, we had a welcome view: all around us, lines of defeated enemy soldiers were falling back towards Port Stanley, quitting the peaks that had cost both sides so many dead and injured. Clearing back through the ground we'd taken during the night, we found a number of dead enemy officers. They'd been shot in the back of the head at close range – executed by their own men.

We set about the grim task of recovering our fallen. I helped pick up Sergeant White. As we laid him on one of the vehicle decks, I saw where the bullet had broken open his skull. I found myself talking to him as I laid him down. Then, the news we'd all been waiting for came over the air: Stanley had fallen – the Argies had put out a white flag. Enemy forces on the Falkland Islands surrendered officially at 2059 hours on 14 June.

When we saw the defeated Argie soldiers at the POW holding areas in Port Stanley, we couldn't believe how many of them there were: a huge, huddled grey mass of men. We'd captured more than 11,000 enemy. You could see the Argies couldn't believe how few of us there were. Stripped of their weapons and kit, the POWs looked a sorry bunch, bedraggled and totally demoralized. The operation to get them back home to the Argentine mainland started straight away.

I was too cold and hungry to feel all that elated. But we'd liberated the Falklands.

You'd think they might let us go home now too, but not a bit of it. Worried the Argies might stage a counterattack, the powers-that-be decided we had to stick around. That was not good news. We were wet, we were cold, we'd seen our comrades getting blown up, shot and burned, and we'd been hoping to get billeted in a nice, warm house in Port Stanley with things we fondly and distantly remembered – like walls, windows, furniture, doors and heating. The house went to 3 Troop. We got a field to the south-east of Port Stanley. We had two options: live on the wagons or scrounge up some tents. Tents! By now, it was cold enough to freeze the wedding tackle off a brass chimp. We were well upset – not least by the idea that 3 Troop were toddling along to the Upland Goose Hotel in town. And drinking the bar dry.

Sitting about in that windswept field freezing our bits off, me and

Pete Fugate decided to do something about improving our food stocks. Starting with a goose hunt. Bearing in mind his performance with the hand grenade at the fish pond, we decided to stick to small arms. It had to be geese – we couldn't shoot the sheep, they belonged to the farmers, and the penguins were much too nice to kill. Neither of us had ever hunted goose before. But that didn't matter: the Falkland Islands were gaggling with geese. And we'd already found out that Upland geese are ridiculously tame. They'll waddle right up to you and say hello.

Pete and I still had our Army-issue Sterling sub-machine guns, but we'd also picked up Argie FN rifles. Mine had a folding stock, very handy for the Scorpion's confined space, not to mention extremely cool. For our big game hunt we took everything we had: the FNs, the SMGs and our Army standard-issue SLRs. When you go after tame geese there's no point in taking any chances. Off we wandered into the local area in search of dinner. Pretty soon, we came on a flock of geese. They were mucking about at the edge of the sea inlet not far from where we were camped. True to form, they gave us a friendly look, then carried on grubbling about in the sea. The nearest birds were only about 15 metres away. You'd have to be blind drunk to miss them – if only.

'You take the one on the left,' I told Pete. 'I'll do that fat fucker over there.' We took aim with the SMGs and let fly with several rapid rounds. The shots reverberated all around the landscape. It was a still day and the sound seemed to carry for miles. I knew I'd hit my goose, but to my amazement, the bullets bounced off its wings and whanged up into the sky. The goose gave us a nonchalant glance, took off and flew away as if nothing had happened. Its mate went with it. 'I hit mine,' I said.

Pete said, 'I hit mine, too – couldn't hardly miss the bugger. Armoured fucking geese – unbelievable!'

When we'd both stopped laughing, we forayed off to find ourselves a new candidate. This was getting embarrassing. Here we were, two highly trained soldiers, part of a heavily outnumbered task force that had just defeated a better-equipped and well-entrenched enemy. And we couldn't even bag ourselves a goose for the pot. Pretty soon, we spotted another target paddling about in the shallows near the shore.

'Right,' I said, 'we're having this one: I'm using the FN, no messing.' I drew a bead on the Upland and put a couple of shots into him. Loads of feathers flew up. He fell back in the water, stone dead. We stood staring down at the corpse for a while. It hadn't occurred to us that once we'd shot the goose, we'd have to wade out into the freezing water to get him.

Pete turned to me. 'Goose or no bloody goose, I'm not going in there – it's way too fucking cold.' He was right. We went and found a big long branch. The tide began pushing the goose slowly towards us. When it got within reach, we hauled it out of the water.

We took our trophy back to the wagons. Then we gutted it, plucked it and stuffed it into a bastardized ammunition tin cooking-pot with some water. Yum. Because of the horrible cold and wet I had a persistent drip on the end of my nose. As I leaned over the pot, it dropped into the stew I immediately got the nickname 'Sniff'. But no one seemed all that bothered about the seasoning.

Pretty soon, a weird fishy smell started coming from the pan. I stared down at the goose and then back up at Pete. 'It looks all right – but it stinks something terrible. What's wrong with it?'

Pete shook his head sadly from side to side. 'It's your cooking, Mike.' Then he got a whiff. 'Fuck, I see what you mean – the fucker smells like rotting fish guts.'

I snuffed out the Hexi blocks to douse the fire. 'Let's try it anyway.'

I lifted our prize out of the pot, laid it on a tin plate and carved off a slice of breast. We were all starving, and the meat looked lovely – creamy and tender and glistening. Just like Christmas. The whole troop gathered round to share the feast. Eagerly, we each pulled a chunk off the breast and stuck it in our mouths. And as one man, we all spat it out again.

'Yeeuuch!' Pete yodelled, retching and gobbing bits of half-chewed goose-meat across the landscape. 'That's the most disgusting thing I've ever tasted in my whole life.' I was too busy spitting out scraps to agree, but he was right – the bloody goose tasted like rancid cod liver oil. I looked round. As far as the eye could see, there were big hairy troopers spitting out lumps of fish-flavoured goose.

'Kelp goose,' someone said, knowingly.

'What?'

'It's been eating kelp – that's why it tastes like rotting seaweed.'

I looked at Pete: we'd gone to all of that effort for nothing. The Uplands weren't tame because they were stupid: they were tame because they knew no one in their right mind would want to eat them.

But our troubles were only just beginning. Paul Stretton came striding up. 'Come here Flynn,' he said, 'and you, Fugate.' He pointed at the festering stew. 'Where did you get that goose?'

'We shot it,' I said. 'It's really, really tasty – would you like to try some?'

He eyeballed me: 'Never mind that: how many shots did you fire trying to kill the fucker?'

I glanced at Pete. I could see he was thinking the same thing as me: that was the kind of loaded Army question it was best not to answer. 'Er,' I said, 'to tell you the truth, in all the excitement I can't remember.'

Stretton glared at me. 'Don't get fucking funny, Flynn – this is serious. Do you two have any idea of all the trouble your little hunting trip has caused?'

'Trouble? What trouble?'

'Your gunfire has put the whole of British forces on immediate alert. Every bugger's stood to, ready to repulse the big Argie counterattack!'

Oh dear.

'Sorry,' said Pete, 'we didn't think about that.'

I could only agree. We were so hungry, thinking hadn't entered into it.

'Listen carefully,' Stretton said. 'I'm only going to say this once. We didn't have this conversation. And you two didn't go out hunting geese. Go and clean your weapons, all of them, right now. And if any bugger from Brigade comes snooping around asking questions, you know nothing, you heard nothing and you're suffering from temporary amnesia – got that?'

We nodded.

'And get rid of that minging goose!'

We took what was left of the Upland, slung it into the sea and sloped off to get our cleaning kit. I understood where Paul was coming from: if Brigade found out it was us who'd caused all the fuss, then it was his neck on the line. Sure enough, a couple of bods came poking around later, wanting to know if we'd heard any shots fired. You never saw so many innocent faces.

To everybody's relief, Argentine leader General Galtieri Castelli resigned on 17 June, three days after the official surrender. Now, with the lucky Falkland islanders free from any threat of compulsory tango lessons, we really could go home.

CHAPTER THIRTEEN

With its own crew doing most of the routine things that had to be done on the *Fearless*, on the long voyage home we started to get a bit bored. A few of us were lying around on our bunks as the ship steamed north, we had nothing to do and the Devil makes work for idle hands. There was myself, Klaus von Fisher, Dave Voyce, Gary Birch, Harry Ford and a few others. The weather was a bit rough and there was a rollocking swell running.

We fell to talking about women. After so many weeks away from female company, the subject was constantly at the top of our minds. Klaus started telling us how the second his feet hit solid ground, he was going to find himself a nice woman and work his wicked way with her.

Harry Ford, who usually had nothing but football and golf on the brain said, 'Oh yes? And how are you going to do that? I mean, what's your best chat-up line?'

That was it, we were off. I said, 'You know what? We need a woman to practice on.'

The others jeered and laughed. 'Yes, there are so many to choose from on a ship full of blokes in the middle of the South Atlantic.'

'No,' Gary Birch said, 'Mike's right. All we need is a substitute. How about the mop?' He jumped off his bunk, flung open the cleaning cupboard and dragged out the mop we used for swabbing the deck. It was the old-fashioned type, with long bits of thick string fastened in a bunch to the end of a wooden pole. He stood the mop up in the corner and we inspected it. As mops went, it didn't strike me as particularly attractive. Its head had been wrung out too many times in the course of cleaning too many floors. It needed to go to a good hairdresser. And it had definitely been dieting too hard. On the other hand, none of us had been near a woman for a long time. If you half-closed your eyes and looked from a certain angle, maybe the mop wasn't all that bad looking.

'What we'll do,' I said, 'is lean Miss Mop up against the lockers there. She's this bird in a bar, we take it in turns to come in, go up to her and give it our best shot.'

'I think she's gorgeous,' Gary piped up. 'Bags going first.' He went down to the end of the bunks, disappeared round the corner, spent a minute or two getting his act together and then sauntered back in. Mr Casual, looking for some action in the Mucky Duck on a Saturday night. He came up and stood next to the mop as if he was going to order a drink at the bar. Then he flicked the mop a sideways glance. 'Hello,' he said in a low voice. 'The way the light catches your hair tonight, you've never looked so wonderful. Can I buy you a drink?'

The mop didn't say anything. But the rest of us were in stitches. 'That,' Dave Voyce said when he'd stopped laughing, 'is the worst fucking chat-up line I've heard in my entire life.'

Gary looked offended. 'That's just where you're wrong, mate. You'd be surprised how often that one works for me.' And with that he leaned in and put his arm around the mop. 'Your place, or mine?'

It was my turn next. I went round the end of the bunks, slicked my hair back and then started strolling towards the mop. When I was close I pretended to bump into her. 'Oh, sorry!' I said, brushing an imaginary spill off the mop's dress. 'Here, let me buy you another.' Miss Mop didn't say yes, but then she didn't say no either. Taking her silence as encouragement, I nestled a bit closer. 'I'm Mike and I'm from Cardiff. Where are you from?' I launched into the whole patter, kept it going until the mop had agreed to come back for coffee.

Next up was Klaus von Fisher. Klaus was one of those people who always went one better. He fell in along the space between the bunks as if he were already drunk, caught sight of the mop and staggered up to it. 'Hello, love,' he slurred. 'Get your coat, you've pulled.' He grabbed hold of the mop, flung it over backwards and started giving it some lip action. He was full-on necking this mop, making extreme moves on her and planting big juicy smackers.

There was a miserable little REME corporal in the mess with us, he looked a bit like Charlie Chaplin only with a Mexican moustache. The guy was a real jobsworth, none of us liked him He hadn't taken any part in the entertainment, and now Klaus was tonguing the mop he jumped to his feet. 'That's disgusting,' he said, 'kissing a filthy mop! You lot are fucking disgusting!'

'Shut the fuck up, Lopez,' someone else said. That was this bloke's nickname, on account of the bandido face fungus. Lopez kept going on at us about how we had to stop chatting up the mop, how disgusting we all were. One of the boys said, 'You know what? He's right. Let's not use the mop as a woman. He's like a woman, except he's got a moustache. Let's shave it off and use him as a woman instead.' Lopez shrank back into his bunk space and started to bleat. Too late. We grabbed hold of him, held him down, got a razor and a pair of scissors and went to work. Off came the Mexican-style facial hair; he looked a lot better without it.

'He's still not as attractive as the mop,' Klaus said when our man was clean-shaven. 'What he needs is a spot of make-up. Some eye-shadow, maybe, and a touch of lippy. Then we can really get to work on him.' Klaus was winding him up, but having seen what he'd done to the mop, Lopez took Klaus von Fisher at face value, he really thought his virtue was at risk. He started yelling and screaming at the top of his voice. Gary said, 'Klaus is only joking – keep your hair on.'

'Bit late for that,' Klaus said. We let Lopez go. In the struggle, he'd come by a small cut on his lip. He stood up. He was so angry he couldn't speak. We were all laughing so hard we couldn't speak. He stormed off and complained to Paul Stretton. Paul came down and asked us what we'd been doing.

'We needed a woman,' Dave said, 'and he was it.'

We could all see Paul was trying hard not to laugh. 'Keep it down,' he said, 'we don't want him taking it any further.'

'OK, Paul.'

'Cheers.'

Any mop in a storm.

The experience of war in the Falklands had been terrifying, exhilarating and gruelling by turn: but not as scary as the letter I got from my mam on the way home. I don't know why, but my mother has a terrible habit of trying to make everything right. The spirit might be generous, but in practice trying to mend things when they're broken doesn't always work. Just before leaving for the Falklands, I'd told Mam that Denise and I had officially separated, and we were waiting to get divorced. To most people, that information would have been final and clear. But while I was away, my mother had gone into overdrive. She was determined to save my marriage, determined to save me from myself. She's a very determined woman.

As part of her grand plan, Mam had got in touch with Denise and suggested she come along and meet me on the quayside at South-ampton when we docked. Mam reasoned that the moment I caught sight of a wife I hadn't seen for the past many weeks and months, then violins would swell in the background, little pink cartoon hearts would appear in the air all around us and we would fall into one another's arms like long lost lovers. Why not? There was only one slight snag: I'd been writing to Rachel during my time in the South Atlantic, and I'd arranged for her to come and meet me at Southampton. Somehow, I'd neglected to tell my mam about this. Or Denise. Or anyone except Rachel.

The *Fearless* was ferrying a large complement of Royal Marines back to the UK. Their home base was at Lympstone in Devon. Before going on up the English Channel to Southampton, the ship was due to dock at Plymouth so that the Marines could disembark. While we were alongside at Devonport, all the mail that had piled up for us during the long weeks at sea came on board. Among the clutch of letters from Rachel there was one from my mam. I opened it. 'Dear Michael,' it began, 'I've spoke to Denise and she's going to come down with us to meet you at the dockside on your return. She's very much looking forward to seeing you again, Michael, and I hope ...' I dropped the letter. My heart rate had just doubled and a prickle of cold sweat had broken out across my shoulders and neck. Jesus, Mary and all the Saints, why couldn't my dear old mam learn to leave bad alone? I'd told her that Denise and I had agreed to divorce before leaving for the Falklands. Why on earth would she be trying to bring Denise and me back together now?

My hands started to shake a bit. My mother and father were going to be there, all five of my sisters, my wife – and my girlfriend! I didn't mind meeting them, I just didn't want to meet them all at the same time in the same place. I'd been in some tight spots in the Falklands, but this was a nightmare scenario all of its own. What the hell was I going to do?

While I was lurching round the ship in a blue funk muttering, 'Oh my God, oh my God!' and imagining all kinds of blood, tears and mayhem when we arrived at Southampton docks, the *Fearless* set sail. I knew this because the ship was bouncing up and down again, which is something I've never really liked all that much about ships – or horses, for that matter. The way things were going, something else was going to bounce up and down when we docked – my nuts. I had to sort something out, sharpish. Perhaps I could go and ask the captain if he'd turn the ship about face and take us back to the Falklands? It was quiet there now. And I'd always liked penguins. Or maybe he'd set me down on the Isle of Wight?

Then I had a sudden flash of inspiration. I'd been on board long enough to know that like all warships, the *Fearless* came equipped with a ship-to-shore radio telephone. It was used for routine exchanges with pilot vessels, coastguards and so on. It was meant for official use, not for sorting out love lives. But I'd heard that crew members could use it in dire emergency. To me this was a dire emergency. Would the Navy see it that way, too? There was only one way to find out. I shot up to the bridge. I wasn't supposed to hang around there, but with everything that was going on no one seemed to notice me. Finally, a young lieutenant looked round and caught my eye. 'Hello,' he said. 'Anything we can do for you?'

'Er, yes,' I said sheepishly, 'as a matter of fact, there is.' I explained the little local difficulty I'd managed to concoct for myself. When I'd ended my tale, he said, 'You've got a problem, young man – come with me.' He took me to the comms room. There, on a table in the middle of the room was a lovely, shiny-black radio telephone. My lifeline to a better, safer world: one that had all the different people I knew neatly placed in different compartments, which is how most men want things to be, except that real life keeps on getting in the way. 'I'm going to give you two minutes on that,' the lieutenant said, pointing, 'but I'm afraid the going rate for a ship-to-shore call is £10 per minute. I'm not overcharging you, by the way: that's how much the air time costs the *Fearless*.'

'Fine,' I told him, 'brilliant, I'll pay it.' In 1982, £20 was a fair amount, but I had many weeks of back pay saved: there's nothing to spend your money on in the Falkland Islands unless you take a fancy to one of the sheep. As luck would have it, I'd kept the number for the nurses' home where Rachel lived. The phone rang. And rang. The seconds ticked by and the cost mounted. Finally, a female voice answered at the other end. The carrier wave induced an echo that made it sound as if she had a bucket on her head. 'Hello,' I said, 'I need to speak to Rachel Mount – it's urgent.'

'I'm afraid she's not working today,' bucket-woman said. 'Can I take a message?'

'Yes,' I gabbled. 'Yes! Can you please tell her Michael Flynn rang? Tell her Michael says she's not to meet him at the docks in Southampton – it could be a bit embarrassing. Can you ask her to meet me at Combermere barracks later on, instead?'

There was a short pause. Then the voice-from-the-bottom-of-the-well said: 'Very well, Michael – I'll make sure she gets the message.'

'Yes, yes!' I urged her silently a couple of dozen times, 'Make sure!'

The *Fearless* steamed on up the English Channel. With every smack of wave against the hull, I was praying, 'Please, please let Rachel get that message.' Visions of the two women meeting swam before my eyes. With my mother as referee. You can tell I'm not all that keen on a scene. Eventually, I bumped into Gary Birch. He gave me a sideways look. 'You all right, Mike? You look a bit green around the gills.'

'No,' I said, 'I'm not all right.' I explained the bind I was in. Gary pretended to be all sympathy. Then a smug grin appeared on his face. 'That'll teach you to keep it in your trousers, mate,' he said, and went off chuckling. Gary didn't know it yet, but the boot was actually on the other marching instrument.

A couple of hours later, the throb of the ship's engines died away and we began nosing slowly up the Solent. It was 0800, and the ship's Tannoy played out a late reveille. I went up on deck. We'd reached the Nab Tower. There were scores of small boats waiting to escort us in. It was an amazing sight, it looked like a kind of reverse Dunkirk. The Duke of Edinburgh and various other dignitaries landed by helicopter on the midships flight deck, went round shaking hands for a while and then disappeared back into the sky where they'd come from. After an early mist it had turned into a fine, sunny day, as if especially arranged from on high for our homecoming. The waves were sparkling, the sky was blue and as we came within sight of land, more and more small boats and yachts festooned in flags and bunting came out to meet us, their decks lined with waving, cheering people. The Royal Marines band played on the forward flight deck as yet more vessels came out in welcome: fire tenders, tugs, all kinds of passenger craft and even people in kayaks and canoes.

Everything looked lovely – but for me there was a dark grey cloud hanging low on the horizon. A tug came bustling out and began to nudge the *Fearless* in towards the quayside. Every bugger on the ship not actually required to dock it was on deck. There were hundreds of us sailors and soldiers craning and jostling to see if our loved ones were waiting. Or in my case, how many of our loved ones were waiting. I wasn't craning and jostling: I was keeping a low profile, crouched behind the other lads. Desperate to remain out of sight, I'd tried to volunteer as one of the essential personnel who had to stay below decks. I'd even offered to work in the galley. The petty officer cook I spoke to waved me away. 'Don't be silly, this is your homecoming, matey, they'll all be waiting for you. Go on – get up there and kiss the girls!'

The crowd on the jetty was huge – there were thousands and thousands of people down there, waving flags, cheering, shouting, crying, laughing and quite often managing all of those things at the same time. It was murder trying to sort out the faces you knew from the massive crowd. There was another Royal Marines band playing on the dock, and it looked as if it had rained red, white and blue bunting. The *Fearless*, and the all other ships were blasting their sirens out repeatedly. It was all very moving. Or at least, it would have been if I could have shaken off the feeling of impending doom.

Suddenly, I spotted a familiar face in the crowd: my mother. Mam was standing next to a big banner two of my sisters were holding. Daubed on it in huge black letters were the words: 'Welcome Home Michael!' I shrank back, sneaking furtive looks at the rest of the crowd. I couldn't see Rachel anywhere. But then, she'd probably be waiting on her own. Then I saw Denise. She was standing next to my dad, peering up at the ship. Looking for me. As long as she was on her own I could sort things out. I'd talk things over with Denise, try and make her stick to the planned divorce. Then she'd go back home. I'd go up to barracks and see Rachel, and we'd all be happy. Or not. I waited nervously on the flight deck. My luck was holding – my family and

Denise were coming on board, but still no sign of Rachel.

A shadow fell across me and I glanced up. It was Gary. There was something nervous and furtive in his manner. It reminded me of me. I sidled up to him. 'What's the matter, Gary? You're looking a bit green around the gills.'

'Very funny,' he said. 'Jane's on the jetty waiting, and so is my fiancée. And they've both brought their families with them.' He looked terrified. Well he might. I'd met his girlfriend Jane a few times in the pub in Windsor, she was no pushover. I looked over Gary's shoulder. Sure enough, Jane was standing with an older woman who was obviously her mother. There were a couple of large men standing with Jane – her brothers. I also knew Gary's fiancée. She wasn't the type to stand for any nonsense, either. There she was on the quayside, surrounded by an escort of heavy-duty Scouse relatives. 'Are they there?' Gary whispered.

'Yes mate,' I told him, 'they're both on the dockside – with armies of relatives, waiting to come on board.' Gary looked as if he'd just shrunk a shirt size. If he could have disappeared down through the metal decking he'd have been happy. I said, 'What are you going to do?'

'Keep out of the way,' he mumbled with a glazed look. 'Hope they all give up waiting for me and go away.' And with that the love-rat scurried off below decks.

I watched as the large opposing parties waiting to meet Gary came on board. Then I saw my own family and Denise coming up the brow. I went down below. Regardless of whether Rachel was there or not, now that the moment had come to meet everyone, I felt really nervous. But not as nervous as Gary: he was really in the shit. I found my way to the big NAAFI bar and sat down to wait. Gary was standing in the middle of the room with a face like a man awaiting execution. I looked up and saw why: Gary's fiancée and her family were coming down the companionway on one side of the bar, while Jane and her relatives were coming down the other. The two groups caught sight of our man and closed on him like the jaws of a vice. His fiancée got there first. Gary pasted a fixed smile on his face, grabbed her round the waist and planted a kiss on her cheek. There was a tap on his shoulder. His head rotated very slowly backwards, as if he knew there was a gigantic grizzly behind him. He might have been better off: Jane was standing behind him instead. One glance was all it had taken for her to understand what was what. As a coming-home gift, Jane had brought Gary a bottle of his favourite tipple, Bacardi rum, all wrapped up in nice shiny paper. She rammed the bottle into his chest. It made a hollow thump. Gary staggered back. 'There you are, you bastard – enjoy it!' She turned on her heel and stalked away. That was the kind of scene I was anxious to avoid.

I was just thinking, 'There but for the grace of God go I' when my own family and Denise came up. They gathered round me. We kissed and hugged and smiled and tried to speak a few words, stopping and then starting and then stopping again. My mam cried a bit, that was really out of character. My dad was beaming from ear to ear. 'Well done, Michael,' he said quietly. 'You boys did a great job. We'll have ourselves a drink down the Fox when you get home.'

'Looking forward to it, Dad.'

My dad still didn't know I'd served in Northern Ireland. But after all that had been said and done, the fact that he was there meant a lot to me. I still needed his approval, and by coming he'd given it.

We made our way down to the quay. By now I was certain Rachel had got the message and I'd stopped worrying. Everything was falling neatly into place. I'd sort things out with Denise, she and my family would all go home and then I could get back on up to Windsor and see Rachel. But as usual, the Army had other plans. As a special gesture of thanks, they'd laid on coaches to take us and our loved ones back to our home barracks. They'd also laid on a special reception. They just hadn't told us how nice they were going to be. I was out of the frying pan and into the fire. If I turned up at the party with my family and Denise in tow, what was Rachel going to think? More importantly, what was she going to do?

When we got a moment to ourselves on the coach, Denise said, 'Michael, I want to try and make a go of our marriage.'

'I'm sorry, Denise. I've been thinking things over while I was away and for me it's gone past that. We agreed to a divorce. I'm ever so sorry, but I'd just like to get on with that. Mam means well, but I really, really don't think it's ever going to work out between us.'

After that, it was a bit of a sad and silent journey to Windsor. When we arrived I went off to get showered and changed into civilian clothing. Rachel had managed to wangle the afternoon off. She'd never met Denise before, and I didn't want them to meet now, with me starring in a replay of the Gary B fiasco. All I could think was, 'I've been away for six months, I can't handle this. Please let it stop happening. I've got to get out of here. I've got to get down the nearest pub and have a pint. Or several.'

Denise was crying in the women's toilets. Her sister, Karen, had her arm around her shoulders. Karen was going out with a mate of mine, Martin Mitchell, I'd introduced them. Denise was just in the middle of saying, 'Michael doesn't want anything to do with me any more,' when in walked Rachel. Women are smarter than men about this kind of stuff – they get the picture right away. Karen looked up, recognized Rachel and shot her a look. Rachel decided her best option was tactical withdrawal. I was in the NAAFI by this time. We managed to steal a few words.

'Hello,' I said, 'is everything all right?'

She leaned and murmured, 'No. I just met Denise in the loo. I'll meet you down the Swan later.'

I turned and went back to join my family and Denise. I took my mam to one side. 'Look, Mam, I didn't want to meet Denise just now. This is all too much, I've got to go.' I kissed Denise on the cheek, gave her a hug and said goodbye. Sometimes, it's really hard to feel like you're doing the right thing in life.

CHAPTER FOURTEEN

With no children and not much in the way of assets between us, Denise and I separated without too much hassle. But although I'd set the whole process going, we'd never succeeded in finalizing the divorce. Rachel and I stayed together for about another eighteen months, then that relationship ended too. So when the army sent me down to Lulworth on a Challenger tank conversion course in the summer of 1983, I was footloose and fancy-free. And ready to accept Rupert McKinney's £10 bet that he could sleep with more women than I could during the six weeks of the course. I know, I know – but we were young then and green and in our salad days – with lashings of extra mayonnaise. And in any case Rupert had no chance of winning the bet. He was up against a professional.

We'd been on the range firing large chunks of high-explosive metal at the extremely beautiful Dorset landscape one day. It was hot and stuffy in the Chieftain tank, we were parched and all we wanted to do was go down to Poole, find a pub and pull some skirt. We jumped out of the tanks, tucked them up in bed for the night and ran for the showers. Pretty soon there was a lively party of lads ready to hit the town. Poole's Health & Safety officers had issued advance public warning of a serious incoming bio-hazard – the toxic fumes from a couple of dozen Blues and Royal troopers drenched in high-octane aftershave. We were guaranteed to stop a girl in her tracks at a distance of fifty paces – if not for the right reason.

All systems go. The only trouble being that one of the tracer shells we'd fired that afternoon had started a heath fire. The grass was dry, and with a stiff breeze fanning it the blaze was in danger of spreading out of control. The range control officer decided we had to get out there and contain it. The duty Corporal of Horse came round asking for volunteers. Everyone studied their toes or looked out of the window. It was six o'clock on the evening of a lovely summer's day. The last thing any of us wanted was to be out on the heath with the 'fire sticks' – long wooden poles with leather flaps on the end – thrashing away at a blaze and losing sweat when we'd just got ourselves all clean and cool, nice and ready. We were straining at the beer leash.

'Look lads,' the Corporal of Horse said, 'if no one's going to volunteer then you'll all have to go. You'll need to get out of those civvies and get your overalls on.' He went out. As soon as he'd left, Rupert dived into his wardrobe, pulled the door shut behind him and pretended he wasn't there. Given his enormous size, in Rupert's case that was quite difficult.

This struck me as a very sound idea. I cleared a space in my own wardrobe, squeezed inside and held the door shut. I could see out through the three little air slots in the partition. A couple of the other lads had seen me using the available features of the terrain to take cover: all of that Army training was coming in handy. Quick as a blink they scuttled inside their own wardrobes. Pretty soon, the duty Corporal of Horse got tired of waiting for everyone to fall in for fire duty. He came into the accommodation and started to hunt us down. Rupert's wardrobe door swung open a fraction, then closed again. The idiot had let it slip.

The Corporal of Horse stopped in front of the door. He reached out, grabbed the handle and yanked it back. There was Rupert, all six feet five inches of him, hiding from extra fire duty in a wardrobe. 'McKinney!' shouted the Corporal of Horse. 'Get your overalls on and get fell in outside!' It may not have been all that grammatical but it was effective: Rupert shot out of the cupboard and started to undo his shirt. Then he stopped.

'Hang on a minute,' he said. 'If I'm getting nabbed, then so is Flynn. And Gaskell. And Dobie – they're all hiding in their wardrobes, too.' The bastard had grassed us up. The Corporal of Horse crashed all the doors back. Sheepishly, we stepped out and started to change.

We were working on the fire when one of the lads came running up. 'There's a Land Rover stuck over the other side of the hill. Female driver. We need to rescue her, she's bogged in near the fire.' The words 'female' and 'stuck' in this context had a certain attractive ring to them. Rescuing a damsel in distress was much more exciting than bashing a heath fire to death. There was no shortage of volunteers, in fact there was a bit of a stampede.

I dived into one of the 4-tonne trucks, fired it up, Rupert jumped in the passenger seat and we raced over there. Sure enough, there was a young, attractive blonde at the wheel of a Land Rover stuck in a marshy spot near the fire. I recognized the major sitting next to her. He was a self-important person if ever there was one. But he wasn't the object of my sudden and keen interest: even the terrible khaki Army uniform she wore couldn't disguise the driver's good looks and curvaceous figure. And there was something about her that promised a bit of a challenge. The kind I enjoyed taking on. 'Hello there,' I said. 'Stuck in a rut?'

'Very funny,' she countered, 'how about pulling us out?' The major stared out across the heath, trying to pretend he wasn't getting rescued from a bog by a bunch of lowly squaddies. We hooked the back end of the stranded vehicle up to the front of mine, engaged reverse and revved up the engine in low ratio. The cable went taut, took the strain and the Land Rover popped up onto firm ground. Major Important was studying a local area map, still pretending none of us was there and we hadn't helped him. The lovely blonde was leaning out of her window, keeping an eye on progress.

I turned to Rupert. I still had the bet on with him. 'I bet you I can get off with her tonight.'

Rupert shook his head. 'No you can't, mate – she's much too good for the likes of you. You've got absolutely no chance.'

'Thank you,' the blonde called.

I climbed down from the cab and strolled over. 'That's all right – any time you need a pull. What's your name?'

'Michelle,' she said with a very slight accent I couldn't place, 'Michelle Wharton. People call me Shelley.'

'Shelley,' I said, 'my name is Michael Flynn. Would you like to go out with me for a drink tonight?'

'No,' she said, 'I can't: I'm going on leave to Wales tomorrow morning. I've got to pack. I'm already late because of this.'

I hit her with my best smile. 'You would like to go out with me, Shelley. I'll come by the women's block and pick you up at eight o'clock.'

She shook her head. 'Thanks, but I don't think so.'

Once we'd beaten the heath fire to death, we got cleaned up and changed, and jumped in the Bedford truck we used to get into town. It had just started rolling towards the gate when I shouted: 'Stop!' Ray Dobie stamped on the brakes. I jumped out.

Ray said, 'What's up, Mike? Where are you going?'

'The blonde. I have to go and see her.'

There were about eight people in the truck, they started taking the piss. 'Come on, Mike, she's already said no. Get back in the van, you're wasting valuable drinking time.'

'No,' I said, 'I'll see you down town later.' I was wondering what had come over me. Ditching the lads on the way to a session was unheard of.

I walked back to the female accommodation block. A WRAC answered the buzzer. 'I'll go and see if Shelley wants to see you,' she said. All of a sudden, Shelley was standing there looking at me.

'I see you don't take "No" for an answer, Michael.'

'Not in your case. You will come and have a drink?'

She hesitated. 'It'll have to be quick – I still have to drive to Wales. Wait there a minute while I put some make-up on.'

We had a drink in a local pub. The drink turned into a meal. Michelle was smart, she was fun and she definitely had my number. But she still had to get to Wales. With things going so well, I didn't want to break it up. I had a sudden flash of inspiration. 'Tell you what: my family live in Cardiff, and I've got weekend leave. If you drop me off on the way, then we can share the driving.'

Shelley thought it over. 'All right then – I suppose that's a good idea.'

'It's a very good idea,' I said. 'See you in the morning.'

'I'm leaving at twelve o'clock sharp. Be there on time – I won't wait.'

The only problem was I had to work the next day. Despite what she'd said, Shelley waited for me. But that meant we didn't get going until four in the afternoon. The drive from Lulworth to Cardiff is never one of the world's easiest. On top of that, it was a Friday evening and the traffic was murderous. 'I'm never going to get to West Wales tonight,' Shelley said as we sat in a traffic jam somewhere outside Bath. 'What shall we do?'

'Don't worry,' I said, 'my sister, Christine, lives in Cardiff She won't mind if we stop overnight.'

Shelley knew a gambit when she saw one. 'Your sister won't mind? Does she have enough room for us both?'

'She has a front room we can bunk down in – if you don't mind that?' What a romantic. Shelley didn't say, 'Yes.' But on the other hand, she didn't say, 'No.' By morning, we knew one another a lot better. And I knew I'd found someone who was worth very much more than a daft bet.

After that first night, we started going steady – or we would have if my training at Lulworth hadn't come to an end and the Army hadn't posted me to Germany. I told Shelley I'd been posted to Detmold. She laughed. 'You think that's bad? Guess where they're sending me?'

'Er, Canada?' I hazarded.

'Worse, in some ways: Benbecula, in the Outer Hebrides.' Benbecula! That was bad. I could see what Shelley meant. You could catch a commercial flight to Canada. But as the base for one of the UK's most important missile-testing ranges, Benbecula was a tightly sealed military zone. The only way of getting there was on an RAF flight, or by a boat service that was also strictly controlled and in any case often didn't run because of the atrocious weather up there.

Shelley was a WRAC computer radar operator, a specialized job. If you wanted to keep a missile-testing range away from prying eyes, where would you put it? On a remote Outer Hebridean island. The MoD wanted Shelley to track its latest missiles up there. But when it came to seeing her, Benbecula was about as hard as it got. It would be a bit of a miracle if we survived it.

But life has a strange way of springing surprises. When I got to Germany, I discovered that Stephen Borja, one of the guys I'd known back in Cardiff had ended up in the Royal Corps of Transport. Even better, he'd been posted to Air Movements at RAF Gütersloh – twenty minutes drive from Detmold camp where I was based.

We met up for a drink one evening at a local bar. Steve asked me how things were going and I told him about Shelley. Or to be more exact, I told him about the problem of not being able to see Shelley. 'Benbecula? No problem, Mike. I can get you up there on the weekend RAF salmon run – leave it to me.' I thought Stephen was pulling my leg, not least because he'd used the words, 'RAF salmon run'. But no: as so often, the truth was stranger than anything you could make up. A tight-knit group at RAF Gütersloh had a nice little piece of private enterprise going. Most weekends, a C-130 Hercules transport aircraft flew the round trip from Gütersloh to Benbecula. It was a routine flight ferrying people and supplies. Steve said there was never any problem getting a seat. But there was some additional, unofficial business going on around the edges: the Hercules left Germany on a Friday afternoon and came back again on Sunday evenings loaded up with fresh, smoked salmon from the local Benbecula fisheries. Money and fish changed hands, the salmon was distributed around the various RAF air bases in Germany, lots of officers – and possibly even some of the non-commissioned officers – got to eat it, and everyone was happy. It was the most amazing break; it meant I'd be able to see Shelley most weekends.

I tend to live life on the expectation that everything will go well until it doesn't. No one on the squadron knew about my weekend jaunts – I was acting strictly without official permission. The weather in the Outer Hebrides can turn from good to terrible in no time at all. If a storm closed in over a weekend and I got stuck on Benbecula, then I was going to have a lot of explaining to do.

Sure enough, one weekend when I'd been with Shelley, an absolute hooligan of a weather system roared in from the north-west: not just your standard Hebridean gale, this one was nudging hurricane force. 'Sorry,' the Benbecula guy in charge of air movements told me when Sunday afternoon came round. 'Looks like the return flight won't be going back today: the wind's much too strong. It's too risky.' I sat down on the nearest chair with a bump. Even for a guy who'd gone AWOL in the US for three months, getting stuck on a remote Scottish island was stretching the imagination. The orderly major would have my guts for garters when I failed to show up for duty on Monday morning. The air movements officer saw my expression. 'You never know though: it depends on how brave the pilot is feeling. And,' he tapped the side of his nose, 'there's a very big consignment of salmon needs shifting on this run.'

So followed the most terrifying flight of my entire life. We took off in a gale that was so strong you could lean on it – just walking into it ate every ounce of strength I had. But the pilot was a brave man. Some might say, foolhardy. There was only one passenger: me. So he let me come and sit up in the cockpit with him. I'm not sure this was an advantage. He turned the planeload of fish and unofficial weekending troopers into the howling wind, pushed the throttles forward a touch and released the brakes. As soon as he did that, the aircraft began to lift off the ground. We'd only moved a few metres down the runway, but I could see him trying to hold the aircraft down. The Herc kept trying to lift her blunt grey nose, bucking in the gale like a horse. The pilot gave up trying to hold it, let the aircraft have its head, tapped the throttle forward and eased back a fraction on the stick. The Herc shot up into the sky like a rocket, leaving such guts as remained to me far, far below on the ground. After that, I started paying much more attention to the weather forecast: if there was any chance it was shaping to blow over the weekend, I stayed put in Germany.

CHAPTER FIFTEEN

Denise had agreed to an amicable divorce, and we both had new partners. In the meantime, Shelley and I had decided to wed. It was more than a year since we'd met and we were still getting on really well. I had the feeling this was the woman who could help me settle down and grow up – be the woman of my life, in short. The nearest town to where Shelley's family lived was Grimsby. We couldn't get married in a church: I wasn't a practising Catholic, but I was still one by upbringing; more to the point, my dad was still a fully-paid up member of the faith. So a second church wedding was out of the question. The idea was for me and Shell to have a quick skirmish at Grimsby registry office, follow that up with a church blessing and then get on with the main business of the reception. We'd taken over a hotel in the middle of town for the occasion.

The date we'd set for the wedding – 25 July – crept ever closer. But in part as a result of my mother's well-meaning intervention, my first wife Denise had never signed the forms that would put a formal, legal end to my first marriage. With only four months to go before a planned wedding to a second wife, I was still married to the first one. That would teach me to try and save money on a solicitor. Denise was living in Feltham. I took the forms, explained that Shelley and I had set a date, and did my best to persuade Denise to sign them.

The first week in June came round and at last Denise signed on the dotted line. But I still had to wait four weeks before the decree absolute became law. All the coaches were booked to bring our families up to the hotel we'd taken over for the occasion; the church, the reception, the honeymoon: it was all paid for, it had all cost a bomb and unless the divorce was finalized in time it would all have to be scrapped and the wedding cancelled. In the end, it came right down to the wire: Shelley and I were getting married on the Saturday. The decree absolute went through with only four days to spare.

A coachload of my relatives who'd come up from Cardiff and surrounding district were staying in the hotel, along with a fair few of Shelley's family. Ray Dobie was my best man, and Rupert McKinney was on the sub's bench. The evening before the wedding, we went down to Cleethorpes on a stag run. Cleethorpes is a lovely old, traditional seaside town, all fish and chips, candy floss and kiss-me-quick hats. And lots of nice pubs.

Shelley's dad, Frank, had worked on the docks all his life. He's on the large side and he enjoys a pint. My father had worked on the roads all his life and he enjoys a pint, too. Although they'd never met before, the two fathers struck up a bit of a rapport.

After a few rounds, everybody started getting really friendly. Rupert got so friendly with Frank, he decided to give him a love-bite. It's his own special way of showing people he likes them. Rupert grabbed hold of Frank, picked him up and started trying to do a vampire impression on his neck. Frank took exception: the wedding was the next day and a love-bite on his neck wouldn't look that good in the photographs. And Shelley's mum would take some convincing he'd got the love-bite from a man. Frank said, 'Get off me, you big silly bugger!' He gave Rupert a friendly push. It would have put a smaller man through the pub wall. Rupert kept on trying to attack Frank's neck. At this point, my dad decided to lend his new pal a bit of a helping hand.

You couldn't really call it a fight, it was more of a friendly tussle, like three bulldozers in a bullring in a pushing match. It ended up with Vince getting a black eye, Frank getting a love-bite on his neck and Rupert getting a few bumps and thumps he was too pissed to notice.

I did my best to break it up, but I couldn't stop laughing. Opting for tactical withdrawal, I got them outside, hailed a cab and we made our way back to the hotel. I made it to bed. My dad didn't even make it back to his room. Early next morning, we found him snoring in the hotel lift. The night porter had been unable to wake him up: he'd been going up and down all night.

We had breakfast and then immediate family members headed for the registry office. Everything went fine there: Ray produced the ring, I put it on Shelley's finger and the clerk said I could kiss the bride. Wonder of wonders, Shell and I were legally married. As we were leaving, Shelley took the ring off – I was supposed to put it on her finger again for the blessing. On the way out, my dad said, 'Did I go up and down in the lift all night?'

'Yes, Dad.'

We went back and reconstituted. Shelley got into her wedding dress, me, Rupert, Ray and the other lads from the regiment climbed into our dress uniforms and off we went to church. The lads formed an arch of swords, Shell and I walked up the aisle to swelling organ music, it was all going really, really well. The priest did his stuff and then he said, 'Now I'm going to bless the rings.' Shelley's chief bridesmaid produced Shelley's ring. Ray Dobie didn't move a muscle. I turned to him.

'Ray, where's the ring?'

Ray looked blank. 'I haven't got the ring.'

I was certain he was winding me up. 'Come on, Ray – give us the ring.'

'No mate,' he shook his head, 'really, I don't have it. I gave it to you at the registry office and you never gave it back.'

I turned to Shelley. 'Have you got the ring, Shelley?'

'Why would I have the ring, Michael?'

The priest was waiting, the whole church was waiting, and there was no ring. The people in the front pews had heard all this. They included Shelley's Aunt Pat. Quick as a flash, Aunty Pat stood up, took off her own wedding ring, came up and handed it to Ray. 'I think,' she said, 'you need this.' Ray gave me the ring and I slid it onto Shelley's finger. And that's how Shelley came to get married in her Aunty Pat's wedding ring. You can imagine how pleased she was.

My dad came up to me at the reception, he had that look in his eye I remembered as a kid, when he'd just caught me doing something naughty. 'All those times you said you were in Germany, Michael, it turns out you were really in Northern Ireland.'

Fuck. What a time and place for him to find out. 'I'm sorry, Dad. It's just that I knew you wouldn't like it if I told you the truth.'

'And your mother and sisters were in on it too.' He took a swallow of his beer. I took a swallow of mine.

'How did you find out?'

He touched the side of his nose. 'A little bird told me.'

'You mean one of my mates. Who was it?'

'No names, no pack-drill. Anyway, your mate didn't know he was letting the cat out of the bag. He thought I already knew about it.' I gazed at my dad. He didn't really look all that angry. In fact, there was the hint of a smile on his face. I suddenly realized my father had known – or suspected – the truth all along.

I reached for his empty glass. 'Fancy another one, Dad?'

He handed it over. 'Why not?'

Shelley and I went to Majorca on honeymoon; that was another disaster. With money tight, I'd booked a package more or less at random from an advert on the television. Every hotel in the resort including ours turned out to be filled with big gangs of lads there on stag runs.

We came back off the perfect romantic honeymoon to find a message from Shelley's mother. Hazel had been reading the local paper and she'd seen an announcement in the Lost and Found column: 'Found: one gold wedding ring, outside Grimsby registry office on 25 July.' Shelley and her wedding ring were happily reunited. But we never solved the mystery of who'd dropped it.

*

A couple of months after we were hitched, Shelley left the Army. We spent some time travelling, mostly in Europe, and it was much better fun than the honeymoon. I went back to the squadron in Germany, the Army rented us a married quarter and that's where we lived for the next couple of years. At the end of 1987, I was promoted Corporal of Horse. Then, in 1988, the regiment posted me to Knightsbridge barracks.

Its streets stuffed with exclusive shops and millionaire homes, Knightsbridge is one of London's most expensive areas. The average pay of a trooper with a family back then was hardly enough to support basic human life. The local rich paid their nannies more than the government paid us.

To make ends meet, a lot of the soldiers based at Knightsbridge took on extra jobs. I got a part-time job driving a dustbin lorry around the Paddington area for a company called Onyx. It was a bit of a rubbish job. Shelley did some cleaning for a doctor's surgery and for a rich businessman who lived nearby.

We thought if we were going to have a family, it made sense to have the children close together. Our first child, Liam, came along in December 1989. Sean followed shortly afterward, in 1990. With Shelley now at home looking after the boys, we struggled even harder to get by.

Knightsbridge barracks is basically a tower block with some admin buildings and stables attached – it doesn't have a garden. But it has a secret weapon when it comes to bringing up small children – Hyde Park. We could more or less fall out the front door into this massive park: there were playgrounds, rowing and swimming in the Serpentine, horses, trees and plenty of nice walks. We had Harrods department store as our supermarket – that sounds expensive, but at the time a pint of milk there cost no more than it did in Tesco. We could catch the bus into the West End with its theatres and cinemas – it was a great place to live. I loved London then and I still do.

There's always a Blues and Royals squadron stationed at Knightsbridge, and there's always a Lifeguards squadron. They alternate duties day for day, and the overwhelming majority of those duties are ceremonial. Ceremonial duties meant dressing up in number one uniform and in boots that had been bulled to an eye-watering shine. It meant pomp, drill and learning about horses. It meant learning to ride. Being a tanky, I didn't really take to all of this right away. Luckily, I had Major Whitespunner and Rick Manning to help me. Rick took me under his wing when I first got to Knightsbridge, he taught me how to run the stables, how to look after the horses, keep the accounts straight, keep everything under tight control.

Horses and I had never been the best of friends. That now had to change. I started taking lessons with a member of the Household Cavalry's permanent riding staff, otherwise known as the Blue Mafia. That's because they wear dark blue uniforms. I was lucky enough to get a good instructor. Slowly, I began to get the hang of riding, until I could be reasonably confident of not falling off. Some months later, when I'd finished riding school, the annual senior show jumping competition up at Thetford came around. Everyone in the Household Cavalry had to enter. As first prize, Harrods had put up a saddle worth £800. Shelley said that would buy us the new double bed we needed, so I'd better win it. If I did win, I had my sights set on a four-star foreign holiday.

But I was up against the massed ranks of born-to-the-saddle Household Cavalry officers. They'd grown up with horses and most of them had learned to ride shortly after they'd learned to walk. I'd only just got the hang of it. But I had a secret weapon, the most important thing of all when it comes to show-jumping – a good horse. Not just a good horse – a push-button horse. As soon as I tried him out, I knew Equerry was special. He did what I wanted him to do almost before I'd asked. In his younger days, Equerry had been a bit of a star. He'd jumped in some of the top tournaments, including the Horse of the Year Show, and regularly come out a winner.

The day of the competition came round. The fences weren't all that high but they were packed close together, with some very nasty turns in between. It came down to which horse and rider could make the hairpins the sharpest and fastest, against the clock and keeping a clear round. I was sitting on Equerry waiting for my turn to go when a Blue Mafia Corporal of Horse named Brian 'Errol' Flynn came up. We might have had the same surnames, but we weren't related.

'Listen, Mike,' he said, pointing at the jumps, 'if you cut through that fence there, pull him sharp round and then take the next fence at a forty-five-degree angle ...'

My gaze followed the obstacles as Errol talked me through the course. 'I can't do all that,' I said when he'd finished. 'It's impossible.'

Errol shook his head. 'You don't have to – let the horse do it. You know Equerry was a top show-jumper in his day, don't underestimate him. Trust him to do the job. Neck rein him hard as you like: he won't mind, for him it'll be just like old times. Treat him like you would a polo pony. He'll come good for you, or my name's not Errol Flynn.'

I studied my touchline coach. He didn't seem to be pulling my leg. 'All right then,' I told him, 'I'll give it my best shot.'

We trotted out into the arena. Equerry's ears went up, he knew what was what. I could feel his excitement and eagerness, it sparked my own. This was what my lovely horse had been born to do, and trained to do, and what he liked doing. I leaned and spoke softly to him. 'Steady, boy. Wait for it.' The bell went, the sweep-second hand started racing round the clock and we were off. Errol had told it right: Equerry flew over every fence. He loved being pulled round, in fact he was into some of the turns almost before I could catch up with him. I heard cheering from the stands and looked up. We'd completed the course with no fences down and in the fastest time so far. 'Good boy,' I told Equerry, 'you did a great job. Now all we have to do is wait and see how the others get on.'

I was standing in the wings holding Equerry's reins when the results were announced. 'And the winner of the 1988 Household Cavalry Senior Show-jumping Tournament is: Corporal of Horse Mick Flynn, on Equerry.' I turned and patted Equerry on the neck. 'We've won! Get in there my son!' I rode Equerry proudly up to the podium. He got a nice blue winner's rosette pinned to his forehead, which I could tell he really liked. I got the beautifully made Harrods saddle. I took it home and showed it to Shelley.

'I won, Shell. What do you think?

Shelley had a gleam in her eye. 'I think it will come in very useful, Michael.'

It did. A couple of weeks later, I got back home from an exercise. Shelley took me upstairs and showed me our lovely new bed. She'd sold the saddle for £250.

CHAPTER SIXTEEN

I'd just been posted back from Knightsbridge to Windsor early in the New Year of 1991 when we heard the regiment was earmarked for a role in Operation Granby. Saddam Hussein's army had invaded Kuwait the previous summer and since then the Iraqi dictator had ignored all attempts to make him withdraw his forces. Granby was the UK's part in the invasion if it came to war.

In typical Army fashion, no sooner had we been warned off about Iraq than we got a new job, codenamed Operation Woodshed. Woodshed was a joint effort with the Metropolitan Police aimed at protecting London's Heathrow airport, and the aircraft that used it, from attack. Especially the aircraft considered at the time to be at greatest risk, the El Al flights to and from Israel.

The first time armour had been deployed at the airport, 'Tanks patrol Heathrow' was front page news. And they were our tanks, or rather light armoured vehicles, which made me feel especially chuffed: the Blues and Royals hadn't yet merged with the Lifeguards to form the Household Cavalry – that would happen a year later.

Our Scimitars and Spartans might look impressive on the TV news, but in reality we knew they were more of a deterrent than anything else. Surrounded on all sides by busy roads, Heathrow is so big and so open it's almost impossible to guard completely against a concerted and well-planned surprise attack. But we kept vigilant and did our best. The El Al flights were always the last to land. That meant we often didn't get off duty until one or two o'clock in the morning. But there was the odd side benefit: sometimes, after work, we got to go on one of the supersonic Concordes, sit in the comfy leather seats and drink the mini bottles of champagne left over from the latest flight. It made a change from the turret of a Scimitar. No stewardesses were harmed in the making of these extra reconnaissance trips.

When our tour of duty at Heathrow airport ended, B Squadron began to train for a new mission. And what a mission: a surprise attack on Kuwait airport, an opening shot if Saddam refused to budge and it came to a ground war. A Tactical Air Landing Operation (TALO), the idea was to land a mixed force of our armour and about 100 men of 3 Para, go in fast and hard, shoot up the Iraqi forces guarding the airfield, seize it, secure it and hold it as a forward strip for follow-on forces.

The raid was the full Freddy Forsyth: very like the 1976 Israeli attack on Entebbe airport, Uganda, when a mixed force of Israeli commandos and armoured vehicles conducted a successful surprise attack on a team of gunmen who had hijacked an Air France Airbus with Israeli citizens on board. For our own raid on Kuwait International, the plan was to have two Scimitars in the back of two C-130 Hercules transport aircraft, come in low and fast, touch down and brake like crazy, roll the vehicles off the tailgates at high speed and go for it guns blazing: the Paras in WMIK Land Rovers armed with .50 cals and twin 7.62mm machine guns, us with our armour. Shock and awe our way to victory.

We practised for the new mission at an airfield in Kent. Over and over again, until I was dreaming about skimming in low over the treetops, steaming out of the back of a Herc, racing for the terminal and gunning for Iraqi troops. If we did it once we must have done it thirty times. The practice runs were hairy enough, but unless the Iraqi defenders were all fast asleep when we landed, the real thing had every chance of being the most almighty firefight. So it wasn't a complete surprise when they cancelled the op. I was gutted – I'd really been looking forward to it.

In the event, the attack on Iraqi forces in Kuwait that began with a massive wave of air strikes on 17 February 1991 was so overwhelming that less than two weeks later the defeated Iraqi forces had quit Kuwait and the war was over. The squadron hadn't really done any actual fighting, which was really disappointing. Combat is what you train for in an armoured regiment. And it had been a long time since the Falklands.

I went back to Windsor and the armoured side of the regiment. From there I deployed with B Squadron, The Blues and Royals on a training exercise to Cyprus. For obvious reasons, trips like these are known as 'sunshine tours'.

Dry and mountainous with handy stretches of plain in between, the Cyprus battle training area gives units a chance to experience something very close to desert conditions. We'd been charging about up there for two weeks, and by the time we'd finished we'd worked up a bit of a thirst. When we got back to Camp Bloodhound, Jimmy Evans, Motty the Welsh Guard and I went out on the town in Paphos. We ended up in what looked from a distance like a nice pub. But as soon as we walked in, we could see it was a bit seedy. We'd already had a few, and because I hadn't had a drink for a fortnight the alcohol went straight to my head.

We'd been drinking for an hour or so when Jimmy, who'd been chatting to a local woman, went upstairs with her for a cup of tea. I was sitting in the bar on the ground floor trying to focus hard on the same spot. The only trouble was, it kept moving. Some time went by and then Motty came in. 'Come on, Mick,' he said, 'we've got to go.' He looked a bit anxious. 'Go where?' I wondered.

Motty said, 'Jimmy's in a bit of trouble. We've got to go outside and give him a hand.' That snapped me out of it. I got up and followed Motty down the dingy corridor that led to the main entrance. There was a hatch to one side at the end where you paid to get in, then a sharp right-angled turn into the entrance hall. As we drew near I could hear all this commotion going on. A few of the local guys who worked at the joint were pushing and shoving Jimmy, shouting very unfriendly things at him in Greek.

'What's going on?' I asked Motty. 'Why are they pushing him around?'

'There was a problem upstairs. They want Jimmy to pay for that cup of tea.'

Just then one of the bouncers hauled back his arm and smacked Jimmy square in the face. Jimmy staggered backwards, hand to his mouth. Another member of B Squadron, Paddy Brown, had come outside to join us by now. Paddy shouted, 'What the fuck are you doing?' at the guy who'd hit Jimmy. The same bouncer drew back his arm again and smacked Paddy square in the kisser, too. 'Right,' I thought, 'this guy's going to wear it.' I stepped in and hit the bouncer as hard as I could. I broke his nose. He went straight down and lay on the deck, out cold. Blood poured out and down his shirt front.

Bouncers come in twos, always remember that. Often, they come in packs. They did now. I saw a shadow flicker to my right and turned. A second bouncer, right on me. He hit me in the chest. I hardly felt it for the drink, adrenalin and anger. I stepped to the right and hit him back as hard as I could in the face. He went down like a skittle and rolled away clutching his eye. I should have gone after him and finished him off.

By now the whole place was in uproar. There were four or five of us fighting the same number of bouncers. So far, honours were about even. Paddy and Jimmy were back in the game, they were trading punches good style with the local boys. The next thing I knew, the bouncer I'd put down was back on his feet again.

I felt a blow in my gut. It didn't hurt much. But then Paddy yelled, 'Mike! Look at your shirt!' I looked down and saw blood seeping out on my clothes. The bouncer had sliced my stomach wide open. Half my stomach bag was hanging out – an ugly grey mess, shot through with purple veins. The sight surprised me. I reached down and tried to push all the tubing back in.

Earlier that same day, I'd been out and bought myself a new pair of summer strides. 'My new chinos,' I thought hazily, 'look at them, they're covered in blood.' I stood in the harsh light, watching as I bled slowly to death. I saw my shadow outlined sharp on the floor. It looked different: hunched up, with one elbow sticking out at an odd angle. I saw the guy who'd knifed me running away in the distance, maybe he was scared of what he'd done. He wasn't half as scared as I was.

He'd stabbed me twice: the first blow had hit me square in the chest, but I'd been lucky: the chest bone had deflected the knife-point to one side. But the second slash had sliced me open from waistband to ribs. I looked down again. There were bits of purple, bits of red, it struck me how unusual it all seemed. I was beginning to get this detached feeling, as if everything around me was moving slowly away. The bouncers were yelling in Greek, there were other voices shouting, 'Get an ambulance! Call an ambulance!' in English. The words seemed somehow muffled, as if they were coming from far, far away.

Paddy and Motty came over to see if they could help me. They couldn't, but I was glad they were there. I went into dying cowboy mode: 'Paddy, mate, I'm dying: if I don't make it, tell my wife I love her …' A right proper John Wayne performance, the whole six-gun. I thought of Liam and Sean, our two lovely boys, and our third child, Gabrielle, who was on the way. 'My kids, Motty – don't forget my kids. Tell my kids I love them, too, will you?'

'Nah mate,' Motty said, 'you're not going to die – you'll be fine. They'll fix you up in hospital right as rain – you'll be out in no time.' From my own first aid training, I remembered this was the correct procedure with the seriously injured: tell them they're going to be all right, keep them talking if you can, maintain their morale: things must be bad if Motty was giving me a pep talk. An ambulance screeched to a halt in a drama of sirens and lights. I felt my guts sag and wobble as they lifted me onto a stretcher and slid me in the back. As we rolled towards the hospital I lay there staring up at the roof. I thought, 'Right, that's it: if I make it off the operating table I'm quitting the Army. Life's too short to be away from the people you love.'

The ambulance took me to Paphos General Hospital. They patched me up, stuck three pints of blood into me and whacked me with a hospital-acquired infection for good measure. But the Cypriot surgeons who operated on the cut must have done a fair job: a few days later I was lying in bed feeling really bad, tubes were coming out of my body from every orifice and I felt I was dying. One afternoon, a local man came into the ward. He looked furtive. He also looked familiar. In fact, now I examined his broken nose, he looked extremely familiar – it was the wanker who'd stabbed me. He was hanging around the bed opposite, pretending to visit someone.

We had a court case coming up – what the fuck did he think he was doing? 'Oi!' I shouted, 'what are you doing in here?' A look of hatred mixed with panic came into his face. He turned his head from side to side, as if he was trying to make up his mind what to do. If he came anywhere near me, I didn't know what I'd do, but I wasn't just going to sit there and take what he dished out. The water jug on the locker might come in handy. But I'd lost a lot of weight and I wasn't in my best fighting form. I shouted, 'Doc! Doctor! In here!'

A doctor came bustling in, looking nice and official in a white coat and stethoscope. 'Mr Flynn – did you call?' As soon as he saw her, the bouncer who'd stabbed me ran away. Happily, I never saw him again.

Thirty minutes later, my troop leader, Josh Innes-Chambers, and Squadron Quartermaster Corporal (SQMC) Vince Maher visited. I said, 'I need to get out of here: there's a cleaner looking after me and the bloke who stabbed me's just been in here.' Vince asked me if I'd like him to stay. 'No,' I said, 'just get me out of here.'

A team of RAF medics came and picked me up at nine o'clock that night when the hospital was nice and quiet. A doctor noticed me go but he didn't say anything. I was still in bad shape, but I had to stay in Cyprus for my trial at Paphos magistrates' court. On the day, the clerk read out the charge sheet – it basically came down to GBH. The prosecution's main evidence against me was the CCTV footage that had been recovered from a camera positioned outside the bar. It showed the first bouncer hitting Jimmy and the whole thing kicking off. Then it showed the rest of the fracas up until the moment when I'd hit the second of the two bouncers. Down he went, clutching at his face. I can't say I felt any remorse as I saw him fall. That was the bastard who'd got back up and come very close to killing me. I was looking forward to seeing that bit, it would prove that I'd acted out of self-defence. The video stopped just before my attacker pulled the knife.

My brief asked the prosecution lawyer why the footage had stopped at the crucial moment. 'No more footage,' the prosecutor told the court, 'the tape broke at that point.' I don't think the Fair Trials International organization operated in those days, which was a pity, I needed it. My defence asked what had happened to the piece of broken tape. The police sergeant present shook his head. 'Not usable,' he said. 'Not available.' The magistrate found me guilty of assault and hit me with a £400 fine. Even though one of them had started the fight in the first place, and a second had tried to kill me with a knife, none of the Cypriot citizens involved suffered any punishment.

CHAPTER SEVENTEEN

Quitting the Army in 1993 wasn't quite as easy as it might have been. I'd just had a really good annual report and been recommended for promotion to staff corporal. Under the rules that then pertained, that meant I didn't qualify for any redundancy. But I had a card up my sleeve, in the shape of my former troop leader from Knightsbridge, Captain Nick Lane Fox. Nick was now the adjutant of the newly formed Household Cavalry regiment. With his help, I managed to get out with some money.

I wasn't too worried about leaving the Army, not least because Shelley and I had bought a three-bedroom house in Grimsby. Having the security of my own place made a big difference, as did the redundancy payment. Getting stabbed really had made me think about life: the number one priority for me now was to spend as much time as I could with my wife and children, watch my three nippers growing up while they were still young. And try to do the same myself. I'm being serious: the camaraderie thing, if you can call it that, the endless rounds of drinking and joking with the lads had been fun, the womanizing in the days when I was still single. But I'd come to realize how much all that stuff had been stopping me from growing up. I really felt that it was time to move on. I knew if I stayed in the Army, a part of me was always going to stand still. Mostly at a bar with a glass in my hand.

Now I was a civilian and living up in Grimsby, the world and all its opportunities were open to me. But there were so many of them – what was I going to do? It happened that my brother-in-law, Tony, was a mad keen angler. Close to national standard. Every spare moment he got, Tony was out there with a rod and line, fishing. I didn't fish at all, in fact I've never fished. But Tony had spotted a gap in the market for bait, and in particular, for maggots. Not in the UK, where they were in plentiful supply, but on the Continent, where there were plenty of anglers but not, Tony told me, anything like enough maggots to go round. 'Very hard to get maggots when you're in Belgium or Holland. People are crying out for them.' Tony had been over on the Continent many times for angling competitions, he ought to know.

'You reckon we could supply them? Do we breed them ourselves? Or buy them in?'

'We should look into it,' Tony said.

I looked. It wasn't a pretty sight. You start off with some road kill or a chicken carcass and leave it in a suitable spot a long way from human habitation. Flies come up and lay eggs in the flesh. You wait for the larvae to hatch, feed them up, dye them a nice colour, then put them in the fridge and Bob's your uncle.

Except it wasn't. There was a whole science to it. Some anglers want maggots that float, for catching surface feeders like chubb. Others want their maggots to go straight down – that depends on the feed you give them. Given all the palaver involved, we decided to buy the maggots in. 'What about transport?' I wondered.

'We each put in the same amount of money and buy ourselves a second-hand Ford Escort van. We buy ourselves a pile of maggots, load them up, hop on the ferry and sell them to angling shops, clubs, anyone who wants them. We'll start in a small way. Do a bit of a recce on the Continent and see how it goes.'

And that's what we did: set off for Belgium one day with 10 gallons of maggots in the back of the van. The first angling outlet we stopped at bought the whole lot: the owner wanted more. Bingo! The next shop was disappointed we had no maggots left. Everywhere we went it was the same story. After that first trip, we saw there wasn't so much of a gap in the market as a blazing great hole. It was also clear that we were going to need a bigger van.

I was so busy setting up the new business with Tony, driving to Holland and Belgium, looking for new customers, I didn't have the time to miss the Army. I didn't feel relief about leaving or envious about my mates who were still in. I stayed in touch with people, but the demands of civilian life – especially the bit where you have to make enough money – swallowed me up.

Once we'd got the hang of it, the business grew arms and legs. More and more orders poured in. We formed a company; we had to buy a second van, then a third and a fourth, hire drivers – the demand for bait seemed to be insatiable. By the end of the first year, we'd sold 4,500 gallons of maggots and turned over £250,000. As we rolled into 1994, everything was going great guns. We were shipping 2,000–3,000 gallons of maggots a week to Germany, Belgium, Holland, Iceland and even to the United States.

It had occurred to both Tony and me that we should bring something back on the vans, and not run them home empty. At the time, the various European currencies worked in our favour. I started buying fishing tackle in Belgium where it was cheap and reasonably well made, shipping it back and then selling it on wholesale to shops in the UK. That new venture started taking off, too.

Everything in the garden was rosy – always a sign that it's time to step back and look your business hard in the eye; think about who's doing what and how they're doing it. I'd hit on the idea of bringing back fishing tackle, Tony had started importing part-worn tyres from garages on the Continent and selling them on to garages in the UK. Before we knew it, these businesses started turning a profit as well.

One day, one of the vans arrived in the yard – one of Tony's, filled up with slightly worn tyres. The driver got called away unexpectedly. He told me he'd be back in an hour or two and he'd unload the Sprinter as soon as he returned. I was busy at the time, but I needed to turn that particular van around as soon as possible: there was a new shipment scheduled out later that evening. I set to work, hauling tyres out of the van and bouncing them on into the warehouse. One tyre hit the concrete floor, rolled, hit the far wall and bounced back. And a stream of what looked at first sight like small brown bricks tumbled out of it.

Odd. I walked over and picked one of them up. It was a packet of some kind, double-wrapped and carefully sealed with tape. I found a knife and cut it open. The second I did that, the smell hit my nose and I stepped back. Someone had spotted an even more lucrative gap in the UK market – for cannabis resin. And judging by the number of blocks I'd discovered in that one tyre, he was well on the way to filling it.

Used tyres have a strong smell. Whether it was strong enough to put the dogs off the scent if Customs & Excise had decided to investigate the load there was no way of knowing. What I do know is I went completely berserk. One by one, I went through the pile of tyres. More than half had sealed bags of resin tucked inside them. By the time I'd finished there was a small mountain of brown packets piled on the floor. I don't know how much they were worth on the street, but it had to be a fuck of a lot of money.

Not to say he was responsible, but the driver of the load never came back. I shovelled the drugs into a couple of garden waste bags, tied them tight, weighted them and threw them in the river Humber. I'd begun worrying about the business recently: Tony's competitive fishing was taking up more and more of his time and there was an ever-increasing amount of red tape and petty officialdom to wade through. And now this.

It was time to move on. Tony and I split the capital and parted on good terms. Shelley and I bought a village shop and post office in the village of Marshchapel near where some of her family lived. The idea was that she would run the post office and shop, with me helping out as and when I could. At the same time, I'd carry on in business for myself. I decided to concentrate on the fishing tackle business, which was still going great guns.

By now, it was 1995. You might think, 'once bitten, twice shy' – but I only took on a partner to save on transportation costs. And he wasn't a business partner, as such. Let me explain: I was selling a lot of imported tackle, which I bought from a Dutchman by the name of Jan. Jan sourced the gear from China. I put on my own mark-up and sold it on. But the tackle wasn't very well made: a lot of it was coming back broken, for refund. At first, Jan refunded me in turn for the duff gear. But as more and more of it came back in, he started refusing to pay. I decided to take matters into my own hands

If Jan could buy from source, what was to stop me doing the same? I heard about an upcoming Chinese fishing tackle trade exhibition, flew to Beijing, had some interesting chats with some very astute Chinese businessmen and spent some very enjoyable evenings warbling over Maotai in Beijing's finest karaoke bars.

I eventually struck a deal on some good-quality, inexpensive gear I knew I could shift at a profit. I was just getting down to serious business with my new supplier, when who should turn up but Jan. Jan wasn't very good at concealing his feelings. And he was pretty annoyed.

'What are you doing here, Mike?'

'Business, Jan. Same as you.'

Rather than lose my custom completely, Jan suggested we share shipping costs. I wasn't shipping anything like a full container-load on each run, so splitting the cost in half made obvious sense.

For the best part of a year, I did a roaring trade. Once again, it was more than I could do to keep up with demand for tackle. But next thing I knew, a large and well-established fishing manufacturer sent me a solicitor's letter. It came right out of the blue. By now, I'd expanded my range of goods to include a 'bed chair'. A bed chair is what upmarket anglers have in their 'carp dome'. A carp dome is basically a luxury tent, and the bed chair is a kind of luxury folding sofa that goes inside it. The angler can set a remote bite alarm, settle

Above Tpr Anthony Dykes.

Left On ops in Northern Ireland, 1979, Glassmullan Camp.

Above Tpr Anthony Thornett

Left 3 Troop, Glassmullan Camp. I'm standing top left. Bottom row, second from right, is Steve Ripton, a.k.a. the 'Screaming Skull'.

Andersonstown police station, 1979. Note the Vauxhall Viva at the front, the first car I ever owned.

View from the main gate. The IRA position was on the upper floor of the barber's shop, next door to the florist.

1982, Ascension Island – Operation Relax.

Ascension Island – view from the landing craft, practising beach assault.

Maintaining armoured vehicles aboard SS Elk.

Departing for the Falklands at dead of night, in secret.

Falkland Islands overwatch position, Port San Carlos.

Lt Mark Coreth's Scorpion destroyed by
an anti-tank mine.

Tap dancing on Argie anti-tank mines.

Home Sweet Home – disembarking vehicles in
the UK.

Kuwait 2003 – church parade one hour prior to the invasion of Iraq.

Me (on the right) and Benny Benson on a Scimitar in Iraq.

Burning oil fields, Iraq.

T-55 destroyed by TOW missile and our Scimitar fire.

T-55 abandoned after strikes from our APDS fire.

Iraq 2003 – setting up satellite comms.

WO2 Dai Rees interrogating captured Iraqi soldiers. Squadron O.C. Major Taylor is at background left.

Iraq 2003 – Lt Alex Tweedie.

Iraq 2003 – Major Taylor breaks the bad news about squadron fatalities.

Bosnia 2003 – on patrol near Banja Luka.

Me in turret of Scimitar, with Tpr Morgan prior to late-night vehicular escapade.

Banja Luka Metal Factory, 2003–4.

Arms find from a small village outside Banja Luka.

Afghanistan 2006 – Lt Ralph Johnson
sleeping.

Camp Bastion, Afghanistan. Left to
right: L/Cpl Andrew Radford CGC,
L/Cpl 'Pez', Lt Tom Long.

Musa Qal'ah overwatch position:
LCoH Jock Anderson.

LCoH Steve McWhirter calling in air strike.

Air strike hits 1km wide of target.

Form-up point prior to clearing Taliban positions at Musa Qal'ah ambush site.

3 Para infantry and D Squadron Scimitars deploying from landing zone and moving forward to forming up point.

Ambush site, Musa Qal'ah – Lt Johnson's destroyed Spartan. Note the 'mouse holes' in the wall behind.

After the ambush – my Scimitar abandoned in a ditch. Note the cage armour.

Taliban IED firing position.

3 Para and D Squadron searching ambush site for missing personnel.

Buckingham Palace with Shelley and Gabrielle after I received the CGC from Prince Charles.

back in the chair for a nice nap and the remote alarm will wake him when he's got a nibble. Call that fishing?

Whatever you call it, my bed chair was selling like hot cakes. The solicitor's letter said my Chinese suppliers had copied it without permission. And as the man selling them, I was in breach of copyright, patent, trademark and everything else they could think of. I'd had no idea there was a problem, but that didn't make any difference to the legal position.

The letter demanded £50,000 in compensation.

Luckily, I'd already sold most of the bed chairs. The company suing me sent their man down to inspect my stock. All he could see was a stack of knackered carp chairs. The upshot was, I destroyed the carp chairs and paid a legal charge of £2,000. Which is a lot better than the £50,000 they'd originally claimed.

I re-sourced my whole range to make sure there was no risk of any more solicitor's letters, and started over. For a few months, everything went back to normal. I was shipping lots of stock, making lots of money and ploughing some of it back in to grow the business. The future looked good. So good, Shelley and I took the children on our first really expensive holiday, to the Bahamas. Before leaving, I paid Jan a large sum of money for the next consignment of fishing gear, including a newly designed bed chair.

Off we went to Nassau. We were having a great time, but after we'd been in the Bahamas for about a week, I noticed the amount of capital in the company trading account was unusually low. I called my secretary. 'How come the accounts are so low?'

Brenda said, 'It's odd you should ask that, Michael: I've been worried about it, too. We've paid for that load of stock you ordered, but none of it has actually arrived.'

The sun seemed to burn a little hotter when she said that, and the noise from the hotel around me seemed to fade into the distance. 'What?'

'Nothing's come in from Jan. We've paid him, but we haven't had a delivery. And he isn't returning my calls.' As soon as she told me that, I knew what had happened. Jan had done a runner with our stock and the money.

I rang our supplier in China. 'Sorry,' he said, 'I believe you when you tell me you've paid Jan, but I'm afraid he hasn't paid us. What he has done is disappear. He's gone off with our money, too.'

I'd lost a tonne of wedge and I wanted it back. The first thing I did was take Jan to court, which cost me more money. The Dutch court found in my favour, but I didn't get a penny back. Jan had used the money he'd defrauded to buy property in Holland for members of his immediate family. Under Dutch law, that meant no one could get at it – not even the court. But that wasn't where the story ended. Some of my staff weren't very happy about being made redundant. They decided to pay Jan a surprise visit. Reason with him forcefully and see if they couldn't persuade him to pay up. They didn't get any actual cash. But it might be they got some satisfaction.

The second betrayal of trust was a blow too far. I sold all my remaining stock, dissolved the company, paid off the staff and quit business. While I'd been getting done over, Shelley had been doing really well in the shop. But managing it on her own was a struggle – it was obvious the place would do much better if we worked together. The business expanded, as did the house, which we enlarged to four bedrooms. And that was what I did for the next three years: got up early in the morning, sorted the newspapers for the delivery boy and minded shop.

It was quiet. Very quiet. No men in stocking masks tried to hold us up with sawn-off shotguns – there's never an armed-robber around to liven things up when you want one. The children grew bigger and went to school, bounced on the trampoline in the back garden and did proper country children things. I made sure we had enough supplies of Blu Tack, paper clips, stamps and tins of baked beans. The months and the years rolled by, and the greatest professional excitement we had was on the days when the paper boy failed to turn up: you'd be amazed how small-minded some people can get if their daily news-paper doesn't arrive exactly on time. Rather than take the horrendous ear-bashing, on those days I'd shoulder the satchel and do the round myself.

And then, one day in 2001, Jimmy Evans invited me to his wedding. Jimmy and I had been friends since 1979. He was slightly younger than me, quiet and he used to read a lot of books: often he'd be reading several at the same time. As a joke one day, the other member of our room, Hugh Davies, and I decided to nick the last five pages out of Jimmy's latest three books. We built a little fire under his bed with the pages. When Jimmy got into bed and was reading his latest novel with his headphones on listening to 'Fat Bottomed Girls' by Queen, I leopard-crawled under his bed and set the bonfire alight. Then I crawled back and got into my bed and pretended to be asleep.

Jimmy shot out of bed shouting 'Fire! Fire! The floor below us must be on fire!' Me and Hugh thought this was hilarious. Hugh walked over with a kettle and put the fire out. Jimmy looked at the remnants of the pages, realized what had happened and started laughing. 'You pair of bastards.' Jimmy could have a laugh at what had happened, he was OK, and now accepted into our room. He became one of my best friends in the years ahead of us.

CHAPTER EIGHTEEN

It was at Jimmy's wedding that Rick Manning first sounded me out about rejoining the Army. It had been a while since I'd seen Rick, but he looked well on Army life: Rick had been the same rank as me when I'd left; now he was captain.

'How's life, Mike?'

'Oh, you know, doing OK. But it's a bit boring.'

'Have you ever thought of coming back in? The regiment needs people.'

At the time I thought Rick must be joking. But then, at a second wedding a few weeks later he raised the matter again. The wedding in question was Harry Ford's. Harry had been with me in the Falklands, we'd formed a kind of unofficial Falklands club with Klaus Fisher, Gary Birch and the other guys who'd been in the campaign. It was a way of keeping in touch, not least for me.

A few months before I got the wedding invitation, I'd been to see Harry in hospital. He'd been teaching at Lulworth Gunnery School when a roller shutter fell on his head and knocked him unconscious. Harry recovered and carried on as normal, but he kept complaining of headaches. The doctor said he thought Harry was pulling the wool and sent him away. It's scary how often medics do that kind of thing. Then half Harry's face froze. They did a scan and discovered a massive abscess on the frontal lobe of his brain. To relieve the pressure they cut some of the nerves in that region – which left

Harry with the old familiar smile on at least half his face.

It was August, and the weather was very warm. Combermere barracks hadn't changed a bit in the years since I'd been away. The accommodation blocks were the same as I'd left them eight years previously, the very same ones I'd moved into as a nineteen-year-old single trooper. We had once pinched a house sign that said Honeysuckle Cottage and placed it outside the D Squadron accommodation block. It was still there; it reminded me of a night long ago at our local, the White Swan. I'd just pulled a new bird. When I asked her where we should go to carry on the evening's fun she said, 'Lets go back to Honeysuckle Cottage.' She was a nice girl, the memory of those days made me smile.

Rick and I had a beer or two and chatted about old times, but I could tell Rick had something more important he wanted to say. 'Mike,' he said eventually, 'have you thought any more about what I said at Jimmy's wedding? I mean, about rejoining the regiment?'

I was so surprised it took me some time to answer. 'Rick,' I said when my wits had caught up, 'I'm forty-one years old. I've been out of the Army for eight, nearly nine years. Do you really think I can come back in and be useful at my age?'

'Listen Mike,' he said, 'we need you. We're really, really short of good NCOs. You're very experienced – hardly anyone in the regiment has seen the action you have. You're not aggressive but you like a fight, and you have the skills to go with it. That's a good combination – in fact, it's invaluable. If you do decide to come back in, I'm certain we can come to some arrangement about your rank. I spoke to Captain Carney at Jimmy's wedding. I'd have to speak to him again, but if you do decide to sign back on then you might be pleasantly surprised.'

I was still speechless. The first thought that came into my mind was 'Shelley'. We had a happy and comfortable life together. Uneventful, granted, in comparison with combat – but it was safe and predictable, and I got to spend time with my family. What would she say if I told her I wanted to go back in?

I turned back to Rick. 'I'll think it over. Talk to Shelley. Sleep on it and let you know.'

'Don't think too long,' he quipped. 'You're not getting any younger.'

I spotted Shelley on the other side of the room and sidled up to her. 'Hi there,' I said. 'How're you doing?'

'All right, thank you very much. How's Rick these days?' It was a loaded question – as usual, Shelley was ahead of the curve: she could tell there was something up just by looking at me.

'Rick's fine. We had a chat.'

'Did you? What about?'

I went for it. 'How would you feel if I rejoined the Army? Rick asked me about signing back on with the regiment. Could you run the shop and the Post Office by yourself?'

Shelley didn't say anything for a few seconds. Then she said, 'Is that what you really want, Michael?'

'Yes,' I said, looking round the crowded room. 'Part of me belongs here.'

'Well,' Shelley said, 'I know cashing Giros and stacking shelves doesn't do it for you.'

'Do you?'

She took my arm. 'Of course I do. It's not quite the same as war, is it?'

'It doesn't have the whiff of cordite.'

'I know', she said, 'that the newspaper round isn't exactly thrilling. Look: if you promise to come home to me every weekend, then maybe we can work something out.'

We both knew the Army means you can't promise anything. But then, sometimes in life you just want things to be true. 'Every weekend,' I said, 'Promise.' I don't think either of us really believed I'd re-enlist. But a couple of days later, I picked up the phone.

Six weeks after that call, I found myself running up a great big, steep, horrible mountainside in Scotland. Gairlochead to be exact, one of the world's least hospitable places in bad weather, unless you like cold, wet and mud. It was only the beginning of October, but already it was freezing. Most days it rained and/or snowed, and when that didn't happen there was sleet. I had the most ginormous heavy pack on my back. I was cold, I was wet through and I missed my family. My lungs were burning and my knees ached. I had chafing burns on my shoulders, back and neck. And big, horrendous blisters on my softy civilian feet. 'This is all a terrible, terrible mistake,' I thought. 'Even worse than doing Charlie's paper round when the boy doesn't turn up on time.' But in spite of all the physical discomfort, deep down where it counted a part of me was enjoying it. I was back where I belonged. And the extra income was extremely welcome.

The Army didn't make me do Phase One (basic infantry) training again, but I did have to retake Phase Two, the training for your specific job and regiment. I was already a gunnery instructor from my previous service. There was a space in D Squadron: Tony Smith, the SCM, asked me if I wanted to fill it. After a few weeks to make sure I could still cut the mustard, the squadron asked me to take a commander's course. I'd left the Army in 1993 as a Corporal of Horse; they'd allowed me to rejoin as an Acting Lance Corporal of Horse. I'd thought it wouldn't matter going back in at a lower rank. In fact, I was hungry for my old status: I wanted to get back up the ladder as fast as possible.

I'd no sooner completed all the courses than the firefighters' strike kicked off in the spring of 2002. The firefighters wanted an increase in their basic pay from £21,531 to £30,000. The local authorities and the government wanted the fire brigade to modernize and reform its working practices. After much argy-bargy, the firefighters held a ballot and came out on strike. So we had to provide emergency cover. Not, sadly, in nice shiny red, modern fire engines. The firefighters kept those under lock and key. We got the aged 'Green Goddess' fire trucks, more properly known as the Bedford RLHZ Self-Propelled Pump.

They were extremely antiquated vehicles – some even dated from the 1950s. But most of us felt right at home driving the Green

Goddesses because they were based on the old Bedford Army lorry. We put out a few cats, rescued a few grannies stuck up trees, that sort of thing. Or it might have been the other way round. What we didn't do was get the call to put out any serious fires. It was peacetime, and the living was easy. I could go home most weekends as promised. Shelley was coping well in the shop, she'd taken on some part-time help in my absence – what could possibly cloud the blue horizon?

Lt Alex Tweedie tipped up into D Squadron as 3 Troop's new commander that summer. Alex had been to Eton and he had a degree from Newcastle University. As soon as I found out his name was 'Tweedie' I went up and spoke to him. 'Mike Flynn, Lieutenant: hello. I think I knew your dad. Was he in the Army?'

'Yes,' Lt Tweedie said, looking a bit surprised. 'My dad's Major Gavin Tweedie, Household Cavalry.' Lt Tweedie was twenty-four years old and fresh out of Sandhurst. He'd only been in the Army for twelve months.

'Well then I do know your dad – he was squadron leader of C Squadron at Detmold when I was stationed there in 1986. I saw you there, too.'

He looked even more surprised. 'Really? Where?'

'There's no particular reason you should remember me. I was one of 500 soldiers on camp. But I remember seeing you from time to time, knocking around the barracks with your brother and the other kids.' Now he was all grown up Alex Tweedie wasn't quite the image of a dashing cavalry officer – he was dark and he was handsome, but he'd missed out on the tall bit.

Lt Tweedie said, 'I don't remember you, I'm afraid. But I do remember we used to bother the troopers when we'd run out of things to do. Small boys and guns. I hope we weren't too much of a nuisance?'

'We never actually met: I was usually lying low, trying to hide from the SCM while I recovered from a Herforder Pils hangover.'

He said, 'The way the squadron operates, with any luck we'll get to know each other now.' We did: by the end of pre-deployment training we'd reached the kind of understanding you want between a senior corporal and a troop leader, where one party knows what the other's going to do before he does it.

A wide social gap used to exist between officers and other ranks in the British Army, especially in the cavalry regiments, which in the past were targeted by the sons of wealthy, aristocratic families. But as the Army has become more professional, most of the 'them and us' stuff has disappeared.

I introduced our new troop leader to David Simpson, 3 Troop's Corporal of Horse. I'd only recently met Dave Simpson, or Simmo, as everyone knew him. Simmo was a very experienced soldier who'd seen action in the First Gulf War. Like me, Simmo enjoys a pint or five, the difference being that when Simmo's had a pint or five he'll argue about almost anything, including whether or not the sun's going to come up the next day.

Under normal circumstances, if Alex Tweedie had had a problem he'd have turned to Simmo for advice. But perhaps because I was older and I'd known his father, as he found his feet in the troop Alex turned to me on the rare occasions that he needed help. I thought it was odd that our paths had crossed again: Alex had been so small when I first saw him, and now here he was in charge.

Christmas 2002 came around, and with it, some welcome leave. We were due back in barracks on 5 January 2003. But then, while the Christmas tree lights were twinkling and we were working our way through the remains of the turkey, I got a phone call. I had to report back for duty two days earlier than scheduled, on 3 January. So did everyone else in D Squadron. The voice on the other end of the line said, 'You probably know why.'

We all knew: it was Iraq all over again. Same war against Saddam Hussein; different day. We'd all seen the TV news reports. United States President George Bush and British Prime Minister Tony Blair had repeatedly told the world that the Iraqi regime under its brutal dictator Saddam Hussein had 'weapons of mass destruction' (WMDs) that could, Blair asserted, 'be ready within forty-five minutes of an order to use them ... He [Saddam] is a threat to his own people and to the region and, if allowed to develop these weapons, a threat to us also.' If the last bit was true, and Saddam had weapons capable of hitting British interests, then it was our job to get out there and fight that threat. The fact that many British people doubted whether Saddam Hussein really did have any weapons of mass destruction wasn't our problem.

Obviously, the best place to train for the hot, dry conditions you get in the Iraqi desert is a cold, lumpy stretch of soaking wet Welsh moorland. We went to Castlemartin, near Tenby, and after that the Brecon Beacons: wet preparation is better than no preparation. I had two young and inexperienced crew in my wagon: twenty-one-year-old Benny Benson, who was a pretty fair gunner, and nineteen-year-old Adie Conlon, who was from Middlesbrough and had the broadest north-eastern accent you've ever heard. It took me a few tries before I could fully understand him, especially when he was talking on the i/c. Then there was his driving. For a tank driver he'd have made a good bat. Time after time, we'd be driving along, I'd spot a big bump coming up in the ground ahead of us, I'd wait for Adie Conlon to avoid it and he'd plough straight in. It was OK for him – Scimitar drivers have a lovely comfy seat, better than a dentist's chair – they can sit there and take the knocks and hardly notice. It isn't quite the same for the two people squashed in the turret.

As the days rolled on it began to look ever-more likely we'd be going to war. Our vehicles were fitted with extra 'under armour' as protection against mines. Once they'd all been reinforced, the Scimitars and the other wagons left for Kuwait on hired civilian ships. When that happened, we knew it was only a matter of time before we joined them.

I was on duty in the guardroom in Combermere barracks when these two new blokes came in. They'd both transferred over to the

Household Cavalry from the Royal Pioneer Corps. The Pioneers do all the Army's unglamorous jobs, like filling up fuel cans and digging latrines. Everyone wants the Pioneers, but nobody wants to be them. As part of yet another cost-saving exercise, the Pioneers had been rolled up with a number of other units to form the Royal Logistic Corps. The new guys had taken the opportunity to jump ship.

The two new men had been assault pioneers, which meant they'd leaned much more towards the infantry side of things. Both qualified instructors, they'd also both been training new recruits at Pirbright barracks. As the evening wore on, we got talking. If he'd wanted to, 'JC' Moses could have made money working as a stand-up comedian. JC was joining A Squadron. He had a natural wit that had been sharpened on the streets of Manchester. But JC's fondest wish was to become a sniper. He was very serious about it: he must have been – his rifle was camouflaged and he had a T-shirt that read: 'One shot, one kill'. Plus all the Gucci kit, like special gloves and shades, elbow pads and all the rest.

The other newcomer was a bit more reserved. Stocky and strongly built, his full name was Matthew Hull, but everyone knew him as Matty. I could tell right away that Matty was a good professional soldier: he took the Army seriously and he wanted to get on in his new regiment. He'd joined the Household Cavalry as a lance corporal, and he was keen to find out more about the kind of soldiering we did and move up the scale.

Like me, Matty was married. When we did work together – aside from the fact that he was good company – my professional respect for him steadily increased: he was a very good instructor on all types of small arms, especially the SA-80.

In February 2003, three members of D Squadron: Corporal of Horse Alan Anderton, Lance Corporal Matty Hull and I deployed to Kuwait as members of the advance invasion team. Matty and I had done specialist courses in range management. We were there, among other things, to map out suitable sites for practice ranges. Alan, who was the squadron radio instructor, was there to help set up the communications network.

We flew out from Brize Norton on a jumbo jet borrowed from Iceland Air. The last time I'd been to war, in the Falklands, they'd sent me off on a huge chartered cruise ship. This time I was travelling on a huge chartered plane. I said goodbye to Shelley. It was only two years since I'd rejoined and here I was back off to battle. So much for coming home every weekend. And no one had any idea how long we'd be out there.

Since I'd first joined the Army in 1978, we'd been trained repeatedly for rolling plain warfare against the massed Communist armies of the Warsaw Pact. But here I was again, part of yet another British Army expeditionary force, getting ready to fight a type of warfare for which we'd hardly trained at all.

This would be the biggest British forces deployment since the Second World War. With a total of some 45,000 personnel, it even made the Falklands task force look puny. After an unusually pleasant flight complete with a movie, we landed in Kuwait City. Then it was into the trucks and on to a huge area of open desert near the Iraq/Kuwaiti border about forty minutes' drive away.

We stepped out of the transport to an amazing sight – and 40-degree heat. We were sitting in the middle of a huge sandpit. With their scrapers and pushers, the Royal Engineers had bulldozed huge berms, or sand walls, to create a massive rectangular containment area, hundreds of metres long on each side. So far, the entrance was just a bloody great gap in one of the sand walls. There were sparse cooking facilities in the form of a single tent, but no showers or latrines. Instead we had 'field roses' – pipes stuck in the sand to pee in, which stink, and not of roses. No buildings – just a big, empty walled space, rapidly filling up with an army of machines and tents.

It might have been better if we'd been properly equipped. In fact, there were people there without any kit; others had the wrong type of kit. It was as hot as a whorehouse in Haiti, but the place was thick with red-faced, sweaty guys clumping about in leather boots and clothes meant for cold, wet northern European weather. There was a strong smell of mothballs: that would be the desert combats that been in storage from the last Gulf War. There weren't even enough armoured vests to go round. Well organized, it wasn't.

We needed all the skills and drills of an old-fashioned expeditionary force, of the kind that we'd developed in conflicts like the Crimea and the Boer War: butchers and carpenters, field cooks and foragers: skills that thanks to all the cutbacks – and the mania for privatization – had been slowly disappearing from the ranks of the British Army.

Although we were NCOs, the three of us shared a great big forty-man tent with those officers who'd also been sent out early. Like me, Matty was keen on keeping fit. Use it or lose it. But it was way too hot to run in the daytime. So I started getting up at 0615 and running round the camp while it was still cool. When you make any noise at all in a big open tent, people tend to hear you and wake up. On the third morning, Matty swung his legs to the floor and said, 'Mike, if it's OK I'll come running with you.'

'You're welcome,' I told him. 'Makes thing easier with a partner.' It became an early morning ritual. We started by circling the perimeter, and then, since Kuwait was deemed a safe area, we began to go further afield, running up and down the sand dunes in the surrounding desert. Legging it up dunes is a short cut to serious fitness. Like me, Matty was competitive: we egged each other on to go as hard as we could.

Thanks to the almost non-existent washing and toilet facilities D& V – diarrhoea and vomiting – broke out in the camp. As always, we did everything we could to make the best of a bad job. We dug proper latrines and installed Portaloos, which helped alleviate the sickness. When the rest of the squadron arrived we began sharpening our weapons, handling drills and prepping the armoured vehicles for combat.

There was one particularly brilliant development: a team of boffins – on $500 per diem – arrived to bore-sight and fit gyros to the Scimitar's gun aiming and target location systems. This was and is the biggest improvement to the weapons platform ever. The new kit meant we could lay a laser on a target, get its precise range, bearing and GPS location and bring down artillery onto that exact spot: mega. Another hugely welcome arrival was a several-tonne consignment of US MREs, or 'meals ready to eat', courtesy of our American neighbours. The MREs made a nice change from our own rations. Not nice, fantastic. In the first place, we didn't have enough compo rations of our own to go round. And one MRE bag had more food in it than the British Army's entire 24-hour ration pack. Besides, MREs came with a bag of Skittles. That's morale for you. In our own ration packs we had Yorkie bars, which melted in the heat. That didn't stop us. The approved Yorkie bar method is: cut one end of the bar open, stick it in your mouth and then suck the contents straight down your throat.

We'd done years and years of training. Now we had a chance to show what we could do in a real fight. That was a fantastic feeling.

CHAPTER NINETEEN

Shortly before dawn on the morning of 20 March 2003, D Squadron, The Blues and Royals rolled over the start line for the invasion of Iraq. Pretty much at full strength, D Squadron was made up of three Sabre Troops of four vehicles apiece: 1 Troop, 2 Troop and 3 Troop. For extra firepower, we also had a Guided Weapons Troop of four Striker vehicles armed with Swingfire anti-tank missiles. SHQ made up a separate troop with a mix of Spartan and Sultan command vehicles. I was in 3 Troop and my call sign was Three Two. I was still only a Lance Corporal of Horse.

Call sign Lightning Three Four, a US forward air controller (FAC), was attached to D Squadron for the push north. A wryly humorous, capable-looking man with a bog-brush haircut, Lightning Three Four was a member of ANGLICO (Air Naval Gunfire Liaison Company), the USMC (United States Marine Corps) unit that specializes in co-ordinating artillery, naval gunfire and close air support (CAS) for US and Allied forces. He had a big fat Humvee bristling with comms gear, and an Hispanic driver whose real name I never found out either.

D Squadron was part of 16 Air Assault Brigade, which was operating in concert with the 1st US Marines Expeditionary Force – in fact we were under US Marines command. The overall British effort was known as Operation Telic. Nobody knew what the word 'Telic' meant, until some wag claimed it stood for: 'Tell everyone leave is cancelled'. When I looked it up, the dictionary said it meant 'purposeful, with an aim'. The Americans called their own ever-so-slightly bigger advance Operation Iraqi Freedom.

Whatever you called it, the overriding strategy was simple. A column lead by the US 3rd Division would swing west and north from Kuwait in a wide, looping left hook, then turn east and north and hit Baghdad hard in the underbelly from the south. From a separate start line a few kilometres further to the north of that front, a combined USMC and UK expeditionary force – that included us – would punch north-north-west on a separate route through the broad, ancient marshlands north and west of Basra. We'd skirt the boggy ground to the east of the huge Hawr al Hammar salt lake where some of the Marsh Arabs still survived despite Saddam Hussein's persecution, leave Nasariyah tumbling in our dust and then press on to Al Amarah, a large town in south-eastern Iraq whose Shi'ite community had resisted Saddam's Sunni-dominated regime from the outset – and paid the cost in blood. As Shock and Awe attacked in tandem along these broad looping axes, other UK forces including the Royal Marines Commandos and 1st Armoured Division would secure the strategically important port of Umm Qasar on the Gulf in order to secure our supply lines, then move on to take and hold Iraq's second-largest city, Basra.

Coalition air power and artillery had been softening up the Iraqi defences for days: as the air strikes and bombardment went in, the ground sometimes actually shook beneath our feet. Now it was our turn to get in there and carry the fight. Everyone was psyched to the eyeballs, including me. This was the first time at war for most of the younger guys, including Matty Hull. One evening, he drew me aside. 'What was it like in the Falklands, Mike? I mean, what's it really like to be under fire?'

Every soldier who has yet to experience a firefight wants to know this. But there's no ready answer. I told him: 'Everyone reacts in their own way. The worst thing you can do is lose your nerve. The best thing you can do is use your training.' Matty thought about it. He was worried about how he'd deal with combat; in a way, he wanted to know what he was made of. From what I'd seen and heard so far, my guess was that Matty Hull would acquit himself just fine.

'There's something else you need to know Matty: I'm bricking it.'

He shook his head. 'No you're not – you're just saying that to make me feel better.'

'No, Matt, I'm not. I really am scared. It's twenty-one years since I was in the Falklands. Anyone who tells you they're not scared is a liar – or daft in the head.'

You can never tell who is going to step up to the mark when the shooting starts, but often it's the quieter ones. The guys who have been chopsing off about how much they're 'up for it' tend to be full of crap once the bullets start to fly. But there's no hard and fast rule – occasionally, one of the biggest bullshitters will turn out to have the coolest head. Nothing matters except the stuff that's inside you, and you can't know how that's going to react until a bullet or a bomb's headed your way. That's what makes going into battle so interesting. My own position as a vehicle commander also made a difference when it came to keeping up a brave face: I had to live up to expectations.

The day before we moved out they called me into the joint US-British Brigade Intelligence cell. It was an amazing sight: there were all of these big plasma screens displaying real-time 'downfeeds' from keyhole satellites, Unmanned Aerial Vehicles (UAVs, or drones), as well as footage shot by specialist RAF Tornado and other surveillance aircraft. Some of the best reports were coming in from elite units far out ahead of us, using the Mark 1 Eyeball and a satellite uplink. It was all extremely impressive, Top Secret stuff that made me glad I was on our side and not Saddam's. My past experience of UK Brigade HQ was four staff officers with binoculars and a dog standing round a map drinking tea. I exaggerate a bit, but all of the super-duper state-of-the-art electronic Intelligence feeding into the system was a definite improvement. Even so, everyone in HQ was on tenterhooks – 7 Royal

Horse Artillery had been shelling the Iraqi border area continuously for a number of hours.

Our primary task in D Squadron was to scout ahead of the main force, spot enemy positions, report their location, strength, type and readiness to fight, and call in artillery, air and ground forces as necessary. Whether in armoured vehicles like the Scimitar or on horseback, scouting is the traditional role of a light cavalry reconnaissance squadron. The whole point about 16 Air Assault is that it can deliver air manoeuvre, air assault and airborne operations at short notice. Born out of the 1999 Defence Review, it is now a rapid reaction force, seizing ground over great distances at high speed – and holding it until relieved by back-up forces.

As the eyes and ears of the main force, the cavalry often has the most up-to-date information about the emerging battlefield. That in turn means you often end up controlling the fight. That's a great job: it was what I'd trained for during most of my Army career and I was straining at the leash to do it. My only regret was that the US Marines were spearheading our own axis of advance. They'd most likely see the lion's share of the action. The words 'mopping up' had even been used when it came to describing our role.

At first light on the morning of 20 March we crossed the border into Iraq. We were now in the spearhead of an advance that would take us through the giant oil fields of Rumaila in south-central Iraq – many of which, Intelligence warned, the Iraqis had mined and intended to set on fire in the case of invasion. Our first objective was to drive the enemy forces out and secure the well heads before they could set them ablaze, with all of the economic and environmental damage that would inevitably cause.

Someone said we were close to where the Garden of Eden had been. That sounded exciting. But all I could see was field after field of nodding mechanical donkeys sucking oil from the earth, mile after mile of electricity pylons marching over flat, endless reaches of grey-brown, scrubby desert and zillions of ditches, canals and other water-

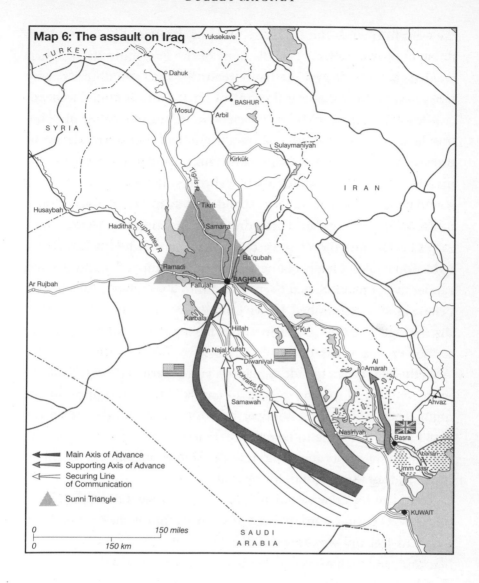

Map 6: The assault on Iraq

ways cut in the dreary, treeless landscape to drain the marshes. At one
point we passed a burst pipeline that had made a shallow black lake of
thick crude oil. The smell was sickening. If that's the Garden of Eden,
Cleethorpes gets my vote every time.

By the end of that first day, we were on the edge of the Rumaila oil
fields. There was a broad waterway ahead of us, about 50 metres wide.

We went firm while the engineers prepped the crossing site and then threw pontoons across. Two platoons of the Parachute Brigade had secured the far side and they were reporting they could hear enemy tanks nearby. Now that was the kind of Intelligence I wanted to hear.

Ahead of us, the USMC had been bombing and shooting anything hostile that reared its head, and Iraqi troops had been surrendering in droves. We saw some US main battle tanks that had been hit but not disabled. There were hundreds of prisoners of war for the MPs to round up and marshal, loads of abandoned weapons and bits of Iraqi uniform lying where they'd been dropped. The young Iraqi conscripts, in particular, just didn't seem to want to know when it came to a fight. You couldn't really blame them: poorly equipped, badly led and randomly supplied, they'd been forced into a war they clearly didn't believe in, shot at, bombed, blown up and they'd had enough. It looked depressingly as if the US Marines were having all the fun, while we got to mop up as advertised.

As the light began to fade, Squadron Headquarters (SHQ) came up on the radio and told us to go firm and laager up – camp – for the night. They said we'd be holding the position for two days. Even so, I told Benny and Adie to take the spare jerry cans off the wagon and refill the near-empty fuel tank. I don't like fuel oil hanging round on the outside of the Scimitar, for obvious reasons.

Confident my crew would get on with refuelling the wagon, I went off to the O Group (Orders Group) to check for operational updates. I had to feel my way towards the tent: we were operating a total blackout, and with everyone so hyped up my main worry was getting shot by one of our own sentries. D Squadron's leader, Major Taylor, started his briefing.

Our orders had changed: instead of overnighting at our present location, we were to move out in one hour. The anticipated Iraqi resistance hadn't materialized. Our new mission was to secure the oil fields at X, and deny the enemy use of the roads at Y and Z. No problem, I'd go back and tell the boys to get ready to roll. I groped my way back through the darkness, listening for sounds of Benny and Adie filling up the Scimitar.

Instead, I heard a low murmur of conversation. As my eyes adjusted, I saw them sitting on the front of the wagon, chatting. While I'd been away, neither of them had lifted a finger. Not only that, now I was back they still didn't seem too bothered: they were sitting up there as large as life, looking down at me as if I was some kind of minor nuisance. This was bad. Very bad. We weren't running a youth club. I needed to impose my authority on these two. Permanently. But in the PC climate that has now infected even the British Army, I wasn't allowed to grab hold of them and bang their heads together. I could shout at them – not too loudly – and put them on extra duties, but if I went by the book then that was about it. Pretty soon, we'll be so hedged about with legal and PC restrictions, British forces will no longer be able to defend the country at all. And if someone wants to behave like a lazy arse, there'll be nothing anyone can do about it – except lose the war. But lots of lawyers will be raking in nice juicy fees at the taxpayer's expense.

I stood there having a slow sense of humour failure. Then something struck me: we were at war now, all bets were off. I'd learned the hard way that in war, preparation often makes the difference between life and death. My crew had to realize we weren't still on Salisbury Plain. The boys sensed my anger. They jumped down off the Scimitar. 'Why haven't you filled up the wagon?' I demanded. 'Our orders have been changed: we've got less than an hour before we've got to move.' They looked at one another without speaking. I thought I detected a bit of a smirk. That did it: I stepped forward and smacked Benny on the chin. He staggered back, but didn't go down. I hit him again and he did. He lay on the ground, holding his nose and looking astonished. Adie had noticed what was happening. He legged it round the other side of the vehicle, picked up a full jerry can of diesel and started shouting, 'Mike, Mike, sorry Mike, we thought we had ages to fill up!'

'Fuck ages,' I shouted. 'Come here!' I chased him round the Scimitar for a bit, Tom and Jerry style. The boy could shift when he wanted to, I'll give him that. We stopped when we were both out of breath. By now Benny was sitting up, holding a fat nose. He looked a bit the worse for wear, but no blood was spilled and not too much physical damage done. When I'd got my breath back, I said: 'Listen, the pair of you: if you ever, ever let me down again when I give you an order you'll be fucking sorry.' And that was it – sorted. I never had a problem from my crew again. They were both good solid lads, all they'd needed was a bit of old-fashioned guidance.

CHAPTER TWENTY

We set out at daybreak as ordered. Towering columns of black smoke clouded the horizon ahead of us, the air growing darker as the pollution settled and spread. It was getting harder and harder to see anything. With some of the wells already burning, it was more important than ever to keep up the momentum, get up there and secure the ground before the Iraqis set every single one ablaze.

I noticed the odd guy on a motorbike to our front, barely visible in the murk. They'd come to within a couple of kilometres, take a good look at us and then race off again, talking into their mobile telephones. There was something wrong about their behaviour. At that stage it hadn't occurred to me they might be dickers – touts like the street rats who'd spotted for the IRA in Northern Ireland. I was definitely out of practice.

Sure enough, a kilometre or two further on up the track we started to get incoming artillery fire. It was raining in from about ten clicks away, but as time went by it was growing increasingly accurate. Some of the shells were falling within 50 metres of us, even though we were moving along quite steadily. That suggested someone was directing the fire. The Iraqis were stationing their artillery, mortars, multi-barrelled rocket launchers and tanks in and around schools, hospitals, sports stadiums, mosques and in heavily populated areas, shooting and scooting, popping out, firing a quick salvo and then scuttling back into cover – a tactic that made it almost impossible to bomb them.

Our troop was following Route Dagger, one of the main routes north to the western side of Basra, 2 Troop was about 4 kilometres away to the east on Route Sword, which ran roughly parallel, 1 Troop was 2 kilometres in the rear, with SHQ and the LAD a further 2 kilometres behind. We're not talking about a nice, solid road here: we're talking lots and lots of earth tracks, some better than others, that quite often do a disappearing act when you least expect it. We were constantly switching from one track to another, trying to stay on the best ground.

By mid-afternoon on the second day we were still about 20 kilometres south-west of Basra. Lt Tweedie's wagon started to play up – it had been having mechanical problems ever since we'd set out. Given the need for speed, Alex decided 3 Troop should split into sections, with the vehicles operating together in two pairs. I took up section with Lt Tweedie. Simmo and Gooders – Corporal of Horse Dave Simpson and Lance Corporal of Horse Rob Goodwin – kept parallel and about 500 metres to our west.

If you had to cast a soldier to play Friar Tuck, Gooders would pretty much fit the bill. He enjoys his food and a bit of a laugh and he doesn't have a nasty bone in his body. Not many people enjoy being shot at, though, and Gooders is one of them.

Within the hour, Gooders and Simmo ran out of northward track. They were forced to veer even further west in an effort to pick up a better route. We'd been coming under sporadic artillery fire since daybreak, but now mortar bombs began to rain in on us, the fire growing ever more accurate. All the time, I was scanning the ground ahead for enemy mortar positions.

Lt Tweedie came up on air and reported that his Scimitar was really struggling: he had no alternative but to stop and get the LAD to fix it. I asked Alex if he wanted me to fall back and join him, or push on another 1,500 metres to see if I could spot the main Basra–Baghdad highway. From the map, I knew the road must be close. Alex told me to push on alone.

In one of those accidents that so easily can happen in war, me, Adie and Benny suddenly found ourselves isolated in the lead Scimitar. A kilometre or so ahead of everyone else, we were now the tip of 16 Air Assault Brigade's spear.

A village came up to our left. About 1 square kilometre in size, it was a ramshackle huddle of low-rise blocks and compounds. It was so old and grey it looked like a picture out of a Bible story. I scanned it on 10x optical magnification in my commander's sight: it definitely wasn't going to win any 'best-kept Iraqi village' awards.

It was slightly cooler than it had been back in Kuwait now, and a bit greener. We began to breast a low ridge of hard sand. As we crested it I saw a bright flash of light followed by a puff of smoke. It had come from beneath a concrete bridge ahead and slightly to the right of our position, at a distance of about 2 kilometres. The bridge sheltering the mortar team spanned a wide, muddy ditch: the whole area we'd entered was criss-crossed with dykes, canals and irrigation channels; the vehicle tracks were all raised above the level of the surrounding waterways, like the canals I'd seen in Holland back in my fishing-bait days.

A second later a mortar bomb exploded about 200 metres to our rear with an almighty bang! We'd run right up onto the Iraqi position. While I was digesting that idea, I spotted a new threat: a Russian-made BMP-1 armoured personnel carrier, armed with a Scorpion-type 73mm gun, a machine gun and anti-tank missiles. It was parked hull down in a shallow dip, a short distance to the left of and covering the mortar team.

I hadn't been lying to Matty Hull: now we were under direct enemy fire, my throat was as dry as a bone and my breathing was fast and hard. The Iraqis under the bridge were popping out a steady stream of mortar bombs. The metal rain was creeping ever-closer to our vehicle. If we didn't do something about it, then any second now they were going to plant one in my commander's hatch. I radioed SHQ: 'Contact mortar! Wait out.' Bennie and Adie were keeping solid, just what we wanted.

We took up a fire position about 1,500 metres south of the bridge. I saw movement in my sights then and upped the magnification. There were at least ten Iraqi soldiers in and around the mortar position. Until then I hadn't spotted them. They wore khaki-coloured combat trousers and baggy black shirts with black headdresses. Most likely fedayeen guerrillas. As I watched, two of them began to climb up onto the bridge. When they'd reached the top, one of them raised a pair of binoculars and started to observe us. The other stuck a walkie-talkie to his ear and began talking into it. They were calling fall of shot, helping their buddies working the tubes down below walk their fire onto us.

I saw another bright orange muzzle flash. This time the shell landed about 150 metres to our rear. A second landed about 100 metres ahead of us, flinging sand and stones up in a grey shower. 'Fuck,' I thought, 'we're bracketed: he can see my line of sight.' The next round was going to hit our vehicle. We had to stop the enemy before he stopped us.

'Benny, let's take those two on the bridge out of play.' We lased the mortar to get a range and a bearing. Benny laid the gun on the enemy. I checked that the aiming mark in my thermal sight was onto the same target. Benny had his index finger on the red button.

I gave him the order. 'Fire!'

'Firing now.' He squeezed the trigger. The Rarden thumped out a clip of three high-explosive rounds. The tracer left a bright orange tail as it flew straight towards the enemy. To the west, Rob Goodwin's Scimitar opened up at the same time, pumping fire into the mortar position and the BMP-1. The Scimitar's new laser aiming and ranging system was deadly accurate: I could see the rounds exploding on and around the Iraqis. A 30mm cannon round travelling at 1,000 metres per second turns a human body to shreds. The Iraqi my binos were trained on disappeared in a cloud of blood and flesh. I'd seen this before in the Falklands, but it was still amazing to watch. And terrible. 'Target!' Benny shouted, much as I had back on the freezing slopes of Mt Kent: 'Got him!' He certainly had. The other Iraqi spotter began to scramble back down off the parapet as fast as he could, with a squirt or two from the machine gun to help him on his way.

The mortar team obviously hadn't enjoyed pieces of their dismembered comrade raining down on them. I could see them racing around dismantling the mortar, trying to move out as fast as possible. 'Switch to automatic, HE,' I said. 'Go on!' Benny was going on all right – he was going berserk. His blood was up, he kept shouting, 'Target!' as he spotted new and better things to fire at. He put bursts of three high-explosive rounds smack into the scurrying figures. At the same time he hosed them down with the co-axial GPMG. More bits of body and metal flew up high into the air. We were definitely having an effect.

Adie had gone quiet.

I switched fire onto the BMP. We hit that too, with a burst of sabot rounds, and as soon as that happened it bugged out. 'Marvellous', I thought. 'But we're spread out all over the place. We need to reconstitute the troop.' As if he were on the same mental wavelength, Alex Tweedie's voice came up in my ears: 'Whisky Three Two this is Whisky Three Zero, send a SITREP.'

'Zero, this is Whisky Three Two. Reference contact mortar position. Myself and call sign Three Three have engaged a mortar position at grid 549740. We have destroyed the mortar position and killed four enemy. They also have casualties. A BMP has now moved to the north and gone into dead ground to myself and call sign Whisky Three Three. We need a fire mission on that location.'

SHQ came back, 'Negative Three Two, the guns are still too far back to support. Suggest . . .' I never did hear what Major Taylor was going to suggest. His words were lost in a new roar of gunfire and explosions from close by.

Things were hotting up. Simmo came up on air. He'd spotted more enemy activity ahead of his location and gone firm to engage it. I heard the distant thump of his Rarden as he pasted a unit of Iraqi infantry. As he did that he came under fire from a Triple-A system. Anti-aircraft artillery, or AAA, was a priority target. It was essential we find the enemy system and knock it out. Gooders, in Whisky Three Three, moved back to support Simmo.

I moved the Scimitar east to see if I could spot the BMP-1 and the Triple-A, sending an update to keep Alex and SHQ in the picture as we rolled: 'Confirm engaged enemy mortar position, at least three enemy dead, damage to the mortar and equipment; enemy BMP is falling back.'

One of our Gazelle scout helicopters buzzed up to join us. I looked up and saw a Lynx coming in low and fast behind. No one had given us the heads up the helis were joining, but with its height advantage and extra firepower the Lynx in particular was just what we needed: an extra set of airborne eyes, and the TOW anti-tank missiles on its pylons might come in handy.

I gave the heli crews a tactical SITREP. Once he'd grasped the picture, the Gazelle's pilot edged closer to the ramshackle village: the BMP-1 had disappeared in that direction and I wanted to know if he could find it and help take it out. But as soon as it came within small-arms range, gunmen concealed in and around the settlement opened fire on the Gazelle. A burst of AK47 rounds slammed through its tail section, just missing the rotor. That was the end of our new ally – he turned about and headed back to base for running repairs. The Lynx pulled back too. But at least we now knew there were enemy troops in the village.

Enemy infantry were firing AK47s at us all the time now. That didn't worry me. But if we met more serious opposition – like, say, a couple of T-55 tanks – we had no immediate back-up. Given the risk, Brigade now imposed a no-go line: no friendly call signs were to move north of an east – west line bisecting the village.

The battle was hardening and quickening in pace. We were still taking small-arms, mortar and artillery fire. I wanted to locate the source of the enemy ordnance and hit back. I radioed SHQ: 'Permission to probe around our position. I'll stay within bounds and make sure we don't get cut off.'

Still marooned back in the rear with the gear, SHQ replied: 'Proceed with caution.'

I jockeyed the Scimitar up to the east and north. Almost immediately, a swarm of black-and-green-clad fedayeen armed with AK47s and RPG-7s scurried across one of the village compounds. With a shock, I realized I wasn't looking at a village square, but the parade ground of a full-scale Iraqi Army barracks. I was itching to open fire, but the barracks adjoined a straggle of civilian homes.

Just then I caught sight of a BM-21 'Grad' 122mm multiple rocket launcher, hidden in a dark stand of palm trees about two clicks to the north-west. An upgrade of the Russian Second World War system the Germans dubbed the 'Stalin Organ', this was extremely bad news. The Grad – the name means 'hail' in Russian – is basically a truck fitted with a bank of forty rocket tubes arranged in four rows of ten. It looks as if someone's been up the builder's yard and strapped a bunch of rainwater pipes to a flat-bed. But the weapon is no joke: each 122mm rocket propels a 20kg high-explosive warhead out to a range of more than 20,000 metres. When that lot starts raining down on you, you need the services of a very good umbrella.

A Grad was the last thing 16 Air Assault needed right now. The Grad's a really fearsome weapon, especially against troop concentrations. But it needs the protection of infantry or heavy armour. This one was all on its ownsome. Nothing the Scimitar couldn't handle with its 30mm. If we could get close enough, the collection of rainwater pipes was a sitting duck.

I wanted to kill it.

Nudging forwards, we came up on a double line of sand berms, spreading east – west for as far as I could see in the swirling smoke. Roughly 2 metres in height, the berms had gaps about 3 metres wide cut into them at irregular intervals. The Iraqis had built them during the 1980–1988 Iran-Iraq War to channel enemy armour into killing grounds. Our briefings had told us that, more often than not, the spaces between and in front of the berms were heavily mined. Waterways weaved in and around the obstructions, further restricting movement. Our little Scimitar was going to have a hard job getting through that lot.

Scanning rapidly, I spotted a main road over to our north running north-west – south-east at a distance of about 4 kilometres: the Basra–Al-Amarah highway. Anywhere else you cared to look front there were spiky green date plantations. After hours of bare open desert it was strange to come up on the lush richness of the trees, and see ordinary people and houses dotted in and around them. At the same time they were a bloody nuisance, providing perfect cover for the enemy. Lines of electricity pylons criss-crossing the landscape added to the confusing picture.

Never mind the scenery, we had something else to worry about. Gunfire rippled orange from a big plantation ahead of us. The Grad had moved north a tad and opened fire. I saw the multiple flashes from the palm trees as the rockets shot up out of the tubes. At more than 4 kilometres, it was too distant for us to engage. Even so I laid the sights on it, took a grid reading and got on the blower to SHQ. Nothing doing. The RHA with the 105mm guns were still too far south to be of use. In which case, I wanted some air support.

We drew a little closer to the berms, keeping an extremely wary eye out. At SHQ, the OC had asked Lightning Three Four to come up in support. The dust-covered Humvee rolled up alongside us a few minutes later. The FAC stuck his head out of the cab and said, 'Hi!'

I was extremely happy to see him: a good forward air controller is one of the most important assets you can have in battle – a 'force multiplier' if ever there was one. But there was a comms problem: the FACs were patched into the coalition air forces radio net, but the Scimitars weren't on it. I had to lean out of the turret and shout so that Lightning Three Four could hear me. The Grad in the plantation was still pumping fire over our heads south towards Basra. I pointed at the orange flashes. 'Do you see that rocket fire?'

He nodded. 'Affirmative. I see that position.'

'Call in air. Let's take that out.'

'I can, and I will.' Lightning Three Four lifted a walkie-talkie radio to his ear and spoke into it. The radio bit was only half the size of a shoe box, but the antenna was about as tall as the Eiffel Tower. Holding it, he looked like something out of an Action Man set.

Allied forces in the Second World War learned the hard way that in the smoke, fog and confusion of war, front-line troops are at extreme risk of friendly fire unless the person controlling close air support (CAS) is an expert. In that war, just about anyone could call up CAS. Our own forces paid for that in much unnecessary death and injury. Nowadays, no one can call in CAS except for a fully qualified FAC. When he was happy the target was a safe distance from all friendly forces, that it was firing at us from enemy lines and confirmed hostile, Lightning Three Four called the 'cab rank'.

A few minutes later, a pair of F-16s came screaming up. Popping out a constant stream of brilliant orange infra-red decoy flares, they wheeled round ready to run in on the Grad. The only problem being, they couldn't actually see it in among the trees. They fired a couple of missiles at the tree line to be going on with. Watching through the binos, I saw the ordnance land a fair distance away from the target.

I was determined to nail the Grad.

I leaned out of the turret and shouted down to Lightning Three Four, trying to help him talk the jets on. He knew where the target was. I knew where it was. From ground level, the bright orange flashes from the launch tubes as the rockets shot out were as plain as day. But the pilots still couldn't see the Grad. No problem: we'd just have to do a better job of talking them on. I jumped out and grabbed the walkie-talkie: 'Reference the village – you see that?'

Back came the flight leader: 'Seen.'

'Roger that. Look east of the village 120 degrees. There's a plantation of palm trees. Do you see the trees?'

'Seen.'

'Great. At the back, northern side of the palm trees: just before you get to the river embankment – there's at least one enemy vehicle firing over our position. Do you see it?'

'Not seen.'

Not seen. I thought, 'Not seen! Why the fuck can't you see it?' I tried talking him on with a different set of landmarks but he kept saying, 'Not seen.' Next to me, Lightning Three Four was getting a bit antsy about his countrymen's inability to see a large Iraqi vehicle shooting rockets at our forces to the south. Short of walking up to the target waving a red flag, it was hard to see how we were going to get the jets to hit it.

Just then, another weapon system opened up from the plantation. From the pattern and rate of fire, I suspected it was a ZSU-23-4. Designed as an anti-aircraft weapon but extremely effective against infantry and light armoured vehicles, the Russian-made ZSU has four 23mm automatic cannon, and a massive rate of fire. ZSUs eat Scimitars for breakfast if they're not eaten first. Whatever it was, we had to kill it – it was probably the same Triple-A system that had fired on Simmo.

It let rip with another burst. The muzzle flashes twinkled a brilliant orange-red in the gloom. You'd have to be wearing a blindfold not to see them. Sure enough, the flight leader came up a second later: 'Enemy seen! Weapon system seen in the trees!'

Marvellous. Now perhaps they could get on and whack the target. The F-16s ran out, looped around and turned in on their firing run. The leader drawled: 'Running in hot, running in hot.' Always a good thing to hear when the air power's on your side. They were firing Maverick anti-armour missiles, big bad beasties that make a horrible mess of plate steel. The flight leader opened up first, then the wingman. Time seems to slow down at moments like this. We watched as the missiles speared towards the target. There was an echoing *kaboom*! as the first one hit, followed almost immediately by a second resounding explosion. I lowered the binos and rubbed my eyes. Both pilots had missed the target by a distance of about 500 metres, hitting a patch of waste ground to the east. A tonne or so of dirt that had been minding its own business got an unexpected high-speed excursion skywards.

Not so marvellous. Next to me, Lightning Three Four was hopping up and down in frustration. I knew exactly how he felt. He was so embarrassed his pilots had missed I almost felt embarrassed for him. But the Iraqis hadn't failed to notice the size of the explosions to their front and left: the ZSU-23–4 and the Grad were starting to scurry away.

With their weapon racks empty, the F-16s rolled out and raced away to the south and east. What did a guy have to do to get some decent air support around here? I moved the Scimitar until I had a slightly better view of the barracks on the edge of the village. Maybe the enemy would make for that. There was a gate with a drop barrier set in the south wall and next to that an Iraqi flag flying from a pole. As I watched, another BMP-1 rolled out through the gate. It swivelled its nose and headed towards us. This was getting interesting. Suppose we moved the Scimitar to a position where we could cut off the BMP-1 and kill him? Yep, that struck me as a good plan.

As we manoeuvred the Scimitar along behind the twin lines of sand berms, the gaps between them suddenly lined up. I saw a T-55 tank through the nearest gap. Fuck! I did a double-take and looked through the sights again. There was no getting round it: there was a bloody great enemy tank directly ahead of us, at a range of between 3 and 4 kilometres. At the same time as I saw the tank, it saw us: the turret slewed round and the gun laid on our position. I called, 'Zero, this is Three Two: contact, tank, wait out!'

I'd been waiting to say those magical words for a long time. I'd practised them so many times in training – at last I'd got to say them for real. Tingling all over like a kid with a new bike, I was buzzing as if I'd been hooked up to an electric current. I was forty-three years old and I'd been waiting to say, 'Contact, tanks!' all my life. Now it had happened – but instead of sitting pretty in a nice big Challenger main battle tank, here I was in a thimble-sized Scimitar, which provided about a tenth of the Challenger's protection and came armed with a pea-shooter gun that was so small, the T-55 probably wouldn't even notice if we hit it.

Just as I was thinking this, the tank opened fire.

The round fell about 500 metres short of our position. Even so, the explosion shook the Scimitar to its metal bones. Adie yelled, 'Mike, we've just been engaged by a tank! By a tank!'

Benny yodeled, 'Tanks! Tanks! Mike, they're firing at us!'

'I fucking know they're firing at us, Benny – Adie just told me. And anyway I noticed. Calm down. Move, before he fires on us again.' We dropped back into cover behind the berm and moved 50 metres to the east. When we stopped again, all the gaps between the berms seemed to line up anew along another previously concealed diagonal. The Iraqis had built the berms with shooting lanes between them. Now they were aligned, I saw two more enemy tanks in a shallow depression about 4 kilometres out and slightly to our west. We scuttled back into cover before the first tank could fire again.

We were still way out on our own ahead of the main force with no back-up other than Lightning Three Four, who wisely was staying out of harm's way behind a berm. And now we were under enemy tank fire. SHQ tasked 2 Troop to come and help us, along with one of the Striker guided weapons vehicles from 4 Troop. It was good news about the Striker: now we'd find out if its Swingfire anti-tank missiles were up to the job.

Looking right, I saw dust rising up in long plumes as our buddies in 2 Troop hurried forward to assist. But because of the rough ground, they'd had to split into two units of two Scimitars. The two lead call signs now closed on us and took up a supporting position about 400 metres to our east. The remaining two Scimitars of 2 Troop would catch up as and when they could.

There was the deep roar of jets from the southern sky. I looked up to see the unmistakable silhouette of an A-10 looming up. A second aircraft came into view behind it. A dedicated tank-killing aircraft, the A-10 was a flying armoury. Designed to knock out modern Russian battle tanks, it ought to make short work of oldster Iraqi T-55s. The A-10 carried Maverick anti-tank missiles, rockets, bombs and other stores, but its trademark weapon was the GAU-8 Avenger 30mm rotary cannon. A seven-barrel Gatling gun, the Avenger fires a concentrated storm of depleted uranium (DU) rounds that can mince armour. At more than 60 rounds per second, its rate of fire is so great it sounds like a giant ripsaw cutting the air. Everyone knows when an A-10 is on the attack – you can hear the deep distinctive roar of its cannon echoing for miles around.

I heard it now. The gunfire came in bursts of 1–2 seconds. Watching front, I was looking forward to fireworks from the rich Iraqi pickings out there. I scanned between the berms looking for secondary explosions, a fireball, or at the very least some smoke from a burning Iraqi tank. Nothing. That was odd. What were the A-10 pilots firing at?

As that thought struck home, the pit of my stomach dropped away. I looked right. The remaining pair of 2 Troop Scimitars were in sight about 2 kilometres away. A great plume of smoke was rising from that location. I heard someone shout on the net, 'This is Whisky Two Two: we're being engaged by A-10s! Check fire! Check fire! Check fire!'

Call sign Whisky Two Two was one of 2 Troop's Scimitars. Its commander was Gerry Gerard. I recognized his voice: 'Check fire! Check fire! Tell those A-10s to stop engaging us!' The 'check fire' command tells every unit and call sign on your side to cease fire immediately, and hold fire until the problem is sorted. Anyone can make the call, but you only make it in a dire emergency. With a terrible sinking feeling, I realized the A-10 pilots weren't patched into the 16 Air Assault Brigade radio net. They were unable to hear Gerry's call.

Christ.

I could hear other friends in 2 Troop calling for help, one voice calling over and into another. Then there was silence. 'Traverse right!' I told Benny. The turret slewed round. I stared through the sights on 10x magnification, trying to see what was happening. One of the Scimitars over there was on fire. Black smoke streaked with long tongues of orange flame guttered from its shattered carcass. The second Scimitar was smouldering. There seemed to be men trying to get out of the vehicles, other figures trying to help them. It looked like a total, horrible mess. The A-10s had lived up to their reputation – at the expense of our own side.

A long finger of red smoke swirled skyward from stricken vehicles. That gave me a flicker of hope: red smoke signified a friendly call sign. When they saw it, the A-10s should break off the attack. To my right, Lightning Three Four was yelling, 'Check fire! Check fire!' into his handset for all he was worth. He had direct contact with the A-10s. Even if they ignored the red smoke, a call from their own FAC ought to make them cease fire.

It didn't.

As I watched, horrified, the A-10s began winging round in the fast, rollercoaster loop that meant they were coming in for a second strafing run.

I had the overwhelming feeling of powerlessness and dismay you get when something terrible's about to happen and there's absolutely nothing you can do to stop it. I could hear new voices on the radio net shouting for help. What was going on over there? The A-10s lined up on the burning Scimitars and rolled out, wings level. The rotary cannon slung under their shark noses roared into life again.

The buzz-saw sound of it seemed to go on and on. A fresh hail of high-explosive armour-piercing bullets smashed into our men and machines. I felt sick. In the face of that devastating aerial assault, the guys didn't have a prayer. I wanted to help them. But how? In all of the smoke and confusion, what was the best thing to do?

The Iraqis decided for me. The three tanks ahead of us had seen the air attacks go in. They could hardly miss the outcome: two of our

Scimitars were on fire, and a full-scale rescue operation was underway. The crew of the recce engineer Spartan attached to 2 Troop was helping men out of the burning vehicles and giving them first aid. While they did that, 1 Troop's Scimitars were securing the immediate area. But everyone at the scene of the attack was focused on the rescue. And with T-55s in the offing, we were seriously outgunned. If the Iraqi tanks broke through our own position and closed from their flank, the rest of 1 Troop and 2 Troop would be easy pickings.

'Traverse left!' I told Benny. The turret swung back round and settled. I looked through the commander's sight and drew in a sharp breath. Two BMP-1s were headed directly towards us. Behind them, in column, were the three T-55s. The Iraqis knew a good chance to strike when they saw one. They'd be stupid not to make the most of our disarray. Already, they were nosing through the gaps between the berms. We were only about 2,500 metres south of them. The intervening ground was criss-crossed with ditches, and we were at the end of the only available track. If they kept coming down that track they'd overrun us and kill us. Then, when we were out of the way, they'd hook round and blow every British vehicle at the scene of the friendly fire attack to pieces.

I grabbed my binos and my radio pack, jumped off the wagon and scrambled up the nearest berm. I needed to see the exact position of the enemy tanks. Dropping flat on the scraggy berm top I scanned the landscape. I hardly needed the binos: the enemy were in plain view, and getting closer with every passing second. I pressed the radio's send button to call it in. There was no signal. Shit! I shook the back-pack radio and tried again. The batteries were flat. That was infuriating. SHQ had to know what was happening; Brigade needed to stay on top of the emerging picture. And the fucking batteries were flat on my pack. I hopped back up onto the wagon, leaned down and shouted: 'Benny! Get on the radio! Tell SHQ three tanks and two BMPs are headed towards this position.' I sang out the grid reading on the Scimitar's Tactical Navigation and Target Location system (TNTLS):

'range 3,000 metres and closing. Tell them we need support like yesterday. And Benny . . .' He looked up. 'If you ever let the radio batteries go flat again, I'll wring your bastard neck. Got that?' Benny nodded and made the call.

Looking left again I could see the rescue operation was in full swing. Lightning Three Four had finally got the A-10s to cease fire: I could see the aircraft pulling clear. I climbed back inside the Scimitar. By now the interior was covered in gun oil and filled with smoke and cordite fumes. There were empty ammunition clips and cartridge cases scattered all over the place, and a fine layer of sand covered everything. It looked like a dog's breakfast. But compared with being up on the berm in the sights of an enemy tank gun, it felt like a home from home.

I switched my attention back onto the enemy armour: they were at 2,500 metres now and still closing. Point-blank range for a 105mm tank gun – but very long range for our 30mm.

We had two choices: we could either turn around and run away, or stay there and try to delay the Iraqi advance. It was a no-brainer. We had to stand and fight. If it had been me, Adie and Benny over there in the smoke and flames, then the guys in 2 Troop would have stood their ground without a thought for their own safety. I had to slow the enemy down at all costs. Otherwise, we'd all end up as barbecued meat.

All of these thoughts flashed through my head in the space of a few seconds. I had a default clip of three APDS (Armour-Piercing Discarding Sabot) rounds loaded ready to fire. 'Sabot' is extremely effective when it comes to destroying enemy armour. A sabot round is a long, thin dart of extremely dense, heavy metal like wolfram carbide or depleted uranium, encased in a plastic or aluminium 'boot' or 'collar'. The boot encasing it means the heavy-metal dart can be fired from a larger calibre gun barrel. When the round is fired, the sabot casing falls away. The difference in size between the sabot and the dart gives the projectile enormous kinetic energy. Travelling at hypersonic speed, the metal arrow strikes a tiny area of the enemy armour, vaporizes it on contact and punches through.

We lined up on the lead enemy tank. Benny opened fire. Watching through the sights, I could see rounds striking all around the T-55, but not hitting it. The tank started firing back. 'Benny,' I shouted, 'hit the fucking target!' We'd fired at least twenty rounds and I still hadn't seen a hit. I wanted to grab the hand controls and aim the gun myself, but that just wasn't possible. Then I saw one of our rounds strike home. Then another and another. Fucking brilliant! Benny had got the range and the correction. One of our APDS rounds struck the T-55's turret ring smack on: good shooting.

When APDS punctures a tank, bad things can happen. Often, the dart dislodges a large chunk of spall from the tank's interior. Whizzing around like a supersonic metal Catherine wheel, the whirling lump of metal turns the crew inside to mincemeat. At the same time, the dart's energy heats the tank up to 2,000°C – about ten times hotter than your average Sunday roast. That carbonizes the crew and cooks off the tank's internal ammo stores. Frightening. The bigger the APDS round, the better. We only had titchy 30mm rounds, but we'd hit our adversary where it hurt, in the gap between the turret and the hull. It might just make him think twice about coming too close.

It did: the lead T-55 stopped dead in its tracks. Hardly daring to believe my eyes, I watched the crew dismount and run away. 'Yes!', I shouted, 'Yes!'

Adie called back, 'Yes what?'

'We stopped them. We stopped the tank!'

That was fucking good news. But there was less good news – the other T-55 and the BMPs had cleared the line of berms. They were fanning out to engage us. I squinted through my thermal sight, which was slaved to Benny's. The enemy was spread out in a flat V-formation, with a second T-55 in the lead. I lined the sight up on the left-hand BMP-1. It was the type fitted with Sagger anti-tank missiles. The Sagger was a really serious threat to our health. But the Rarden would chew up a BMP and spit it out any day of the week. The BMP was sitting at a slightly oblique angle. I could see some of its side armour. 'Next target traverse left, BMP!' I told Benny. 'Loaded. Go on.' Benny opened fire. All three shells smacked into the side of the enemy vehicle. Benny was definitely getting the hang of this. I gave the fucker a burst from the machine gun for good measure. The BMP-1's side armour buckled and it started coughing oily grey smoke. Its hatches flew open, the crew started jumping out and running away.

What about the second tank? After a slight pause, it had started to roll forward again. The enemy had lost us.

It was payback time.

CHAPTER TWENTY-ONE

The Iraqis were drawn to the blazing wreckage east of us like moths to a flame. We had no heavy armour in support, there was still no artillery on task and no helicopters. But in one way, our luck was in: except for the BMP–1 we'd just knocked out, the Iraqis had so far been very cautious. In their position, I'd have been looking to race around and whack us much faster than they were. I manoeuvred a short way to the east and sneaked another peek at the enemy. The tanks were down our throats, now, less than 1,500 metres away. Even to the naked eye, they looked huge.

I was just wondering what to do when the Striker that had been ordered to join us rolled up out of the smoke. Lance Corporal of Horse Nobby Telling's head was sticking up out of the turret. The Striker halted about 80 metres away. 'All right, mate?' I shouted.

'Yes. You?'

'Marvellous.'

'What's up?'

'Tanks, Nobby. The nearest one's behind that berm to your right a bit and east. See it?'

'Can't hardly miss it. Fucker's right on top of us.'

I nodded at the rack of anti-tank missiles mounted on the rear of his hull. 'Think you can hit it?'

'If we can't, then we're in the wrong business. Only got two missiles left, though. And they really are close: best if we sep-sight.'

Based on the same basic chassis, from a distance the Striker looks like a Scimitar without the main gun. But when it comes to killing tanks, the Striker is a much more dangerous animal: in place of the Rarden cannon, it mounts five Swingfire anti-tank missiles in a rack of armoured launcher rails on its rear deck, with another five kept inside under armour. The Swingfire missile has a 7kg HEAT (High-Explosive Anti-Tank) warhead. It can do main battle tanks serious damage. I was looking forward to seeing that happening.

Quick as a flash, Nobby and his crew 'sep-sighted' – dismounted the Swingfire's sighting unit and set it up on the berm. The Swingfire missile takes its name from the fact that it can execute a 90-degree turn after firing. That allows the launch vehicle – and the gunner – to remain in cover. Nobby's gunner, Steve Chin, lay down behind the berm, switched on the Swingfire's sight unit and laid the aiming mark on the target. When he was happy with the sight picture, he squeezed the trigger.

There was a loud roar from the tail-end of the rocket as the pro-pellant ignited. The Swingfire is a relatively low-velocity weapon, so we were able to track it by eye. The missile shot up out of its launcher, made a stonking 90-degree turn as advertised and then streaked towards the enemy tank. At the last moment, it veered to the right and completely demolished a nearby bunker. Which Steve had mistaken for the tank.

Hmmm.

With no artillery and no fixed wing close air support available, Brigade had also tasked an Army Air Corps Lynx to come up and assist us. The Lynx came armed with TOW missiles that had the power to punch through more than eighteen inches of rolled armour. There was a low droning sound. I glanced back and saw the helicopter beetling towards us through the haze. As it drew near, the Lynx pulled into the hover. I told Adie to tuck us well in behind the nearest berm. We'd take a little breather while our helicopter friends had a crack at the foe.

The TOW missile is wire-guided: to aim it, the gunner needs clear line of sight. That meant the Lynx either had to climb above the tangle of power lines that lay between it and the T-55, or get right down beneath them. The pilot went for the second option, dropping the helicopter vertically until it was turning and burning directly above us. Its skids were almost brushing the top of our antennae. The noise from its rotors was deafening. The downwash threw up more dust, sand and grit and dumped it inside the Scimitar.

Just then, I heard the roar of a new Swingfire launch and looked front. Steve Chin was having another pop. The missile streaked towards the second tank. It hit the T-55's turret square on and punched through into the crew compartment. The ammo stores exploded in a mass of smoke, flame and supersonic hot shrapnel. The blazing wreckage turned into a fireworks display.

Two down. One to go.

The Lynx gunner was still trying to line up on the third tank. I'd told him where it was, but he was having trouble spotting it. The Iraqi camouflage was absolutely first-class: the T-55s were the exact same colour as the landscape. Unless they fired or moved, they were very, very difficult to spot in the undulating terrain – especially from the air. Smoke from the burning vehicles made things even more difficult.

No probs, I'd just have to talk him on as before. We stuck our nose out from behind the berm. There was the T-55, still rolling towards us. Beyond it, the remaining BMP-1 appeared to have stopped. 'Reference enemy tanks,' I said. 'Palm trees at one o'clock. Tank and BMP-1 immediately to the right of the palm trees.'

The Lynx pilot came back to me almost at once: 'Target not identified.'

I tried again, 'Enemy tanks, reference palm trees at one o'clock, just to the right of the palm trees . . .'

'Not seen. Target not identified.'

This was a bit frustrating. As in, I wanted to catch hold of the skids, climb into the cockpit and point out the target myself. 'You must be able to see them. They're hull down, immediately to the right of the palm trees . . .'

'Not seen.'

There was only one thing for it. I called the loitering helicopter: 'I'll mark the target for you: watch my trace.' Then I told Adie, 'Drive us up onto the nearest berm.' Adie gave it some welly and the Scimitar lurched up the slope.

The second we popped up into view, the remaining T-55 opened fire. The shell hit the ground directly in front of us. The world rocked. There was a deafening explosion and a massive fountain of sand and stones flew up into the air. The debris flew all over the wagon, at the same time lashing a sharp shower of stones across the hovering Lynx. The Iraqi tank commander had been waiting. He'd guessed which berm we'd show up on, ranged it accurately and it was only by the purest luck that he hadn't blown us to pieces.

But the T-55 had fired a round. If we could lay some tracer on him while he reloaded, maybe the Lynx crew would be able to see and engage him. The tank was stationary. We had our sights smack on it. And he was still busy shovelling another shell in the gun. The deal wasn't going to get any better than that.

'Fire!'

Benny squirted off a burst of 30mm sabot. The rounds hit the T-55 plumb on the turret, ricocheted off and spiralled away into the air. What I call well and truly marked. 'Back down!' I told Adie. There was a crunch of reverse gear and we popped back down behind the sand heap. Things had gone a bit quiet overhead. I looked up. Our trace had marked the tank's position all right, but the Lynx had pulled away and withdrawn to a safe distance. Given the stone storm that had just engulfed it, I could understand why.

I jockeyed us along to a new position. The third tank had my most recent range and bearing: no point reappearing in the same place, the idea was to make things as hard as I could for him. There was a lull. We dusted ourselves down a bit. The enemy seemed to have stopped firing. When I edged us back out into one of the berm gaps again, the T-55 was retreating north into better cover. Not that surprising. Its commander could see one of the T-55s in his troop wrecked and burning near by, a second tank abandoned and a BMP-1 knocked out and billowing smoke into the bargain.

To the east, I could see the MERT (Medical Emergency Response Team) Chinook picking up 2 Troop's casualties. For the moment, we were out of immediate danger. I was feeling all warm and cheerful about that when Nobby Telling came up again. 'We're off, mate. We're fresh out of missiles, and the sight unit's malfunctioned. We'll reload and get back to you as soon as possible.'

Amen to that. I made another careful scan of the landscape ahead through the binos. A sand-coloured object moved in the distance, stopped and then started again. The object had a gun barrel sticking out of it. Another T-55, coming up to reinforce his friends. I kept watching. I didn't want to feel cold in the heat of the moment. But there were three more new tanks coming up to join the one that I'd just spotted. Again, they were at a range of less than 3,000 metres.

Nobby had disappeared. But now another of 4 Troop's Strikers drew up next to us. Corporal of Horse Lyndon Heaton was in command. I jumped out, ran across and gave him a QBO: quick battle orders. Heaton listened as I brought him up to speed. We'd hit and disabled a number of enemy tanks and armoured vehicles, but there were at least four more T-55s to our immediate front. Heaton didn't need telling what was needed. There was no time to dismount and separate the sights as before. If he tried to do that, the Iraqis would be on us and through us. He pointed the Striker's nose at a berm, rolled up it and skidded to a halt.

The Swingfire gunner took aim and fired. The missile looped out of the launcher, sizzled across the landscape and hit one of the new enemy tanks smack on. It exploded in a ball of smoke and flame. 'Back up that berm, Adie,' I said, 'let's give them covering fire.' The other three Iraqi tanks were still rumbling towards us. I opened up on the right-hand one with APDS. We were firing at the extreme of the Rarden's capability. In all gunnery, accuracy of fire decreases as range increases, a phenomenon known as 'dispersion'. Each type of shell – HE, sabot or whatever – has its own dispersion rate. By watching our fall of shot through the binos and then adjusting, I was able to get some rounds on the enemy.

Heaton's gunner fired another two missiles. Both missed. 'We're out of ammo,' Heaton radioed. 'We need to resupply. Have fun.' He dressed the Striker back off the berm and trundled away in Nobby's wake.

We seemed to be all alone again – this was getting to be a bit of a bad habit. But we couldn't just sit there in cover waiting for the Iraqis to encircle us. We needed to keep track of the threat. 'Fuck it,' I muttered, 'there's only one thing for it.' Aloud, I said, 'Adie, we need to go back up. There's more tanks. Drive us up that berm to the left.'

Adie said, 'Do we really have to go back up on that berm, Mike? Why can't we just stay behind it, and you go up and take a look?'

'No,' I said. 'I've told you what we're going to do – we've got to deal with those other three tanks. We have to fix their position, and the best way to do that is by attracting their fire.' We drove over the berm and fired at the closest T-55. He fired back. 'Quick! Reverse!' I said. 'And be careful of that bloody ditch – pull a bit of right stick.' There was a drainage ditch to our left, right next to the berm in question. We were too close to it. Much too close. I wanted Adie to get us out and clear of the drop before he did anything else.

'Adie, reverse right stick.'

He started to reverse.

'Pull right stick!' I shouted. 'Right fucking stick' Nothing happened. I tried again: 'Adie! Pull right stick!' He yanked back on the left stick. The Scimitar lurched round. I glanced back. Our rear end was hanging right out over a vertical 1.5-metre drop. If we fell off, then the Scimitar would flip upside down and the impact would kill us. And even if that didn't kill us, we'd be lying upside down in a ditch like a stranded beetle in several feet of filthy water, waiting for a T-55 tank to wander up and finish us off.

I could feel the whole wagon teetering. If any of us leaned just a fraction to the left we were going to tip over and go in. Fury seized me. We were here to fight a war, not remake *The Italian Job*. 'You fucking idiot!' I yelled. 'Take us forward! And PULL RIGHT STICK!'

'We can't go forward,' Adie said. 'That's towards the enemy!' After the near miss, he didn't want to expose the vehicle to more enemy tank fire. 'If you don't go forward I'll fucking kill you myself! Go forward!'

For some reason I had the overwhelming conviction the Iraqis weren't going to hit us that day. The idea they might land a shell on us never even entered my brain. The overriding feeling I had was: 'We have to use all of our training for real. Otherwise, what's the point of it?' I'm not sure Adie fully shared my enthusiasm, but he crunched the transmission into forward gear. The tracks bit and we slewed a metre or two away from the yawning drop. I was sweating, and not just because of the smoke and heat. The Scimitar lurched forward 5 metres. I said, 'Now reverse and pull right stick. RIGHT STICK!' He reversed, pulled the right steering stick and this time the Scimitar backed clear into safety.

I couldn't see any sign of the Lynx, but our own job remained the same: to stop the enemy tanks outflanking us and causing an even bigger fuck-fest. How could we do that in our little Scimitar? Then something struck me – something that might give us a chance. The enemy tank was firing HE. Which was almost lobbing a high-explosive watermelon at us. So there was an interval of several seconds between the muzzle flash from the tank's barrel and the round exploding. Which we could use to engage them. How many seconds? There was only one way to find out.

'Right,' I told Adie. 'What we're going to do is show ourselves up on the berm again and let them open fire on us. Then I'm going to count how long we've got between flash and impact.'

'What!' he shouted. 'Why the fucking hell would we want to do that?'

'Because we can fire back at him while his own round is still in the air.' We were firing sabot, which meant our rounds travelled three times faster than their shells.

There was a silence while we all paused to reflect on the wisdom of this ploy. The squadron 2IC, Captain Nick Hayward came up on the radio: 'Whisky Three Two, stay within your limit of exploitation. Do not go beyond your northing. Repeat, do not go beyond your northing.' I checked the TNTLS. We were already right on the line. If we crossed it, we'd be into the 'kill box', or no-go box, and risk coming under fire from friendly forces.

'Let's go, Adie. Foot down.' We roared up onto the berm. The nearest tank was squatting a few thousand metres away. It looked like a fat metal toad. One that had been waiting for the fly to land, and here we were on cue. It opened fire. As soon as I saw the muzzle flash I started to count: 'One thousand, two thousand, three thousand, four thousand, five thousand, six thousand ...' The round landed 5 metres in front of us. The explosion was so massive it shook the whole berm. The Scimitar shuddered and rocked on its tracks. Adie screamed. It rained sand and gravel for a bit; loads of it went down my neck. I'd been sending SHQ more or less continual SITREPs as we took on the T-55s. The shell had exploded while I was right in the middle of making a report. At least now the 2i/c and the others knew I wasn't exaggerating.

That one had been mighty, mighty close: about as close as it gets. Adie was a little uncomfortable with the proximity: 'Mike,' he shouted. 'We've been hit, we've been hit!'

'Shut up, Adie. We haven't been hit – we're fine. 'Reverse! No sticks!' We shot back down behind the berm and sat there like a scalded cat. A couple of seconds later, a new enemy shell exploded harmlessly above us on the berm. 'OK,' I told the boys, 'that's the drill: we're going to motor up and down along the berms, pop up at different positions each time and wait till one of the fuckers opens fire. It takes six seconds for the round to reach us. Then we're going to fire back at him in that time and then reverse down. Got that?' There was a deafening silence. Then Adie found his voice: 'You're fucking mad!'

'You're fucking doing it!' My blood was up. No way was some fucking enemy going to fire at me and I wasn't going to fire back. 'Drive us up onto that berm on the right there: I want to see where the nearest tank is now.'

We trundled along a couple of dunes, pointed the Scimitar's nose at the huge heap of sand and revved the engine. We shimmied up into view – just enough to get our gun and sights onto the target. A bright orange flash leapt from the T-55's gun. The shell exploded some distance off to our right. 'Engage that tank Benny!' I shouted. Benny fired three rounds off quickly. That took about three seconds. But now we knew the enemy tank's exact position. 'Reverse, Adie!' I didn't need to tell him twice. The enemy shell exploded a little above us to the right. Another miss, our luck was holding.

The Lynx was like the Cheshire Cat: it kept appearing and disappearing when you least expected it. I heard its rotors thudding again and glanced up to see it weaving around to our left. Maybe this time he'd get a missile away. Maybe. 'Up again, Adie!' I said. We drove up onto a new berm. Benny put a quick burst of tracer on the right-hand tank. The rounds bounced off its main armour and ballooned up into the air. Right away we popped back down. 'Target visual,' the Lynx gunner said. Thank fuck for that. He lined up on the T-55 and engaged it with TOW. The first missile flew past the tank we'd marked and exploded in the sand beside it. The second went straight in through the T-55's side armour. It went up like a whore's knickers after payment: fast. Its turret blew off and shot up into the sky, followed by a bright orange-yellow column of fire, like a massive torch burning straight up into the sky. The fire turned to black smoke, pouring out in a thick mass that immediately engulfed the stricken vehicle. The other three Iraqi tanks stopped dead in their tracks. Took a look at the mess. And then started retreating. Marvellous.

I sent SHQ an update: 'Four tanks and one BMP destroyed, three tanks still alive but retreating.' In all of the excitement, I might just have miscounted.

I took a deep breath. We'd had a very exciting few minutes. To calm us all down, I said to Benny, 'Get the kettle on, Ben – it's about time we had a cup of tea.'

Benny thought I was taking the piss. 'Cup of tea!' he shouted. 'Fucking cup of tea! We're in the middle of a fucking tank range, and we're the target!'

'No,' I told him, 'really: I'm parched. Get the kettle on and we'll have a brew.' He looked at me daggers, but he bent down to get the boiling vessel going. While he was doing that I called up the Lynx pilot: 'Do you fancy a cup of tea?'

'Yes – but not here!' And with that he turned, put his nose down and sloped off back towards base.

The squadron 2IC came up in my headset: 'Did I just hear you correctly? Did you just offer that pilot a cup of tea?'

'Yes – we all need it.'

'Whisky Three Two, pull back now. Collect ammunition.'

I looked down at my watch and did a double-take. It was definitely time we had a break. We'd been in contact for more than two hours and fired a total of 190 shells from our main armament. To me, it had felt like a few minutes. The fall back and resupply order was a good call: for all SHQ knew, I only had about a dozen rounds left. In fact, I always carried at least 100 extra shells. Even so, we were getting short. I felt tired, elated, hungry, thirsty and lucky to be alive. And crushed into little bits by the loss of a friend.

As we fell back to resupply I learned that all the casualties injured in the A-10 attack had been extracted and saved except one: no one had been able to get into Matty Hull's blazing Scimitar. Its aluminium body had caught fire and begun to melt. We'd killed four Iraqi tanks and a BMP-1, that was one thing. But we had one man dead and several injured. We'd also lost two Scimitars. And the dead man had been a friend. There was still a score to settle. And once we'd reloaded, I looked forward to settling it.

CHAPTER TWENTY-TWO

We spent two days resupplying, resting and reconstituting the squadron. We were mourning the death of Matty Hull, a good mate and a first-rate soldier. Three men were seriously injured: 2 Troop's leader, Alex McEwen, Trooper Alan Tudbull and Trooper Chris Finney. Immediately after the A-10 struck Finney got out of the driver's cab. Realizing Alan was in a bad way and couldn't get out by himself, he tried to reach him. The flames and smoke beat him back. Finney tried another angle of approach but again the blaze was too much for him. Climbing onto the vehicle, he grabbed Tudbull under the armpits, hauled him out of the gunner's hatch and started pulling him to safety. As he did that an A-10 opened fire for the second time. Despite being shot in the arse, Finney brought Tudbull to safety. Later, Chris was awarded the George Cross for his action.

We'd lost 20 per cent of our firepower, but there was still a war to be fought, so on the third day we rose again and pressed north. Because I knew the ground, I was retasked to move back into the same area we'd fought over two days before. That was still the forward line of battle. We had Lightning Three Four for company again. I don't mind admitting that when the A-10s had been attacking I'd been glad to have him hanging around: my Scimitar looked exactly like Matty's, so our American pal had probably saved our lives. All American vehicles carry a 'blue force tracker' – a transponder that indicates they're friendly to own call signs. Without it, the A-10s would probably have swatted us, too. We need to get every vehicle in the British Army fitted with the blue force tracking system, and not solely the command vehicles.

The US armed forces were equally devastated when they learned of Matty Hull's death. Not least among them Lightning Three Four. He was particularly upset because, although he'd repeatedly told the A-10s to check fire after the first attack, they'd apparently not heard him. Prior to the invasion, to avert blue-on-blues, all coalition vehicles had been fitted with large Day-Glo orange recognition panels. These were supposed to help coalition pilots recognize friendlies. Matty's Scimitar had had one of these orange panels bolted to the top of the rear deck. But as soon as you move in the desert you make dust, especially in an armoured vehicle; in reality, the panels were more or less permanently covered in a grey film.

There's an old Army saying: 'If there's any doubt, there's no doubt: you don't open fire.' But none of us blamed the Americans. Even in the age of technology, war is anything but an exact science. In combat, mistakes happen all the time. The thing is to learn from the error and make sure it never happens again.

Later in the campaign, I noticed that many Iraqis had tied orange tarpaulins across the bonnets of their supply trucks. That suggested they'd noticed our own recognition system, and they were exploiting it in an effort to trick coalition pilots. In war things are usually more complicated than they first appear. In war, things just get seriously fucked up.

We headed north on our new mission. As before, we needed to know the enemy's strength and disposition on the axis of advance. My troop leader Lt Alex Tweedie's wagon started to break down almost from the off, Simmo and Gooders had to veer west to find a better track, and then Tweedie's wagon ground to a halt. He was furious, especially with the REME, who'd promised him they'd fixed the engine.

Same problems, different day: we were once again the furthest forward call sign on the field of battle. But the big difference now was that most of 16 Air Assault Brigade had closed up with us enough to provide support, including the RHA's much-needed guns. Great to have that game-changing battlefield instrument, artillery, back on call. All Allied air ops had been cancelled while aircrew were rebriefed and retrained in the aftermath of Matty Hull's death. This was the first day coalition air power was back on line. We had helicopters up in support as before, but more of them.

We pushed forward until we came up with the same double line of berms where we'd had our previous contact with the Iraqis. But this time round, we were about a kilometre further to the east. We found ourselves a good location for an OP, tucked in and got the Scimitar nicely concealed in a hull-down position.

I could still see the two burned-out Scimitars of 2 Troop to the east, the wrecked Iraqi tanks to the north and great, black scorch marks on the ground where the enemy vehicles had gone up in flames. The same Iraqi Army barracks was also still there at the same location on the edge of the village: no one had moved it. I sat slightly to the east of our previous position in the fold of land, keeping a careful eye on the surrounding area through the periscope. The berm lines ran east – west ahead of us, then there was a stretch of open ground about 3,000 metres wide crossed by more of the eternal drainage ditches and power lines. There was a reasonably good track running out from the barracks to the south-east, and there beyond everything in the distance to the north, the main Basra–Baghdad road.

We were playing cat-and-mouse with the Iraqis again. Only this time, I was hoping to be the cat. We sat and we sat, in hiding. There was a steady stream of civilian vehicles travelling along the highway towards Baghdad, no doubt in an effort to escape the fierce fighting we'd just heard was going on in Basra.

It started to get hot. Squadrons of enemy flies woke up and began to bother us. We'd been watching the compound for about two hours when a couple of Iraqi Army trucks turned off the main highway to the north-east, crossed right-to-left in front of us, headed for the gate in the north-eastern corner of the barracks and disappeared inside. Great stuff, I was beginning to get seriously bored. I told Lightning Three Four what I'd seen. He took a long squint through his binos. 'Roger, agreed. Enemy vehicles inside that barracks. Let's see if we can get some air on that.'

We struck lucky with a pair of F-16s. Or so we thought. Then we learned that only one of the F-16s was actually armed – with a 2,000lb bomb. That was not lucky. Or even suitable. I piped up on the net so that everyone could hear me: 'This is Whisky Three Two – let's not drop a 2,000lb bomb on that enemy barracks. It's right on the edge of a village. There are women and children in close proximity. The risk of collateral damage is too great. If we're going to hit it, let's use line-of-sight guided missiles, otherwise there'll be carnage.'

I wasn't just being mimsy: a 2,000lb bomb would pretty much reduce the whole village to rubble, and the shrapnel and blast from it risked hitting passing civilian vehicles on the highway into the bargain. SHQ came back up: 'Are you sure we can't use the 2,000-pounder?' They wanted to destroy the barracks. So did I, but not take the rest of Iraq with it.

'I'm certain – it can't be done.'

The Boss, Alex Tweedie, accepted my call. The Falcons pulled away.

A few minutes later, one of the trucks I'd seen going into the barracks came back out. It started beetling around some 3 kilometres to the east and ahead of our position. All of a sudden, it stopped. Watching through the commander's sight, I saw its crew unloading what looked like a tank shell. Now, why would they be unloading a tank shell in a big empty stretch of open desert? Then I saw why.

The desert wasn't empty. Far from it. There was a T-55 tank parked hull down about 10 metres from the truck. With only its turret showing. Even as I watched it seemed to disappear in the heat haze. I did a slow traverse: there were four more enemy tanks parked near the first, all equally well concealed. And they'd just been resupplied with ammunition. I called it in: 'This is Whisky Three Two: I see five enemy tanks in front of me. There may be a troop of T-55s at grid position 489521. Wait out.' I felt a cold finger slide up my spine. The Iraqis were back in strength. And it looked as if they were up for a fresh round of battle.

I watched the first truck bustle 300 metres over to the west and then stop again. At that location I could see at least five more tanks. That made ten in total, even with my maths. Speck-like figures in black dishdashas scurried and hurried around them, ferrying ammunition and supplies. I called SHQ again: 'Update to my last message: I now see a squadron of T-55 tanks – ten vehicles minimum.' I kept watching. The more I looked, the more tanks I spotted. A forest of tank barrels seemed to be growing from the dust-brown desert.

I started to count. Then I made a rough estimate and rounded down. It took a while. When I'd reached the end of the calculation I sat for a moment, quietly stunned. I could hardly believe it. There were scores of Iraqi tanks out there: not a troop, a squadron or even a regiment: more like an entire armoured division.

I keyed the mike: 'Zero, this is Whisky Three Two: I can now clearly identify at least 200 enemy tanks 3 kilometres north of my position.' There might just have been a touch of awe in my voice. There was certainly a short silence. Then the OC said, 'Whisky Three Two, this is Whisky Zero Alpha: confirm you have 200 tanks to your northing?'

'I'm not joking, Boss: I can confirm at least 200 tanks, mixed in with command vehicles and other armour. Oh, and a fair bit of infantry.'

We'd found the whole Iraqi 4th Armoured Division. The thing to do now was to destroy it. That meant I'd have to change hats and act as a forward artillery controller. Call down the guns on the enemy's head. We'd also have to play cat-and-mouse with the Iraqi armour again, only now there were a few more tanks lined up on the opposing team. Make that a few hundred more enemy tanks.

We scurried up onto a berm. I got Benny to lase a T-55 in the middle of the throng, took a range and read-out and called Golf One One, 7th

Royal Horse Artillery's forward observation officer (FOO). While I did that, Adie backed us down off the berm. Amazingly, none of the enemy had spotted us in time to open fire.

'Golf One One, this is Whisky Three Two: fire mission, grid 489521. Direction 64 mils, enemy armour in open, neutralize when ready for three minutes.'

The guns officer came straight back at me: I could hear the edge of excitement in his voice. This was probably the first time he'd engaged enemy armour in a real battle. 'Whisky Three Two, this is Golf One One. Confirm fire mission grid 489521, direction 64 mils, enemy armoured division. Over?'

'Golf One One, this is Whisky Three Two, confirm fire mission grid 489521. Fire when ready.'

'Whisky Three Two, this is Golf One One: shot three-four.'

'Shot three-four' meant the battery he controlled would fire the salvo in thirty-four seconds. Thirty-four seconds later, I heard the FOO report: 'Shot over.' That meant the rounds had been fired. Then came the high-pitched descending whine of the incoming shells. A second later, they started exploding on and among the Iraqi tanks. The noise was incredible. Dodging up and down off the berms, I called in a further three fire missions, walking the barrage along the enemy line. The laser sighting system on the Scimitar is so good there was no need to adjust fire: the rounds were landing on the tanks and other vehicles ranged out there with deadly accuracy. But some of the tanks had spotted us directing fire. They started to fire back, the explosions sending great gouts of earth up from the sand around us. Enemy mortars also began lobbing searching fire in our general direction.

Battle was joined. It was to last all day.

As soon as the second salvo of shells hit, all hell let loose in the barren, undulating stretch of no man's land between us and the enemy tanks. Hundreds of Iraqi heads popped up out of the ground, followed by bodies that started running around in every direction. In seconds, the place was seething with enemy troops. They'd all been entrenched and invisible. Now they were running round in plain sight like headless chickens. Make that soon-to-be headless chickens.

Lightning Three Four lased the milling enemy and shouted a new target grid across to me: 'We have infantry at 490520 – fire mission.'

I passed the grid on to the guns: 'Fire mission: Iraqi infantry, grid 490520 . . .' The guns officer acknowledged the target and grid. When we'd run through the standard procedure, I made the final call: 'Roger Golf One One, confirm target grid. Neutralize when ready.'

'Whisky Three Two, this is Golf One One, ready five-six.' He'd be ready to open fire on the new target in fifty-six seconds.

Monitoring the radio traffic back in SHQ, the sharp voice of Zero Alpha, aka D Squadron's OC Major Richard Taylor, cut into my enjoyment of the shell show: 'Whisky Three Two, confirm the grid. Confirm your target grid!'

The snap of urgency in his voice made me sit up and stare at the TNTLS. Ice water replaced the blood in my veins. The target grid I'd just relayed from Lightning Three Four was less than 200 metres away from our own location. Lesson one, day one: don't call in an artillery strike on your own head. 'Hello Zero, this is Whisky Three Two Check fire! Check fire!' I looked across and caught Lightning Three Four's eye. 'You gave us the wrong fucking target grid!'

He glanced at his read-outs. Then he looked back up at me. His face had gone white. 'Sorry!' he said. 'Sorry.'

'You gave our grid, not the enemy's,' I snarled.

'I know,' he said, 'I'm sorry.'

Sorry! In about fifteen seconds from now, eighteen 105mm guns were going to unleash their combined weight of fire. On us. I smacked down on the chest pressel switch. There was no rush – it was just that unless we could stop the barrage in the next few seconds, we were going to wear it. 'Golf One One, this is Whisky Three Two: Check fire! Check fire! Check fire!' Every single unit in 16 Air Assault Brigade had already checked fire. But I had to make sure. There was an eerie silence, punctuated by the odd crump of an Iraqi tank gun.

Major Taylor came back up on air. 'Whisky Three Two, this is Zero Alpha: in future, I want you to double-check your fire mission grids. Understood?'

'Roger,' I said, 'totally my fault. From now on I will double-check.' I heaved a sigh of relief. If it hadn't been for the OC, we'd have been wearing a salvo of 105mm shells.

By last light, the combined weight of 16 Air Assault Brigade's guns and coalition air sorties had reduced large chunks of Iraqi 4th Armoured to smoking metal. Our call sign, Whisky Three Two, ended up directing the greatest number of rounds fired in the whole of the second Iraq war.

We got orders to fall back 5 kilometres and laager up. We moved south the required distance, made ourselves comfortable, brewed up a pot of tea and had a bite to eat. Five clicks was a long way. The order to pull back that far could only mean one thing: a monster air strike was headed in. Sure enough, when darkness fell the fast movers came in, squadrons of them, screaming through the night air. It was more Armageddon than air strike: the jets carpet-bombed every square metre of the enemy's position. As we lay there that night trying to sleep, the ground shuddered continually beneath us. It was like being an ant on a drum skin. The Iraqis might be the enemy, but under that relentless onslaught, a part of me felt for them.

Next morning we went back up north to do a battle damage assessment (BDA). The whole area that had been bombed overnight was a smoking, devastated mess. There were smashed and burned out Iraqi tanks and trucks as far as the eye could see, many of them still burning. The dead bodies had been removed, but there were piles of Iraqi kit, ammunition, weapons and equipment lying everywhere. On top of that and to add to the confusion, the surviving Iraqi troops were surrendering in droves. We were tasked to support our infantry in mopping them up. There seemed to be a never-ending stream of prisoners of war.

When we'd dealt with the immediate flood, Major Taylor came up and joined us. He jumped on my Scimitar and asked if he could hitch a ride. He wanted to video the damage our 30mm APDS rounds had done to the first of the T-55s we'd hit. No problem, there are worse things to do in war than ferry round military tourists. So off we trundled for an official shufti. Pretty soon, we came on the Iraqi tank. We jumped down and went up to examine the damage. Several of our sabot rounds had punched through the T-55's armour, one through the base of its turret race as I'd thought. That one had served our purpose, convincing the frightened crew to jump out and run away. We were seriously impressed that the Rarden's APDS rounds could do that: not bad considering the T-55's armour was a minimum of 10cm thick and our shells only a little broader in diameter than your thumb.

We looped south to pick up the track and head back through the village to our own lines. On the northern outskirts, a villager came running towards us. He wore a dishdasha that had once been white and a dirty, old, blue knitted cotton cap on his head. His hands were raised and he was shouting: 'Stop, stop!' My first thought was, 'Here we go – they're Shi'ites: the Iraqi Army's stolen everything they had, they've got no food, I bet he's trying to beg.' I couldn't have been more wrong – the Iraqi wanted to warn us that we were about to drive into a minefield.

I looked down. Two tiny sand-coloured buttons were sticking up out of the ground directly in front of us. They were less than 3 metres away. I jumped out, got down on my hands and knees, took out my bayonet and prodded towards the objects with extreme caution. They weren't buttons: they were the prongs of Italian-made anti-tank mines. Sticking up and waiting to give us the good news. Not to mention launching Major Taylor, who'd been sitting on the Scimitar's front decks, into the upper atmosphere. The battle had gone well for us so far, but this was a warning: we had to keep our eyes open wide all the time. Another couple of metres and we'd all have been history.

The villager had been standing watching us. Once we'd cleared through the minefield, I went up, shook his hand, thanked him and told the boys to give him every scrap of food we had on the wagon. He staggered back towards the village, weighed down under a massive bag of goodies, as happy as Larry. Driving with much increased care and attention, we headed south to rejoin the rest of the squadron.

CHAPTER TWENTY-THREE

With the Iraqi 4th Armoured Division out of the running, we were ordered to put in protection on 16 Air Assault Brigade's eastern flank. I was lead vehicle in a composite troop made up of two Scimitars, the Striker commanded by Nobby Telling that had helped us back at the village, and call sign Lightning Three Five, a shiny, new, replacement US forward air controller. Three Five had a big fat squat Humvee and a Hispanic driver, just like Lightning Three Four. Maybe they issued them that way. Our troop leader, Lt Alex Tweedie, was behind me in the second Scimitar: finally, its ropey engine had been fixed.

Alex's call sign was still the same: Three Zero.

We were heading north towards Al Amarah on Route Sword. We could hear 1 Troop's intermittent updates on the radio detailing the enemy situation to our front – they had been observing enemy activity north of Basra for three days without rest and were pretty much dead on their feet. We were going to relieve them. It had turned out to be less of an overwatch and more of a running contact: whenever they got the urge, Iraqi dissidents were engaging l Troop with RPGs and AK47s.

With the imminent threat of attack, we were driving what we call 'closed down, hatches open'. Instead of having their heads up out clear of the hatches steering by direct vision, our drivers were shuttered inside the vehicles guiding them by periscope. It reduced the chances of anyone stopping a bullet or getting hit by a lump of shrapnel. But driving under those circumstances severely restricts your field of view.

A ditch about 4 metres wide came up on our right – one of the hundreds of waterways that help drain and contain the marshy land-scape. We now had to make a sharp right turn to cross it, over a thin strip of hard baked clay that bridged the two sides. Adie Conlon was still my driver: despite his occasional lapses on the steering sticks, Adie made the 90-degree turn without any problem.

But Alex Tweedie's driver made the turn a fraction too soon. The Scimitar's right-hand track slipped over the edge of the ditch. The vehicle slid 2 metres down the steep-sided bank, flipped and landed upside down in 1.5 metres of water and stinking mud. In the Striker immediately behind Three Zero, Nobby Telling was the first to see what had happened. His voice sounded sharp in my headset: 'Whisky Three Two, Whisky Three Zero's gone in! Three Zero's gone in the ditch!'

I shouted 'Stop!' We shuddered to a halt.

I looked back.

The Scimitar had turned turtle. Both sets of tracks were sticking up in the air. The turret was completely submerged. There was water lapping round the tracks. The wagon looked unreal – like a big metal terrapin stranded on its back.

I radioed SHQ: 'Three Zero has overturned in a ditch full of water. We need One Four Bravo here now.' One Four Bravo was the Samaritan ambulance. We were working so far ahead of the main force, it had a doctor on board. We needed it here yesterday. The stranded Scimitar's three-man crew, gunner Karl Shearer, driver Chalky White and com-mander Alex Tweedie were trapped under five feet of water and 8 tonnes of metal. My first thought was to rescue them. My second thought was that we were now totally vulnerable, wide open to ambush and attack. 'Put out local defence!' I yelled.

I leapt out of the wagon, ran to the edge of the ditch and jumped in. As I ran I saw Chalky White surface. He'd managed to wriggle out through the gap between the gun trough and the hull – good lad. He pulled himself up onto solid ground. I landed with an almighty splash in the water. It came up to the top of my shoulders. 'Chalky! Chalky!' I shouted. 'How are the other two? Alex and Karl?' Chalky didn't seem to hear me. He was staring and his features were set, in deep shock.

I ducked under. The water was foul: thick with filth, weed and silt. My heart was hammering and not just from the exertion – if we couldn't get those other two men out of there right away, they were dead. I felt my way around the turret, trying to find a gap where I could get at a hatch. There was no gap.

With the weight of the Scimitar on its top there was no way to reach the trapped men. There was a splash to my left. I looked round and saw Nobby in the water with me. I banged on the hull with my fist. There was no reply. The armoured vest I had on wasn't helping that much. I went back up for air. Like Nobby, I was covered from head to toe in grey mud and long green strands of clinging weed. 'Benny,' I shouted. 'Send an update! Tell SHQ we need the air ambulance!' Benny gave me the thumbs up: he'd already done that, the MERT Puma and the Samaritan ambulance were already en route.

We had to get that Scimitar off its back. 'Get the Hustle Kit!' I shouted. 'Throw it down to me!' The 'Hustle Kit' is a system of wire ropes about 15 metres long with strops and hooks on the end that allows heavy-lift helicopters to pick up and move light armoured vehicles. I attached one of the Hustle Kit's strops to the lower end of the semi-submerged Scimitar and handed the free end to someone on the bank. That done, I climbed out of the stinking grey-brown cesspit. 'Adie,' I called, 'move our vehicle back so we can attach the Hustle Kit. You get on one side of the ditch. Get Nobby's Striker on the other.'

By now everyone was out of their vehicles and trying to help as best they could. With Nobby's help I attached two of the Hustle Kit's cables to the front and rear ends of the stranded Scimitar. When we'd done that we hauled the cables across to either side of the ditch. We clipped one cable to my Scimitar on the south side of the ditch and the other to Nobby's Striker on the northern bank. Standing between the two vehicles, I told the drivers to reverse.

It worked. The wire ropes went bar taut. The trapped Scimitar started lifting out of the water, pivoting on its right side. As it broke free a body fell out of the commander's hatch: Alex Tweedie. His eyes were staring wide. His mouth was plugged with mud and he looked dead. Something fell away inside me when I saw that. I shouted to the lads on the bank: 'Pull the troop leader out! Pull him out!' They grabbed Alex by the shoulders and hauled him across to the bank. A couple of other blokes caught hold of him, dragged him up onto dry land and began resuscitation. By now, Alex had probably been underwater for five minutes.

I jumped back into the ditch. The vehicle was still on its side, the gunner's hatch was still beneath the water. I put my head back in the filthy mess. I knew exactly where the gunner's hatch catch was. I grabbed it and pulled back. The hatch should have opened easily. It didn't. I caught the lip with the fingers of both hands, braced my legs and hauled up with all of my strength. The hatch refused to budge. The vehicle's angle and the weight of all the mud were jamming it shut.

I glanced up. If the Hustle Kit snapped then the Scimitar would fall back and crush me. Best be quick, then. I stuck my head and shoulders in through the commander's hatch. Karl was slumped sideways in the turret, lying at an angle across his seat. His eyes were grey-white and staring in the murk. I leaned closer: there was mud in his mouth and nose. With the help of another pair of hands that suddenly appeared in the darkness beside me, I dragged him out. When he was up on dry land we clambered back out of the ditch. A couple of the guys started trying to resuscitate Karl. Two of the other lads and Lightning Three Five's crew had already set to work resuscitating Alex. I knelt down beside him. 'How's it going?'

The three who'd been working on Alex shook their heads. 'Nothing'

'Get out of the way,' I said. 'Let me do it.' The fear that Alex might die made me furiously angry. We'd all learnt mouth-to-mouth resuscitation on 'Resussy Annie', the lifelike training dummy we used to get a realistic sense of how to give the kiss of life. But I was sure I could do it better. At least in theory. Now I was doing it for real, I wanted it to work more than anything I'd wanted for a long time. The others moved back. Alex still had no pulse and no breathing. I cleared all of the remaining mud out of his mouth, throat and nose and started doing the 'six to one' on him: six heart compressions to one breath. There was no response. I kept going.

Every fibre in my body wanted Alex to live. But whatever I did, the staring wide fish eyes stayed the same. I gazed into them. They were milky-grey, almost opaque. When I saw that my hope faded. I shouted at him: 'Fucking well breathe, Alex! You are not going to die in this shit-hole!' He gave no sign of life. There was no point pummelling the heart out of a dead man. But a part of me refused to accept that he was gone. I pushed down on his chest for the last time. A gout of filthy water mixed with mud and mucus shot out of his mouth and he coughed. Christ, he was alive! He coughed more silt up out of his lungs. I turned him, pulled the shit out of his mouth and then put him back on his back again to check his breathing.

Hope flooded back into me. We'd get him out of there and into hospital and he'd live. Alex coughed again – it sounded terrible, watery and racking. His pulse was beating now, but it was very faint. We pulled back his shirt to check him for injuries. His ribs looked odd, misshapen, they were probably broken. Karl Shearer was lying beside Alex. They were still trying to save him, but Karl hadn't responded to treatment. He was already dead.

There was a roar of engines as help arrived: the Samaritan with the doctor in One Four Bravo, D Squadron's Corporal-Major Dai Rees in Three Three Alpha and the LAD recovery Spartan. Dai Rees began to set up better all-round defence double-quick. A unit of 3 Para's anti-tank section had been deployed a couple of kilometres away when the accident happened. I hadn't realized it before, but they'd also come up to help while I'd been busy. The Paras were the perfect force to have if the Iraqis decided to try their luck.

The doc jumped off the Samaritan and made a quick assessment: 'Tweedie's breathing,' he said, 'the other one's dead.'

I said; 'Karl Shearer.'

'Yes,' he said, 'sorry – I didn't know him.' He was working frantically on Alex. 'He's only got one working lung – the other one's collapsed. The working lung is full of water. We need to drain it.' Action to his words, he pushed a massive needle in through Alex's ribcage and attached a tube to it. Grey water immediately began to dribble from the plastic mouth. Alex's chest heaved and his breathing grew louder. But it was still very shallow – laboured and stuttering. We needed to get him to a hospital, and for that we needed the Medical Emergency Response Team.

The MERT in the Puma air ambulance was circling overhead, but the pilot wouldn't land until we could guarantee the area was secure. We hadn't been able to clear and secure the area before because we'd been too busy trying to save lives. The Catch-22 meant we'd lost valuable time; time that might make the difference to a man's life. The Paras and Dai Rees were on the case now, rapidly securing the area. I knew there was no point risking the MERT before we'd made sure there were no mines. But the delay made me hopping mad. If I could, I'd have reached up and pulled the Puma to earth with my bare hands.

Chalky White was still in extreme shock. He kept repeating: 'It was my fault – I clipped the corner. It was my fault.' I remembered he'd done the same thing at the corner of another canal a few days before. That time, the Scimitar's track had slipped over the edge of the bank but Chalky had managed to recover the vehicle before it went in.

'It wasn't your fault, Chalky,' I told him. 'You couldn't see the turn – it was an accident.'

I've said driving a Scimitar isn't easy at the best of times. Driving by periscope is really difficult: all you have to look through is a small vision block. Plus, being at war we had big thermal recognition panels stuck on the vehicle's front end: those reduced the driver's vision even further, as did the LAW anti-tank missiles and all the other extra kit strapped to the hull. The rule is, the commander takes responsibility: he's higher up; he has his head out of the turret; he can see better; and if he thinks the driver is going too fast or is about to make a mistake, then it's his job to give a warning.

The MERT landed. The onboard team rushed over and got to work on Alex. They confirmed what the first doc had said: Karl Shearer was dead, but if we could get him to a hospital fast enough then Alex Tweedie might live. You didn't need medical training to see it was a big 'might'. After my initial elation when he'd started to breathe again, I could see Alex was really struggling. But he was breathing on his own, and as long as that was happening there had to be hope. I watched the Puma lift away, hoping to God that he'd pull through.

After initial treatment in Iraq they flew Alex back to the UK for specialist care in an Edinburgh hospital. Not being a member of his immediate family, it was difficult for me to find out what was happening. I didn't know it then, but a friend of Alex's who'd known him since they were kids was a doctor in the same hospital. We found out later she was going to Alex when she was off duty, sitting by his bedside and talking to him, in the hope of bringing him out of his coma. Sadly, she never succeeded.

Some days later, a message came through from Brigade: Alex Tweedie had caught pneumonia. He died in that same hospital with his family around him.

The Tweedies invited six of us in 3 Troop to the funeral. It meant flying back to the UK from theatre, which was highly unusual, but I wanted to do that: I wanted to pay Alex my last respects. When the day came round I put on my best suit with a heavy heart.

The setting was beautiful – the village of Minto, near Hawick, in the Scottish Borders. The houses are all very similar; one of the locals told me it was a planned village that had been built by some wealthy lord in the nineteenth century. The parish church sits on a small hill. From the graveyard there was a wonderful view down a long grassy glen shrouded with tall, dark green larch trees. There was a lake at one end, and at its head stood a big mansion. The river Teviot ran near by, and there were hills and crags all around. Everything was green and in flower; it was one of those lovely, restful views you only seem to get in Great Britain.

There were low grey clouds scudding by overhead, but every now and then a bright beam of sunlight lanced through a break and shone down on the cemetery, making everything sparkle and gleam. We stood at the graveside and bowed our heads. Alex's family came up and paid their respects. The regimental state trumpeters played the last post, the mournful notes floating out and away down the glen. When the last trumpet cry had faded, a piper in full dress tartan struck up with a *pibroch*, the plaintive lament laying a comrade-in-arms to his final rest. In war, as in life, good people die all the time. But that doesn't make their loss any easier to bear.

CHAPTER TWENTY-FOUR

Sometimes, the Iraqi Army put up dogged and courageous resistance. Mostly, it didn't. So the battle to defeat Saddam Hussein was pretty much over in three weeks. Coalition forces had gone into Iraq on 20 March 2003. On 2 May, speaking from the flight deck of the aircraft carrier USS *Abraham Lincoln* under a banner reading 'Mission Accomplished', US President George Bush announced: 'Major combat operations in Iraq have ended.'

The claim turned out to be a little bit premature. Still, with the immediate fighting apparently at an end, D Squadron was set to doing what we call 'bone tasks'. My least favourite was sitting in the Scimitars on the Basra–Baghdad road in the sweltering heat, monitoring the traffic flow.

We were doing the same thing one day on the outskirts of Al Amarah. The weather was exceptionally hot – so hot that we were complaining. We had to rotate the vehicles so that one crew spent ten minutes on the roadblock, then that vehicle went back into shade and another took its place. Ten minutes was the max in the broiling sun.

After an hour or so, a middle-aged Iraqi man came up and asked to speak to 'the commander'. I debussed and asked what he wanted. He was a grizzled-looking type with a few days of stubble, dressed in Western-style if seriously trashed shirt and trousers, and with that great Iraqi favourite, knackered old plastic sandals on his feet. Our visitor's English was exceptionally good.

'Sir, I have a problem,' he told me.

'What's that?'

'Every night, the Ba'ath Party come to my house. They take all our food. I have nothing left to feed my family. They say they are still supporting Saddam Hussein; they say they know where Saddam Hussein is.' I looked at him. He seemed like a reasonably honest bloke. The first bit of his statement wasn't all that electrifying. The second bit definitely was.

'Fantastic,' I said. 'If you can find out where Saddam Hussein is hiding, me and you are really going to get along.' And he stood to get a lot richer: at the time, there was a $25 million bounty on the fugitive dictator's head. It wouldn't do my own life chances any harm, either. The Iraqi man said, 'I can't talk to you here: if they see me talking to you like this, they will kill me. You must come to my village, we can talk quietly in my house.'

As soon as he said that I thought, 'This is a come-on. This is going to be a trap.' But I couldn't pass up the chance. 'I tell you what,' I said, 'I've got a better idea: why don't we pretend to arrest you, and then they'll think you're only talking to us because we've taken you in?'

He still wasn't happy. 'No, they will still kill me just for talking with you.'

It happened we had a CIMIC (Civil-Military Co-operation) unit with us at the time. It was made up of mixed civilian and military specialists whose task in Iraq was to create goodwill. If we built up security, created a good infrastructure, provided civil engineers and so on, the argument went we'd get more support for our presence in country. If the locals wanted something, CIMIC was the outfit that could wave the magic wand.

I asked our potential informant to wait a tick and strolled over to have a chat with the CIMIC commander, an American captain. The captain came up with what seemed like a good suggestion: 'We'll go into the man's village and set up as normal. We'll rig up the loud-speakers, set out our stall and invite people to come along and talk.

Usually we get a crowd of about forty people, sometimes more – depends on what goodies we're handing out that day. We'll ask lots of the men what the village needs and all, that way your informant won't stand out. You should get a chance to find out what he knows.' I referred it up to Brigade, always a good idea in these situations.

'Fantastic,' Major Taylor said in turn. 'You go in with CIMIC and act as local protection. They can ask about the water, the schooling and all of that, and you can ask about the baddies. And if you do get a lead on Saddam, then we'll all be in clover.'

Never mind the clover – I could feel a yacht coming on.

We rolled into the man's village a day later – a few blocks of cement houses, surrounded by rich agricultural land, green and well tended. By now, mostly because of the three-day contact with the Iraqi 4th Armoured Division, I'd gained a bit of a reputation for attracting trouble. I had the four Scimitars of 3 Troop, but now we had an extra call sign attached to us, commanded by Corporal of Horse Wayne Foster. I'd known Wayne since he was a young trooper, when I'd been a Corporal of Horse in Knightsbridge in 1982. He'd heard all about my little exploits on the front line.

'Look who's here: Bullet Magnet. If there's any drama on this oper-ation, Mike, I'll fucking shoot you myself!'

I laughed. 'There won't be any dramas, Wayne – this is a nice easy task: we're just going to go for a little drive into the village and sit around while CIMIC open up shop. Then I'm going to listen to what the man has to say and we'll leg it back out again.'

It all started off as planned. We drove into the village, blocked the main routes in and out and watched as CIMIC set out their stall. The village was a rambling track – you couldn't call it a street – with low-rise concrete and mud buildings to either side. About halfway down was a rough square, again of beaten earth. There was no working sewage system, so effluent just lay on the surface. In the heat, the smell was overpowering.

The CIMIC team got busy on the loudspeakers and started giving out freebies. The kids came up first. They looked dirt poor – getting a few sweets and a new T-shirt each was probably the best thing that had happened to them all year. They were followed by a trickle of adults. The CIMIC captain and his team began to buttonhole people and interview them. One was our potential informant. Great. Everything was going just fine. A small crowd gathered in the square. Then a bigger crowd. Fifteen minutes later, there were more than 500 people milling around us.

Some of the men were carrying AK47s. Make that most of them. This wasn't very long after Saddam's overthrow. Iraqi civilians were permitted to carry small arms – as long as they didn't turn them on any of us. But we knew from other British Army units in and around the town that Al Amarah was a stronghold of anti-coalition activity: there had been plenty of contacts, some of them serious. And the firefights were gradually increasing in ferocity. As the crowd increased, more and more Iraqi policemen arrived, also armed. Many of the Iraqi police at the time were Ba'ath Party members, and fully paid-up supporters of Saddam Hussein.

With that, we got a shooter. The man had climbed up into the gallery of a minaret overlooking the square. He'd rested the barrel of an AK47 on the parapet and he was showing signs of opening fire. That wasn't a problem – if he did start anything we'd send him on his way up to heavenly glory, minaret or no minaret. The problem was the CIMIC detachment, whose safety was in our hands.

Wayne Foster was in the next-door wagon. He looked daggers at me. 'Drama? What drama?' I said. I went across to the captain, happily handing out sweeties without a care in the world.

'Don't look round, Captain, but we seem to have a little bit of a situation developing here.' His eyes flared in alarm. 'It's no big deal,' I said hurriedly. 'Just a poser with an AK up in the tower there. It probably isn't going to kick off. But we need to get you out of the village under our guard, just in case. Stay put and don't do anything until we sort this out; it'll only take a minute.'

I've never seen a team of people pack up and leave so fast. Within five minutes, the entire CIMIC unit had dismantled all its gear, shoved it on the 4x4s and disappeared towards the western horizon in a cloud of dust. Leaving us in the middle of an increasingly restive crowd of armed Iraqis.

Happily, we managed to extract in good order without a fight. About 8 kilometres out of the village, we caught up with the CIMIC convoy. 'What the fuck was all that about?' I asked the captain. 'You were supposed to come out with us. Not eight bloody kilometres ahead of us. We couldn't see you for dust!'

He shrugged. 'You think we were going to hang around in there with all of those guys pointing guns at us?' I wanted to grab him by the shirt front and shake his bloody head off. 'Listen, Captain,' I said, 'we're supposed to be protecting you. How can we do that if you fuck off without notice?' The captain turned and walked away. He didn't want to hear it.

I stopped him. 'Supposing you'd run into a different problem once you were outside the village? Something more serious than what happened in there? And we weren't there to give close protection? Whose fault would it have been if you'd got whacked?'

The captain just looked at me. He had nothing to say. We escorted the team back to base. But we didn't find Saddam Hussein. And that was the end of CIMIC's local public engagement programme – from that day forward they stayed in camp, well behind the safety of the Hesco blast walls and the armed guards.

By now we'd been in Iraq for the best part of three months. Many Iraqis had initially welcomed coalition troops as liberators. But when they discovered we were going to stay, some people started viewing us as an occupying force.

Resistance began to intensify. The Sunni rump of Saddam Hussein's army and police force, nearly all of whom the US administration had dismissed, hated us because they'd lost their jobs and their power over the Shi'ite majority. Meanwhile, the Shi'ite extremists led by Moqtada al-Sadr and others viewed us as infidels who had no business being in a Muslim country.

Both factions lived in and around Al Amarah. The town was getting a reputation as a hotbed of insurgent activity. Two weeks before we were supposed to finish our tour of duty, Brigade ordered D Squadron to get up there and help keep the peace. The HQ element of the 1st Queen's Dragoon Guards earmarked to relieve us was already in Iraq for the handover. The security problems meant we had to forget our scheduled leave and stay in Iraq for another two months.

We settled into an old Iraqi Air Force base a few miles from Al Amarah town centre, rechristening it Camp Carnie. Our primary mission now was to find the weapons of mass destruction US President George Bush and Britain's Prime Minister Tony Blair had assured us were in Iraq. Since this was the whole reason we were at war in Iraq in the first place, we were under constant pressure to find WMDs. We never found any.

The nearest we got was a gigantic SCUD missile we chanced on. It was parked on a trailer in the entrance tunnel to a football stadium, and so had been invisible to aerial recon. Close to, the SCUD looked pretty threatening: a sinister cigar tube about 11 metres long and 1 metre in diameter, with a nasty-looking point at the end. But when the experts examined it, they were disappointed: the SCUD had no nuclear or biological capability, just a common-or-garden HE warhead.

Our other orders were to protect the Al Amarah oil fields, make occasional security patrols and act as QRF (Quick Reaction Force) in support of nearby units. It was 24 June 2003 and roasting hot – on one operation the temperature touched 60°C. On that particular day, 3 Troop was acting as second-element QRF.

All of a sudden we got the call: a platoon of 1 Para was pinned down in Majar al-Kabir, a large and religiously conservative Shi'ite village some 25 kilometres south of Al Amarah. The brief said the Paras were under fire from most of the town, in deep shit and down to their last few rounds of ammunition. Acting as primary QRF, 2 Troop had already gone in to try and help the Paras. But 2 Troop's Scimitars had also come under heavy fire and were pinned down.

We had all our kit to hand, the vehicles were standing ready. All we had to do was slap on our body armour, jump in the wagons and go. As we were racing to get ready, I heard the unmistakable thumping of a Chinook helicopter. It hurtled in over our heads, made a tight turn and set down hard inside the camp. Medics raced up and started lifting casualties out of the cabin. I counted seven stretchers. There was some heavy, heavy shit going down in Majar al-Kabir – we had to get there fast. Adie was driving for me, but my replacement gunner, Trooper Nicko Nixon was on duty. Benny Benson had returned to the UK for treatment to a broken hand sustained while carrying out maintenance on the vehicle. I buttonholed Adie: 'Where the fuck's Nicko? Have you seen him?'

Adie shrugged. 'Dai Rees has put him on guard duty.'

'Guard duty! What the fuck for? He's supposed to be on standby QRF!' Adie shrugged. I was already angry at Dai Rees. And now this.

After one of the battles we'd been involved in, I'd picked up an AK47. Thinking it would make a good extra emergency weapon, I'd stowed it in one of the Scimitar's back bins. But while I'd been back in the UK to attend Alex Tweedie's funeral, one of the lads maintaining the wagon in my absence had found the AK and handed it in. I returned to Iraq and carried on with normal duties. On the second day back, I came in off patrol. I was knackered: physically exhausted, dehydrated and dazed with the heat: it was the hottest day I'd ever known. Rees was waiting for me at Camp Carnie. 'Flynn,' he said, 'as a punishment for keeping that unauthorized AK47 in your back bin, I've got a little job for you. You're to go round all the tents in camp and pull up all the weeds. Report back to me when you've done it.' I was forty-three years old, I had just come in off a three-day patrol in murderous heat and I was being ordered to weed the camp. If you want to destroy morale in an army, that's the way to do it.

I still had no gunner. I grabbed a passing trooper. 'Jump in – you're gunning for me!'

'What – me?'

'Yes, you.' His name was George Samson.

I ran to the vehicle with the crew; I stopped short. I couldn't believe my eyes. Adie had taken almost all the 30mm ammunition out of the Scimitar and packed it up in the special heat-shielded boxes ready for handover to the incoming squadron. I asked Adie why? He said, 'The SCM, Dai Rees, told me to get it ready for inspection.'

We started to throw the ammo back into the turret, some of it still in its boxes. As we drove towards the incident I was ripping open the boxes, unpacking the 30mm and 7.62mm ammunition and throwing the packaging out of the turret. 'Fuck his accounting,' I thought. It was a bit like Rorke's Drift, where the quartermaster made the men sign for the ammunition as they were being attacked.

Because of the 25-kilometre distance between Majar al-Kabir and Brigade, my wagon was acting as radio link. I started ripping the lids off the ammo boxes and unpacking shells, listening to the radio traffic as it relayed what sounded like a very confused picture. It was. And very bad: hundreds of locals armed with RPG-7s, heavy machine guns, AK47s and pistols had the Paras pinned down in and around the centre of Majar al-Kabir. The casualties I'd seen back in camp were members of the Paras own QRF. From what I could make out, they'd been injured when the Chinook that had been trying to insert them had come under heavy fire.

We stopped on the outskirts to take stock. The town was right on the banks of the Tigris River. Saddam Hussein had drained the marshes around here in revenge for an uprising.

The Para commander gave the troop leader Lt Archie Burton a quick update. None of it was good. 'We're down to our last couple of rounds. If we don't get immediate assistance we'll be overrun.'

It was around noon. The temperature inside the wagon was life-threatening. I'd loaded the 30mm main armament with HE rounds. Movement was torture. The ammo felt heavy as lead. Sweat was dripping off the rim of my helmet and splashing on my armoured vest. It was running down my face and dripping off my chin, trickling down behind my ears, beading down my neck in rivulets. I could hardly chug the warm water down fast enough. Next to me, I could see George was in the same state. When I asked, Adie said he was OK.

We drove into the edge of town. Immediately we came under sniper fire. I spotted one of the gunmen at an upper-storey window. He was only sixteen or seventeen, but he had an AK47 and he was firing at us, one burst after another, the bullets whizzing round the wagon. Then a couple of rounds thumped into our hull. Enough.

'See that sniper, George? Right and up, at the window there?'

'Yes. Seen.'

'Great. Take him out.'

Samson laid the GPMG on the sniper and opened fire. The Gimpy rattled off a couple of bursts and then stopped. One of the mounting bolts had worked loose, causing the gun to jam. We switched to the main armament. George was a good shot. He put three 30mm HE rounds into the top-storey window where the gunfire was still coming from. That entire section of the building disintegrated. The firing stopped.

There were other figures sneaking behind the low parapet that ran along the front of the block. They were taking pot shots at us and then ducking back down into cover. I looked down the track that formed the main street. The town police station was about 200 metres south of us on the west side. Our new troop commander, Lt Archie Burton, was the battle casualty replacement (BCR) for Lt Tweedie. Archie was directly behind me. Dave Simpson and Rob Goodwin were in the other two Scimitars about 150 metres to our right. A sign scrawled in big English letters on a concrete wall near by read: 'Where is Iraq's freedom?'

No idea, mate.

As far as I could see, most of the gunmen were in the south-west side of town. I could see 2 Troop over there, doing its best to cover the beleaguered Paras as they withdrew. We advanced towards them in line abreast, all four Scimitars continually changing position so as not to get pinned down.

Just then, an old woman in a baggy black chador came out of a side alley about 20 metres ahead of us. She was leading a donkey on a short length of rope. Shells whizzed and fizzed around her head, but Donkey-woman took absolutely no notice. There was a small square behind and to the left of her. On the far side, I suddenly noticed three men armed with RPGs and AK47s. They wore black dishdashas and green belt kit. One of the group raised his RPG-7 and took aim at us. Both the woman and her animal were now directly in the line of fire.

We had no cage armour fitted: if a rocket-propelled grenade hit us, we were dead. 'George,' I said, 'fire at those gunmen! And try not to kill the local.' George let rip with the Rarden. Three rounds of 30mm HE slammed into the opposition, shredding them.

Simmo's wagon rolled up alongside. It opened up on another group of gunmen near the first group with co-ax machine gun. The donkey was smack in the way. It took a burst of 7.62mm, staggered back, gazed around for a second in surprise and then fell to the ground. Donkey-woman looked down at it. She tugged at the rope. No response. She bent down and started yelling in the donkey's ear, you didn't need to speak Arabic to get the gist. A bullet hit the side of the turret and whanged off. More rounds buzzed close overhead. Most of Majar al-Kabir's male population was out on the streets trying to kill us, and we were trying to kill them back. It was a chador, not an invisibility cloak.

Donkey-woman scuttled round and kicked the animal's rump. She could have kicked it till kingdom come, but the donkey was no more. It had a large number of full metal jacket slugs embedded in its previously working bits. It had ceased to be. It was an ex-donkey. It had passed on to greener and less violent pastures.

There was a lull in the firing. Over the radio, I heard Brigade request we report any dead or injured at the town's police station. The police station was one of the dilapidated, low-rise, flat-roofed buildings we could see on the other side of the main drag. It sat in a patch of scrubby ground opposite a bust-up school. All the glass in the windows had been shot out. The back of the building was on fire. The front wall, below a small turret where a torn Iraqi flag was flying, was covered in fresh bullet scars.

The machine gun was still jammed in its cradle. How irritating was that? I'd told Adie to make sure the 7/16th spanner we needed for adjusting the mountings was always to hand in the turret, the nuts tended to vibrate loose with prolonged firing. As now. I reached for the spanner to tighten the bolts up before the gun jumped out of its mounting and landed on my lap. No spanner. 'Adie,' I said quietly, 'where's the gun-spanner?' There was a deafening silence from the front seat. 'Adie!' I snapped. 'Where's the fucking spanner?'

'I put it in the toolbox,' he said, in a small voice. The toolbox was on the outside of the vehicle. Where we couldn't now get at it without coming under direct fire.

'I told you to make sure the spanner is always in the turret, Conlon. The gun's falling to bits and we can't fix it.'

There was another silence. I said, 'Get out of the cab and fetch the fucking spanner!'

'What?'

'You heard me – get out and fetch the bloody gun-spanner.'

Adie dived out of the hole. As he did that, half the gunmen in town opened up again. AK47 rounds pinged off the Scimitar, I've never seen anyone move so fast, not even a CIMIC team. Adie snatched the gun-spanner from the front bin, scrambled back up onto the wagon and launched himself in through the driver's hatch. He never forgot to keep the spanner handy in the turret again.

By now, the firefight was tailing off. As we withdrew, I learned that six Royal Military Policemen had come under fire in the police station and then been killed defending it. Their deaths were a terrible blow. It was also a wake-up call for British forces in theatre. We'd been lax, driving around Al Amarah and district with our hatches open. But after Majar al-Kabir and the deaths of those six men, everything changed. Like it or not, we were still at war.

Not long after the contact in Majar al-Kabir, the squadron had a visit from the Chief of the General Staff, General Sir Mike Jackson. 'Jacko,' as everybody seemed to call him, had a reputation as a good bloke. We were making the best of our rough-and-ready accommodation in Camp Carnie, using whatever came to hand to increase comfort. General Jackson rolled up in style with his entourage, which included some heavy-duty close protection. As the one of the highest-value coalition targets in Iraq, he needed it.

We expected it was going to be the usual thing when there's a general visiting: we'd line up on parade, then he'd walk along the ranks and say a few morale-building words to the lucky few. But Jacko wasn't built like that. He told all of his aides to go off and have a cup of tea, ordered us to dismiss, pulled up one of the used ammunition crates we used as chairs and invited us to gather round. General Jackson was a busy man. His allotted span with D Squadron that day was twenty minutes. Two hours later, he was still there, bantering with everyone good-style. Our troop's turn came round, and I found myself sitting next to him.

'How have you been getting on? What sort of war have you been having?'

Well, quite eventful, but I didn't have time to tell him the half of it. 'This is Mike Flynn,' one of the lads said. 'We call him "The Beast of Basra". Mike found the Iraqi 4th Armoured Division and destroyed it all on his own.' Jackson laughed. He'd heard about the engagement, but he was interested to know the details. I told him a bit about what had happened. We got on well, perhaps because I was nearer his own age than anyone else there. Just before he left he called me to one side: 'Corporal Flynn,' he said, 'if you ever get any problems, or if you ever need anything, give me a ring.'

Some months later, I was getting ready to leave Bosnia when I received a letter inviting me to Buckingham Palace. I'd been awarded the Conspicuous Gallantry Cross. The letter contained my invitation and three tickets. But it said no more tickets would be made available under any circumstances. I have a wife and three children. And we all wanted to be there. I called Buckingham Palace, explained the problem and asked for an extra ticket. 'No,' said the cut-glass voice on the other end, 'as the letter makes clear to you, we never issue any extra tickets. We've just had to turn down the First Sea Lord for the same reason. We can't have too many people at the investiture, there simply isn't the room. I'm afraid we have to be quite strict about it.'

'Right,' I thought, 'General Mike Jackson once told me if I had any problems, I should call him.' I rang military directory enquiries and found the General's telephone number. His aide-de-camp, a major, answered.

'Corporal of Horse Flynn. I met General Jackson in . . .'

He cut me short. 'Corporal Flynn? That's amazing! General Jackson was at a dinner only yesterday and he mentioned your name.'

'Really? Why?'

'He was commenting on the fact that if you're anything to go by, then age isn't anything to worry about when it comes to active duty.'

'Fantastic,' I said. 'Now here's the thing: General Jackson told me if I ever had a problem, I was to give him a call.'

'All right. What's the problem?' I explained the little local difficulty about the ticket.

'Leave that with me,' the major said, 'I'll speak with the General.'

A few days later, I was standing in the Ops Room in Banja Luka. The door flew open and the colonel of the Ghurka unit we were attached to came flying in. 'Who is Corporal Flynn?' he demanded. I looked up from what I was doing: 'Colonel, that's me.'

'Glad to meet you. I've just had General Jackson's ADC on the phone. The General wants to talk to you. Is he a friend of yours? Are you related?'

'Neither,' I smiled, 'but we have met.'

'He wants you to ring him. You've got to go and ring him now on my phone.'

I followed the colonel through into his office. The line to the UK was clear as a bell. The major said, 'Morning, Corporal of Horse. We can't get you another ticket for the award ceremony for love nor money. But what we have done is arrange a day's work experience for your son that day. At Buckingham Palace.' He meant Liam, my elder son, who was sixteen at the time.

Work experience at Buckingham Palace. Now that's what I call leverage.

Some time later, when I was in Afghanistan for the second time, one of my troop came up to me, clutching a fat hardback.

'Did you know there's a whole load of stuff about you in General Mike Jackson's book?'

The book had only recently come out 'No, I haven't read it.'

'Well, there is. There's a whole lot of stuff about you getting the CGC in Iraq and the MC in that ambush outside Musa Qal'ah. There's Jacko meeting you in Al Amarah, the lot. You should read it.'

When we got back to the UK, I got hold of a copy. It wasn't a wind-up, it was true: General Jackson had mentioned me in his book. Not to be outdone by a mere four-star, I've now gone and mentioned him in mine.

When I came back from Iraq there was a vacancy open for a Corporal of Horse to go on a six-month tour of Bosnia as part of a composite, reinforced troop. Nobody wanted to go. Most, if not all, of the available people had already been there and done the Balkans. With the Iraq War only recently finished, if they had to be part of a peacekeeping force most people wanted to go to Basra as a way of widening their experience.

I'd ticked the Iraq box now, but I'd never been to Bosnia. D Squadron's leader, Major Taylor, called me in and asked if I'd like to go to Banja Luka as a Corporal of Horse. I stalled, on the grounds I needed to talk to my family. When I got home that evening, I pulled up a bottle of wine and Shelley and I had a chat. 'If I go out to Bosnia, then I'll get promoted. But I'll be leaving again in six weeks from now, and I'll be out there for at least six months. What do you think?'

'I think the promotion is a good idea, Michael. And I can tell you want to go. So you should go.'

I went back to Major Taylor and told him the news. In his usual laid-back style, he said how pleased he was. Major Taylor was an easy-going, laissez-faire sort of leader, until you made a mistake; at which he could turn round and chew you up into very small pieces.

CHAPTER TWENTY-FIVE

According to the unofficial military guide book, Banja Luka is about the size of Maidenhead, and filled with beautiful women and criminal deviants. By the time we got there in October 2003, the reconstituted state of Republika Srbska had spent several years trying to clean up its act: repair the property wrecked in the civil war, improve relations between the various communities, and so on. As the capital of the country in all but name, Banja Luka was very important in all this, which was why we were going there.

We landed by RAF passenger jet at the airfield on the northern outskirts of the city. As we drove in for the first time through a ramble of light industrial units and housing blocks, Banja Luka struck me as being very similar to Detmold, or any of a thousand other modern towns in Germany.

But then, as we drove further in, I could see that this was not just your bog-standard middle-European burg. It was a lovely, picturesque place, built around a river in a broad, triangular-shaped valley surrounded by rolling, wooded hills on all sides. The mountains sit beyond. It has lots of parks and green spaces, broad, tree-lined boulevards, fine old houses sited along the river and some not-all-that-bad new development in and around the centre. The Vrbas River meanders through the heart of town, splitting the community in two.

Life seemed pretty relaxed, considering recent events: there were dozens of pavement cafés with customers watching the world go by, couples strolling hand in hand in the warm autumnal weather and parents pushing small children along in buggies. After all the news reports during the war showing bullet-trashed buildings and dead people lying in the streets, I was surprised to find the city so sedate and pleasant-looking. We drove past a group of men playing chess in one of the small, tree-shaded side-parks that ran off the main drag. A little further down the street men were playing chess in a playground. The more we drove, the more groups of men we saw playing chess in the open air. There were never any women playing. Maybe the men were afraid that if they did let them play, the women would win.

The number of large and important-looking buildings brought home the fact that Banja Luka hosted most of the government institutions. Just under 90 per cent of the town's roughly 200,000-strong population was Serb, the rest were Bosnian Muslims and Croats.

Along with some grand houses and flats, the river frontage was mostly grass and trees with running and cycling tracks, and there were a number of excellent-looking pubs and restaurants. I intended checking them out at the earliest opportunity: especially with the exchange rate so much in our favour.

The composite Household Cavalry contingent consisted of some thirty men. We'd be patrolling under the banner of SFOR, the UN-sanctioned Stabilisation Force that operated throughout the Former Republic of Yugoslavia (FRY).

We set up home in our luxurious new quarters, a huddle of Corimecs placed inside the perimeter fence of a disused metal factory. I shared with Corporal of Horse Glynn Jones. Glynn was the Ricky Gervais of the Household Cavalry: dry-as-a-bone and close-to-the-bone humour, delivered deadpan style. We also had a couple of offices inside the factory proper. The plant still had all its old foundry and metal rolling equipment in place, but the machinery was lying idle. In the days of the old Communist regime led by Marshal Tito, the factory had been state owned and subsidized. Now, its new owner was making more money renting it out to SFOR than he could ever have done trying to operate the ageing plant commercially.

From the Intelligence brief, I knew more Bosnians than you could shake a stick at were mixed up in the counterfeit goods trade. Knocking out dodgy CDs, DVDs, cigarettes, alcohol, clothing, you name it – the city and the whole region was swimming in fake brands that undermined legitimate trade, and were buggering the country's chances of joining the EU.

Our Intelligence captain for the tour – known as 'Inch-high Private Eye' on account of his small stature and dogged gumshoe ways – had ambitions to clean up Dodge. Inch-high stood about five-feet-six in his stocking feet, but he made up for the lack of physical height in other ways. He was razor sharp, he was always extremely fit and he always did his best for the men under his command.

Since there were no longer any firefights for us to referee, Inch-high set us to watching a few of the local counterfeiters. The particular gang we started to shadow was suspected of fuelling the trade in illegal Scotch whisky, French brandy, English gin and anything else they thought they could get away with. When you examined the counterfeit bottles that had been seized in earlier raids, you could see that the labels were all very odd-looking: amateurishly executed and quite often pasted on skew-whiff. But then, when it's late in a shadowy night club and you want a drink, who's looking?

We'd been detailed to suss out this one particular nightclub. Sure enough, we saw many crates of illegal hooch being delivered there late one evening The Scotch wasn't travelling all the way from Scotland, that's for sure. It was coming from a small light industrial unit on the edge of town, where a bunch of the local boys were knocking the stuff out in a homemade still.

I decided to go and have a chat with the nightclub's owner. Four of us went in: me, with my nice new Corporal of Horse stripes on my uniform, and three troopers. We were all wearing dark sunglasses; we found the idea of trying to keep a low profile in our uniforms and in a socking great armoured Land Rover so laughable we'd decided to wear the shades as a joke. Two of my lads were carrying SA-80s, the fourth man and I had Browning 9mm pistols.

The interior of the nightclub was gloomy and cavernous, but it was nicely done out – if you like in-your-face modern Bosnian glitz. A very long bar ran down the left-hand side of the room with a mirror and about 100 optics of dodgy booze behind it. The dance floor over towards the back had a complex overhead lighting rig, complete with a glitter ball. It reminded me of the Cardiff Top Rank club. The rest of the space was taken up with black-upholstered chairs and tables and the occasional well-used sofa. It smelled of cheap whisky, stale beer and several thousand nights of cigarette smoke.

When we arrived there were at least two dozen people in the place: four or five decorative young women, a sprinkling of 'ten-pinters' (much less attractive women) and the usual assortment of Serbian hard nuts. The instant they caught sight of us, about half the inmates got up and walked out.

There was a big, burly figure standing watching us. Flanked by two bodyguards, the guy was straight out of Central Casting. About six-feet-one, with a broad, heavily muscled build, a hard, square jawed face and close-cropped hair, he looked like a Russian bear in a bad mood. He wore a beautifully cut Armani suit, which may or may not have been fake, a silk tie, hand-made shoes and a wristwatch that was roughly the size of Big Ben. It was a statement chronometer if ever there was one, and the statement said: 'I'm rich and bad and powerful – don't mess with me.' He looked as if he took steroids all morning and then worked out in the gym all afternoon. I immediately thought, 'Ivan the Terrible.' A thousand-to-one said he was the joint's owner. Our man blanked us totally. We stood there like spare ushers at a wedding for a minute or two. When it dawned on them we weren't going to leave any time soon, one of the burly goons who'd been glowering at us stepped forward.

'Can I help you?'

'Yes,' I said, 'we'd like to talk to the club's owner.'

The lackey shook his head. 'Sorry, the boss won't want to talk to you.'

I could understand that: the last thing these guys wanted was anyone disrupting their lucrative trade selling counterfeit booze to unwitting punters at a huge mark-up. Still, I quite fancied talking to Mr Big – after all, that was the job in hand.

I said, 'If your boss doesn't speak to us now, we're going to come in here every day. We're going to sit here armed and in uniform. Which might spoil the beautiful ambience you've created and scare off all your customers.' The goon looked me up and down. For a moment I thought he was going to call my bluff. I gave him my best smile. 'I've got eight more armed men outside. It's either a quick chat with the boss, or they come in, too.'

The guy turned his back on us and walked away. I ambled up to the bar and sat down on one of the stools. My three troopers followed suit. More customers stood up and left. We were pretty much down to us and the bouncers. The barman said in a surly voice, 'You want anything?'

'Thank you – we'll all have a coffee.' Most places we visited the coffee or soft drinks were on the house. Not here. No problem; we'd pay for it. The local currency wasn't worth the paper it was printed on, anyway. We made our coffees last for half an hour. From time to time a punter would walk in, catch sight of us lot sitting at the bar and walk straight out again. There was no question we were bad for business. At last, the same bouncer came back up. 'All right,' he said, 'the boss will meet you here in two days. But it must be at ten in the morning.' I smiled at him again. 'No problem. We'll be here.'

We left the bar. Lt Nick Bacon, who'd been 2 Troop commander in Iraq, was now my troop commander in Bosnia. I was driving the Land Rover, with Lt Bacon in the commander's seat. As we neared the camp at the old metal factory, a man ran out into the road in front us. He couldn't speak a word of English, but he looked shocked. He was hopping from foot to foot, pointing at the river to our immediate right. We got out and saw a woman in the water. She was trapped under the far bank, caught up in the overhanging branches there. A sick feeling gripped my stomach, and Alex Tweedie flashed into my mind's eye, back in that ditch in Iraq. I took my pistol out and handed it to Lt Bacon. 'We need to get an ambulance and some help,' I said. Then I jumped in.

The water was ice cold. It knocked the breath clean out of me. The river deepened, so I had to start swimming – thankfully, the current wasn't all that strong. As I got near the stranded woman I came back into depth. I stood up, caught her by the shoulders and started dragging her up onto the bank. I kept seeing Alex in my head.

While I'd been in the water, the Bosnian man had run round and crossed a footbridge a short distance upriver. He was joined by another, and they reached down now and helped me pull the woman out onto dry land. It was a struggle; the poor thing was heavy, with her heavy woollen coat completely waterlogged. Long grey hair straggled out in a fan around her head. She looked terrible. While I was freezing, shivering with cold, she was unconcious. Her skin was dead pale and her lips were tinged with blue. We laid her on her back. It was hard to tell if she was breathing. I bent to start resuscitation, pinching her nose and clearing the muck from her airways.

Then I stopped. There was an overpowering smell coming from her mouth, poisonous and sweet at the same time, like a mixture of perfume and detergent. I didn't want to risk giving her full mouth-to-mouth resuscitation – whatever was causing the horrible smell might be dangerous. Instead, I made a seal around her mouth with my hands and then breathed down hard into her lungs Almost at once she started coughing and spluttering and spewing water.

Lt Bacon brought the Land Rover round and climbed out to lend a hand. As we lifted her to her feet, she tried to struggle free and jump back into the river. We had to restrain her. Then she bent double and started to vomit. We laid her down in the back of the Land Rover and made her as comfortable as possible. I signed to one of the Bosnian men to climb in and sit with her. There was a fair chance we'd need someone to translate when we got her to hospital. As soon as we got going, the woman was sick again, and the same overpowering chemical smell filled the air. It was all we could do not to vomit with her. We drove to the A&E department of Banja Luka hospital.

The hospital was made up of grey, old-style Commie blocks. Run-down wasn't in it. The place was a real mess. She was moaning and her eyelids were fluttering. We carried her inside and laid her on a trolley I found standing just inside the main doors. There was abso-lutely no one around, no receptionist, no nurses, nothing. I called along a corridor a few times: 'Hello? Is anybody there?' Eventually, a middle-aged doctor appeared. She spoke some English, but the Bosnian guy stepped in, rattling off the story at a rate of knots.

A weary look on her face, the doctor asked us to sit to one side. A few minutes later, she came back. 'The old lady has drunk at least two litres of methylated spirits mixed with plum brandy. All her vital organs are poisoned beyond help. She will take two days to die, but she will die and there is nothing that can be done about it. You have saved her life for nothing – only for her to suffer.'

Oh fuck.

'Why did she do it?'

'Her husband died and she has no one left. It was the war. No money, no children, nothing.' The doctor shrugged her shoulders and walked away. I stared after her. No wonder the woman had tried to chuck herself back in the river. Just as the doctor had said, the woman died in agony two days later. All I'd actually done was prolong her suffering.

We went back to the nightclub for the scheduled meeting. Sure enough, the guy I'd pinged and dubbed 'Ivan the Terrible' turned out to be the big boss. He told me his name was Bogdanovic. For the meeting, Bogdanovic wore a black T-shirt, black trousers and shiny black Italian shoes. We sat down and started to talk; Bogdanovic was very good at talking, mostly about himself. He owned this club and several other bars and clubs in Banja Luka. Ivan, as I still preferred to call him, spoke very good English, except for an amusing habit of missing out all the words 'the' and 'a'. We both knew that I knew he was a crook and a scumbag, but he was likeable with it.

Close to, I could see Ivan was wearing a lot of his wealth. He had several heavy, solid gold neck chains and bracelets, his watch was gold – for all I knew, the highly attractive blonde hanging off his shoulder had a solid gold heart.

The guy was the whole nine yards: he might as well have been carrying a placard that read 'Serbian Mafia'. He snapped his fingers and the blonde disappeared. He snapped them again and a handsome brunette arrived with a tray of coffees. He was snappy like that. I got a strong feeling he liked to hear the sound of his own voice: he could have talked for the Former Republic of Yugoslavia. He started telling me what a great leader Marshal Tito had been, how Yugoslavia had fallen apart with Tito's death and look what a mess it was in now. I left off agreeing that the country was in a mess, or saying that I was looking at a big part of the problem right in front of me.

After half an hour or so of his verbal diarrhoea, we got down to business. 'You have to stop doing this,' I told him, pointing at the regiments of counterfeit booze optics. 'Selling illegal alcohol. If you don't stop, we'll have to ask the police to come round and close you down.'

He looked at me with sad, regretful eyes. 'You like skiing?' he asked. It was better than owning up to being a criminal.

'I love skiing,' I said, 'but you still have to stop dealing in illegal booze.'

'You will come skiing with me,' he declared. 'I have chalet near Sarajevo you will like very much.'

He went on like this until I stopped him. 'Very, very nice of you – but you must understand we can't accept. Conflict of interest.' The funny thing was that the squadron had been trying to organize a skiing trip: his offer of free accommodation, ski gear and lift passes was very attractive. But NATO forces were supposed to be spending money in the local economy – not ligging off its gangsters. A pity to miss the chance of freebie accommodation, but there you go.

My report on the illegal drinks trade and the key role I thought Ivan the Terrible played in that was handed in to the Int cell a few days later. I thought no more about it and moved on to other things. I was due my two weeks off for R&R, so I went back home to see Shell and the kids. I was lucky to get leave. Everyone else was going stir crazy in those Corimecs.

While I was away, three of the troopers in Glynn Jones's troop – Morgan, Greenwood and Barnes – decided they were going to break out of the concentration camp otherwise known as the Banja Luka metal factory. The rules stated they were only allowed two cans of beer per day per man at the 'Effi' – the multi-national European equivalent of the NAAFI. But using their skills and a bit of gentle persuasion, the three of them had managed to get hold of some extra beer cards. A lot of extra beer cards. On which they proceeded to get trolleyed. They then decided to liberate the big, brand-new Nissan 4x4 patrol vehicle on camp and take it for a drive downtown. It was snowing. They had more drinks and a couple of dances in the Banja Luka Irish Bar. Then they set off back.

The entrance to the camp was at the bottom of a massive hill. Now an icy massive hill. Two hundred metres from the gate the driver lost control and wrote off the lovely new Nissan in the ditch. Thinking on their feet, as in: 'Why should we all take the rap? One of us can take the blame, he'll get his reward later,' Barnes stayed behind with the jeep, slightly battered and a fair bit the worse for drink.

The other two scaled the 4.5-metre double-perimeter fence topped with razor wire. And got into bed as if nothing had happened. It's amazing what you can do when you're pissed and in trouble. Unfortunately for them, the duty guard noticed the pair of them trying to break in. Not only that, various CCTV cameras had recorded the three of them leaving the camp without permission in the first place. I came back off leave to find that all three troopers had got sixty days' incarceration in Colchester corrective facility and a £900 fine each. An expensive night out in Banja Luka.

A few days later I was lying in bed when I heard a shot. Thinking it was just one of the locals out celebrating a birthday, I ignored it. I had the place to myself that morning. There were two Canadian Intelligence officers in the room next door, and above them two Gurkha warrant officers. I'd grown quite pally with one of the Gurkhas, Prem. When I'd got back in after another meeting with Ivan the Terrible, I stopped off and had a chat with him. There was a battlefield tour to Sarajevo the next day and Prem wanted to know if I'd go with him. The transport arrived at five o'clock in the morning. There was no way I'd make it with the amount of champagne I'd drunk, courtesy of Ivan. But I convinced Prem to go anyway.

Next thing I knew, someone started shouting and hammering on the door of the room. It sounded like one of the Canadians. That was odd. It was his room. Why didn't he just let himself in? Next thing, I heard the Canadian kicking the door down. Still half-asleep, I jumped out of bed and hauled on a pair of trousers. While I was getting dressed he bashed on my door. I opened it. The guy was white-faced and shaking, plainly in shock. 'He's dead,' he shouted, 'he's dead!'

He led me next door. There were two bunks against the far wall and his colleague was sprawled on the floor directly in front of them. There was a large pool of blood around his head and a pistol lying next to him. He'd blown the top of his head off. Only the day before, he'd complained of a head cold. 'Get some Lemsips,' I told him, 'they're good for colds.' Instead, he'd gone and killed himself.

I looked up. There was a hole in the ceiling immediately above the body. Prem! I raced up the stairs and tried his door. It was locked. I knocked and shouted, but there was no answer. I stood there for a second. Prem was a good guy – I didn't want him to be lying in there with a gunshot wound. I kicked the door in. The room was empty. Then I remembered – he'd gone on the tour. Which was just as well: the dead man's bullet had come up through the floor, gone straight through the middle of Prem's mattress and exited out through the ceiling. If he hadn't gone on the trip, he'd have taken a .45 slug through the body.

Glynn himself had returned to Windsor on his R&R. The SCM Paul Thomas – Tommo – had also been looking forward to going home. Instead, he was now told to remain for the full six months of the tour. He was really, really delighted. At the time, Tommo and I didn't see eye to eye. Glynn's replacement and my new room-mate was Staff Corporal Johnny Pass (JP).

The fact is, we were all cooped up in what was effectively an open prison. We needed to get out and do something. But what? Inch-high Private Eye, ever the realist, organized another battlefield tour of Sarajevo. We stayed at the IFOR camp there, which unlike the metal factory had an open drinking policy. As in no rationing. It also had lots of forces from other nationalities, including a sprinkling of females.

We were in the camp's American bar, when one of my troop, Trooper Biddlestone, met an American girl who asked him back for a cup of tea. He came to check with me first. 'All right, off you go. I know how long it can take to boil a kettle – but be back for seven in the morning.' Tommo got wind of the fact that I'd let one of my troop sleep some-where other than in our designated quarters. 'Why have you given Trooper Biddlestone permission to stay out?' he demanded.

'We've got to cut the boys some slack, Tommo. It's because we've kept them hemmed in the whole time that things like the Nissan incident are happening in the first place. You need to take a chill pill.' Tommo obviously still wasn't happy. He wouldn't let it go, and the more he went on the angrier I grew. I'm a great believer in the idea that if you treat people like adults, they behave like adults.

The four of us went back to the room we were sharing: Tommo, a Royal Marines sergeant who'd just arrived to teach us to ski, JP and me. The argument between me and Tommo kept rumbling. The Corimec was boiling hot. I stripped my clothes off and got into the sleeping bag. I was lying there minding my own business when Tommo finally went off on one. He ordered me to go and find Biddlestone.

'Fuck off!' I said. 'How the fuck am I going to find him in the female American accommodation? I'd have to knock on every single door.'

'I don't care!' Tommo yelled. 'Fucking find him!'

'Make me!'

'I will fucking make you!'

He leapt out of bed starkers and lumbered towards me. I jumped off the top bunk and tried to wrestle on my boxer shorts, but I was so angry I couldn't get the fucking things on. Tommo was now almost on me. I got ready to smack him. JP grabbed hold of my arms. 'Fucking stop it, the pair of you.'

Tommo shouted, 'Let him go!'

JP let go. I flew at Tommo Stark bollock-naked, we set about thumping each other. Anxious to keep up the reputation of the Royal Marines when it came to a spot of in-the-buff aggro, the sergeant took a flying leap off his bunk and made it a three-way match. We writhed around on the floor in a seething mass, trying to knock lumps off each other while JP looked on in amazement.

The commotion had not gone unnoticed. Suddenly, the door swung open. Inch-high was standing there in his greatcoat. He took in the sight of his four senior NCOs naked Corimec wrestling, closed the door quietly and walked away. 'Nobody,' he told the duty guard corporal outside, 'is to go near the Seniors' room until I give permission.'

The fight duly broke up. In the morning, sporting black eyes and thick lips, Tommo and I shook hands. From that time on we got along a lot better.

A week or two later, I was up in the mountains near Sarajevo with my whole troop of twenty guys, skiing. We'd gone ahead and organized our own trip. All of a sudden, a posse of skidoos swooped in around me and parked up in a flurry of powder snow. It was like something out of a Bond movie.

A big, blocky figure stepped off the swankiest machine and ambled towards me. Ivan the Terrible, complete and unalloyed and larger than life, in top-of-the range skiwear, supertastic snow goggles and snazzy salopettes. Even his skiwear was black. Either he'd been following me or this was a remarkable coincidence. 'Michael,' he said, slapping me on the back like a long-lost friend. 'You will come with me.'

I looked around. None of the guys I was skiing with were anywhere to be seen. Skiing's like that – you tend to get split up. After turning the offer down a couple of times, I finally gave in and got on the back of his skidoo. What was the worst that could happen? I didn't want to think about the worst; always look on the bright side. The entourage revved up and we shot off. A short, high-speed snow journey later we pulled into the forecourt of a five-star hotel. 'This *my* hotel,' Ivan proudly announced as we settled into the plush sofas.

Out came the beers and the *raki*; the really smooth stuff, not the usual rotgut. We fell to talking again, which is to say he talked most of the time and I listened. Business, he told me, was good. 'Plenty people go my bars. Spend money.'

'Listen, Ivan,' I said. 'You've got to stop all these illegal operations.' He started to bluster but I interrupted him. 'No, you really do have to cut it out: we're onto you. The alcohol is one thing, but we also know now that you're dealing drugs. We can't and won't allow that. I'm telling you, if you don't stop the drugs trading right now, then all your clubs and pubs are going to get busted and closed down.'

Of course, I was winging it to scare him. I didn't even know if there would be any operational busts. The genial expression on his face didn't falter.

'When will this happen?'

'Soon.'

'How soon?'

'Very soon.'

When in doubt, change the subject. Ivan handed me another *raki*. 'Michael, you must organize for top English DJ to come and work in my clubs. Can you try and get me Boy George?'

I laughed. 'Of course I will.'

Two days later, Inch-high Private Eye called me in for a briefing. 'The police are determined to clamp down on the narcotics trade: they're going to be staging a few uninvited visits.' I looked down the list of properties to be raided. Three of Ivan the Terrible's joints figured near the top. I wondered if he'd taken any notice of what I'd said. 'Your troop will be on QRF in barracks,' Inch-high said, 'ready to crash out, in case there's any escalation.' We sat waiting on QRF, but the raids passed off without trouble.

Next morning, I was out on patrol. I was dying to know if the police had hit any of Ivan's clubs. Judging by the fact that the biggest was still open for business, my guess was they hadn't. We poled inside. No sooner had I crossed the threshold than Ivan came up to me, arms wide and all of his gold teeth on show at the same time. He grabbed me in a mighty bear hug and just about managed to lift me off the floor. That takes some doing.

When he'd put me down again, I opened my mouth to speak. 'My friend!' he roared before I could get a word in edgeways. 'My bestest, bestest friend! You have saved me! You save my business!'

He thought I'd tipped him off about the raids. Now Ivan assumed I was his inside man. When I'd just been going for it in an opportunistic, law-enforcement kind of way. Hoping he'd be a good boy. Instead, I'd scored an own goal: he'd taken me at face value, moved all his drugs out and hidden them before the raids went in. The police had found no cocaine or marijuana on any of Ivan's premises. But they'd found plenty on Ivan's competitors. Who were now facing closure, fines and in some cases, prison.

I'd become instant royalty – nothing was too good for me. I could have any drink, any meal, anything I wanted, any time. 'What size are you, what size are you?' he cried. 'You must have best suit.' He snapped his fingers. One of his men came forward with a tape measure. He had obvious intentions on my inside leg.

I stepped back a pace and shook my head. 'No suit. Thank you.'

'I would like to come to Britain,' Ivan declared. 'I want to open English pubs, I have seen English pubs all over the world, I like them very much. I will do English theme pubs in Bosnia, it will be great success.'

He snapped his fingers. I braced: they still weren't getting anywhere near my inside leg. All that happened was a brunette beauty turned up with some drinks.

'Not on duty, thanks,' I said, 'but I wouldn't mind having a coffee.' He snapped and the coffee came about ten seconds later.

'I will need passport for Britain,' Ivan said. 'I need friend to sponsor me. You will be friend, yes?' I stalled him and went straight back to Inch-high Private Fye.

When I'd explained, Inch-high said, 'Your relationship with this man is useful. It might help us get on top of Bosnia's narcotics trade. Our own researches suggest he has strong links to the Russian Mafia. You might like to maintain contact with him and continue to report. But if you're going to sponsor him, you'll have to put up a £150,000 guarantee that when this guy gets to the UK, he doesn't do a runner. Or commit any crimes. Can you stand that?'

I stared at Inch-high to see if he was joking. 'I can't stand 150 pence at the moment.'

I went back to Ivan and told him I couldn't afford to underwrite his British reconnaissance trip. 'No problem, Mick!' he roared. 'You tell me bank account, I give you money and you give me money back when I return to Bosnia.' It was clear that £150,000 meant nothing to him; it was just another snap of the fingers. It occurred to me that in my own little way, I was agent handling for Army Intelligence. Only without the extra pay. Or any of the relevant training. But I was in line for an Armani suit. And my whole troop got taken skiing again, only this time they stayed at Ivan's five-star hotel. And anything they asked for came free.

That evening, I took Ben Vesty, the new troop leader who'd just flown in to take over from me, and twelve members of my troop out to dinner in one of Banja Luka's better restaurants. Vesty came from one of Britain's wealthiest families: he was used to deluxe. Still, we had to do the best we could with the local amenities. We trooped into the place and found a large table. IFOR rules stipulated we had to be in uniform, so we stood out just a bit from the crowd. We'd just ordered when Ivan appeared, beaming like a genie someone had just rubbed up the right way. 'Ah, my very good friend Michael,' he boomed, 'this also my restaurant. Everything is on house!' I hadn't known this was yet another part of his empire, but I can't say I was all that surprised.

Ivan sat down without an invitation, slapped me on the back and ordered champagne all round. I didn't see him snap any fingers, but a few minutes later a bevy of good-looking women appeared out of nowhere and sat down with us. I could see Ben Vesty looking between Ivan and me, staring at the women and the entourage of goons hanging around and wondering what the hell was going on. I was trying to protest that we couldn't accept any more of his hospitality, but Ivan drove through that and piled on the goodies. The lads were getting their arms around the girls, it was a terrific meal and we all had a superb evening.

As we left the restaurant, Vesty turned to me. 'What a fantastic night. What a really nice guy your friend Bogdanovic is. He told me he owns half the hotels and restaurants in town.'

'Yes, I bet he did.'

'He's a real entrepreneur,' said Vesty, approvingly. 'Absolutely terrific.'

'Yes,' I agreed, with a straight face. 'He's certainly terrific.' I didn't tell him Ivan was the very same Mr Local Mafia whose details figured so prominently on the Int Cell's criminal watch list.

Later that day, Ben Vesty reported for his first Int briefing. I sat down next to him. In waltzed Inch-high Private Eye and fired up the overhead projector. 'Right,' he said, 'orders and updates. Not least for the benefit of our new arrival, Lt Vesty, I'll go through the most wanted criminals in Banja Luka.' He shot Ben a bit of a charged look.

The first photograph up on the screen was of Ivan the Terrible. It had been taken the evening before. In a restaurant. On one side of Ivan, next to his lovely blonde personal assistant, was me. On the other side of Banja Luka's Most Wanted – with one arm around the lovely blonde personal assistant – was new Troop Leader Ben Vesty. His other arm was around Ivan the Terrible. Vesty and Ivan looked close. Very close.

I leaned across to him and whispered: 'Vesty, *you* are in my pocket ...'

When the brief was over he rounded on me: 'What the fuck's going on, Corporal of Horse? Are you trying to get me thrown out, or what?' I could hardly stop laughing long enough to answer.

Apart from being cooped up like chickens, Bosnia was a pretty easy gig for us. But it wasn't all plain sailing. Rolling up the counterfeit goods trade wasn't enough for Inch-high Private Eye. He wanted to help the various UK and US agencies track down Serbia's most wanted. Especially General Ratko Mladić and his former ally, Radovan Karadžić.

I was all for it. In July 1995, troops allegedly under Mladić's command had overrun the so-called UN safe area of Srebrenica. Because it was supposed to be safe, thousands of Muslim civilians had taken refuge there. A Dutch peacekeeping contingent had the job of protecting them. Overcoming the Dutch, Mladić's men expelled more than 40,000 refugees. An estimated 8,300 Muslim men and boys were taken out into the local forests and executed. On 24 July 1995, the International Criminal Tribunal for the former Yugoslavia (ICTY) indicted Mladić and Karadžić on charges of war crimes. The United States government had put up a $5 million reward for the capture of the two men. No one had collected on it yet – but there was still time.

The other thing that Inch-high wanted to do was find out who had shot dead the chief inspector of the Banja Luka police, back in 1997. So now, as regular soldiers, we were being asked to hunt down wanted war criminals and open a criminal cold case. It's a varied life in the British Army these days, and no mistake.

We started with the basic step of asking around the town's clubs and bars. It immediately became clear that a fair number of people in Banja Luka knew exactly why the chief inspector had been shot dead – for trying to stamp out the local drugs trade. Not only that, they knew – or said they knew – who'd committed the murder. They just weren't willing to tell us. They said that co-operating with the inquiry might have a terminally damaging effect on their own health. And they were probably right.

I went for a meeting with Banja Luka's new head of anti-narcotics. He was a large man in casual clothes surrounded by officers who looked like recycled hippies: long-haired, dressed in odd, ill-fitting clothes, obviously doing their best to blend in with the town's drug users and dealers. Perhaps a little too obviously. After we'd been chatting for a while, the chief held up his hand. Pointing at my uniform, he said: 'As long as you are dressed like that, you won't even scratch the surface of this case.' I took the dismissal as a challenge.

One casual chat at a time, one detail adding to another, we built up a list of suspects and then began to narrow it down. Against all expectations, we were making good progress.

At the same time, we were trying to get a lead on Radovan Karadžić. I talked to Ivan and he agreed to help, on the strict understanding that our conversation hadn't taken place. He told me I needed to talk to a 'friend'. I met the friend, who introduced me to another 'friend' and so on, until one day, I found myself invited to meet a Serbian man who was supposedly Karadžić's right-hand man in Banja Luka. Up until then, my informant had proved reliable. And Karadžić was still at the top of the ICTY's most wanted list. All of a sudden, everyone got seriously interested – especially Inch-high. I told him where and when I was meeting the Serb. The Household Cavalry's commanding officer, Lt Col Charlie Clee, was with us at the time. The colonel and Inch-high decided they'd come to the meeting. As always in a meet of that kind, we had a dozen of the boys armed and ready on standby, in case the Serbs tried to pull anything.

We met Mr Big at his office. It was on the upper floor of a decrepit, unassuming block that looked as if it might once have been a small shopping centre. Bodyguards were posted all over the place, all dressed in identical black, three-quarter-length leather coats. A couple of them came up. They let us keep our pistols, but frisked us to make sure we weren't wired for sound. When they were satisfied we were clean, we had to pass through a metal detector and then undergo two separate electronic scans for bugging or tracking devices. There was a pretty young secretary typing at a desk in the corner. She was the only member of the Serb contingent not wearing black leather. She smiled at us – at least someone was friendly.

There were wooden shutters over the windows to thwart listening devices. When they'd done frisking and sweeping us, a gentleman the size and shape of a bus came out of the adjoining office. He, too, wore a three-quarter-length black leather coat. He led us upstairs, knocked at the door of a second office and we went in. An even bigger man was sitting behind a broad, heavy desk. In this place, size obviously mattered. The man wore a black turtleneck sweater and a black three-quarter-length leather coat. If only we'd known, we could have adopted the correct dress code for the meeting and blended in. The garden shed who'd shown us in told us to sit down, and then took up station just inside the door.

The Boss's desk had a double-headed Serbian eagle standing on it. There was another eagle with two heads squatting on a plinth in the corner. Looking round, I saw that there were double-headed eagles everywhere, the place looked like a Serbian eagle sanctuary. To rub in the message, there were a very large number of Serbian flags pinned up and plastered around the room. I was beginning to suspect Mr Big was a bit of a Serb nationalist, I'm quick on the uptake like that. More seriously, it was clear that whatever his game, our man was a serious player. Perhaps he really was one of Karadžić's best mates. Either that, or he was Banja Luka's answer to Walter Mitty.

Mr Big didn't give us any useful information about the murder of the chief inspector or about the present location of Radovan Karadžić. Instead, he tried to pump us. 'How long are you going to be in town?'

I shrugged.

'The current UN commitment,' Inch-high told him, 'is open-ended.' He had a way with words, did Inch-high.

'What will you do to stop drugs getting into Banja Luka?'

Talk about a loaded question. And one that told you everything about what he was into. Inch-high rose to the occasion again: 'Work with local law enforcement agencies to stem and ultimately stamp out the trade.' Mr Big's questions told us he had a lot of fingers in a lot of pies.

Colonel Clee asked: 'Do you have any information for us about the massacre at Srebrenica?'

The Serb stared at him for a moment. Then the hint of a smile came on his thick lips. 'I was there,' he said.

'You were there?'

He shrugged. 'Of course. I know who killed the Muslims. But that was in the war.' His voice changed, and a cold note came into it. 'They weren't human beings. They were the enemy.' I got the feeling he was telling the truth: he knew who'd done the killing at Srebrenica, all right – unless I was very much mistaken, he knew because he'd been directly involved in it. The Boss put his social mask back on and made a visible effort to relax. 'I have heard he has been here in Banja Luka. Recently.'

'Who has?' Inch-high's voice was sharp.

'Radovan.'

'Karadžić? Here in town? When? Where is he now?'

Mr Big chuckled. 'I don't know where he is hiding. But Radovan is clever. He will be hard to catch.'

We were wasting our time – he was taking the piss. We said our goodbyes and left. Karadžić is currently on trial in The Hague. Mladić is still on the run.

After investigating for a few weeks, we'd narrowed the list of suspects in the murder investigation down to one. A major league Serbian businessman, the chief suspect was an even bigger fish than my very good friend Ivan. He must have been a big fish: his codename was 'Mackerel'. Which is quite a small fish, but it's also the French slang for 'pimp'. French Intelligence had provided some of the initial info on him. According to the Int reports, Mackerel not only owned a string of top-class hotels throughout the Balkans, but also had close financial relationships with members of the Bosnian government. The Intelligence strongly suggested he'd financed the hotels with money that had either been extorted and stolen from Bosnian Muslims or laundered from the drugs trade.

Why were we so certain this man should stand trial for murder? The biggest breakthrough came when we tracked down a woman who'd been working in the bar where the chief inspector was shot. The woman told us that three men had jumped the chief, overpowered him and wrestled him to the floor. Mackerel had swaggered up and placed a foot on the victim's head. Then one of the goons had pulled out a pistol and shot the chief inspector three times through the head – at point-blank range. Our eyewitness bravely gave us a sworn statement and agreed to testify in open court. At the police station, she immediately identified the Mackerel from police photographs.

Prosecuting the rich and well connected is always a challenge. But with Bosnia still in a state of transition and the judicial system less than it might be, getting a conviction was going to be really hard. Nevertheless, our evidence was so strong the case was officially reopened. The dossier we'd compiled passed up through the hierarchy to the US-led war crimes commission. Later, Inch-high told me the Bosnian government's failure to bring Mladić, Karadžić and the Mackerel to trial had hindered Bosnia's attempt to join the EU.

What happened to Ivan the Terrible? The closer I got to him, the greater my own risk of personal and professional compromise. As the tour came to an end, I gradually began to distance myself from him, citing duty as a reason for passing up his many invitations. But Ivan didn't give up easily. When I got back home to Windsor, a letter arrived. It had been delivered to our base at the Banja Luka metal factory and forwarded from there. Ivan wanted to know how much progress I'd made setting things up for his recce trip of English pubs. He explained that he was going to uncover the secrets of their success, set up a chain of clones in Bosnia and add them to his collection of joints. I passed the ball back to Int. If I'd gone into partnership with Ivan, I'd probably have made a shedload of money – most of it the proceeds of trafficking in cocaine, cannabis and illegal hooch. I'd also very likely have gone to jail.

When we got back from Bosnia we were told that we'd be deploying as the enemy force (OPFOR) at BATUS in Canada for five months. Only this time, I had no intention of going AWOL. But just before I was due to leave, my younger son Sean came to Shelley. 'My leg's aching, Mum. It's really sore.' Shelley took Sean to see the doctor: 'It's only growing pains; plus the fact that he's doing so many hours swimming every week.' Aged fifteen, Sean was ranked seventeenth fastest at butterfly stroke in England.

The next day, Shelley went swimming with Sean. She looked at him and saw that the muscles in his right thigh were withering away.

'How's your leg, Sean?'

'Like I said – it hurts.'

Shelley took him to see a different doctor. He immediately booked Sean in for an emergency MRI scan at the local hospital. The scan showed our worst fears: he had what looked like a tumour. All sorts of thoughts went through my mind: if Sean had cancer in his bone marrow, then the outlook was very bleak. Nothing in the world scares you as much as one of your children being diagnosed with a serious illness.

That was on the Friday. I was due to fly out to Canada for five months on the Monday. By now, Johnny Pass had taken over as D Squadron SCM. I told JP the full story. 'Go home,' he said. 'Sort it out.' We took Sean to a specialist hospital in Birmingham. The relief Shell and I felt when they told us the tumour was benign was just incredible. They drilled into Sean's bone, removed the lump and he made a full recovery. These days, he's bigger than ever.

Scare over, I flew out and joined the rest of the squadron at BATUS.

CHAPTER TWENTY-SIX

I came back from Canada in October 2005 and resumed normal duties. But we found it more and more difficult to get hold of the basic Army equipment we needed for day-to-day training: things like boots, combat jackets and socks. The only time we'd noticed this before was in the run-up to the Iraq War. We suspected something similar was brewing.

Sure enough, we then got the nod: the British were about to take responsibility for the new offensive in Afghanistan. In a place I'd never heard of: Helmand province. When they told me where we were going, I wondered, only half-joking, 'Is that where the mayonnaise comes from?' But Helmand's porous southern border with the extremist-controlled badlands of northern Pakistan gives the insurgents attacking NATO forces a safe haven. And we weren't talking mayonnaise – we were talking marijuana. And opium.

The brief said the Taliban in Helmand were up to their necks in the drugs business, and they didn't like foreigners getting in the way. Helmand produced more than 50 per cent of the world's raw opium, earning an estimated £2 billion a year. Brutal chaos, with no working army, police force or justice system, suited the Taliban just fine. We'd be deploying as part of Operation Herrick 4, with D Squadron attached to the 3rd Battalion, The Parachute Regiment, and both units part of 16 Air Assault Brigade.

We trained at Sennybridge, Brecon, and Thetford, Norfolk, where

I met two of the officers who'd be going out with the troop: Lt Ralph Johnson and Lt Tom Long. Johnson was one of those guys you take to on first meeting. A well-built, stocky South African, he was a soldier's soldier, with no bullshit. We weren't bosom buddies, but I found him easy to work with.

Then the rumour mill said 3 Troop was getting a new leader. No sooner had Lt Long arrived than we were both sent as instructors to a leadership course in Fremington, Devon. It involved what was laughingly called 'adventure training'. One of the adventures turned out to be running through ankle-deep mud flats. I thought our new lieutenant looked a bit on the podgy side and that I'd therefore beat him easily on the run. I was wrong: Tom Long was super-fit. I found myself struggling home behind him. I soon found out why – Long played rugby at club level, and he was a qualified physical fitness instructor.

Most officers listen to what their senior NCOs have to say, offer their own view and then reach a decision based on both viewpoints. Tom Long listens to what you have to say and then does exactly what he wants. It's one kind of leadership. At first, it grated. But as we spent time together running the troop, my view changed. On the night before we were due to fly out, I decided, 'This guy knows what he's talking about. I'd gladly follow him into battle.'

Always the acid test.

A couple of weeks later, we found ourselves at Camp Bastion. At the time it was a desert airfield surrounded by a base about the size of the Trowbridge Green council estate I'd grown up in. We moved into a long tent with eight ten-man rooms branching off on either side of a central corridor. Our first stop after settling in was the Operational Mentoring and Liaison Team (OMLT), a ten-minute ride away at Camp Tombstone. Here, International Security Assistance force (ISAF) personnel with first-hand experience of combat in Afghanistan train both the British military and members of the Afghan National Army.

16 Air Assault Brigade is a lean, mean fighting machine– a little too

lean, when you think that Helmand province is about the size of Switzerland and easily as mountainous. It has become the battleground of choice for Islamic extremist guerrillas of all kinds: Brits, Saudis, Kuwaitis, Yemenis, Chechnyans, Pakistanis and your bog-standard home-grown Afghan variety. Wherever they come from, they fight under the white banner of the Taliban. Some are hardcore veteran fighters, with the tattoo of a Hind-D helicopter gunship on the thumb joint of the right hand to prove it. The symbol shows they fought – and defeated – the Russians. But most are foot soldiers who fight by the day, for a fistful of dollars and a handful of rice. And at Musa Qal'ah, they were fighting like demons.

CHAPTER TWENTY-SEVEN

Northern Helmand Province, Afghanistan
1 August 2006

The Scimitar jolted to a halt less than 2 metres from the cliff edge –
and from my head. Realizing the light from the Cyalume glow-stick
on my helmet had disappeared, Leechy-not-from-Manchester had
made the right call and slammed on the brakes. With all of a second
to spare.

I hauled myself back up onto solid ground, picked up a stone,
walked cautiously up to the cliff and chucked it over the edge. Many
seconds later, when I'd given up expecting to hear anything, there was
a faint clatter from far below. That was some drop.

I went round to the driver's side. 'Wait there,' I told Leechy, 'and
whatever you do, don't move the wagon an inch forward!' I walked
back to the second vehicle in the column. Our troop leader, Lt Long,
leaned out of his hatch. 'There's a fucking great cliff just up ahead,
Boss,' I told him. 'I know because I just fell over it. Might be a good
idea if we go firm until daylight or the moon comes up?'

'That sounds like a plan,' said Long. 'Are you OK?'

My back was still hurting, but hey, I could have been strawberry
jam. 'Bit jarred, that's all. Luckily, I hit a ledge on the way down.'

It was all really strange. One minute earlier, I'd nearly killed myself,
and the entire column had come close to rolling over the edge after

me in a big lemming nosedive. I warned everyone else of the danger, then we went into all-round defence, brewed up some tea, ate, crawled into our sleeping bags and tried to snatch a few hours shut-eye. I can't speak for anyone else, but by now it was two o'clock in the morning: for my tired eyes, snooze time was long overdue. We'd been ahead of time but the darkness and danger had now made us late. The resupply op was due in at Musa Qal'ah in a little less than five hours. It couldn't wait. But it might have to.

The rest of the night passed without incident, except for when a dozen or so wild Afghan dogs turned up looking to filch food. There are wild dogs all over Afghanistan. They're lean, and mean. They travel in packs, they're smart, they co-operate well and if they thought they could get away with it they'd catch and eat a human being. Maybe they do. But that wasn't why they worried me. At night, before they go to lay IEDs or mines, the Taliban will often send a couple of semi-trained mutts in to see if we've set up a reactive OP. Nine times out of ten, the dogs catch our scent on the air and their barking warns the insurgents to stay clear.

When the light began to break we broke camp and moved on. Glancing over the cliff edge, I could see it was a good job we'd stopped – the valley I'd partially fallen into looked scarily deep. The feature was massive, but it wasn't even marked on our maps. Following north along the line of the valley, we began to pick up the telltale signs of prior Russian activity: traces of legacy minefields, old trenches, deep ancient tank tracks and the odd piece of rusting ordnance. Corporal of Horse JC Moses took up the lead in his Spartan. He might have been a good sniper, but when it came to information technology JC was a total nightmare. He was hideous with the latest version of the Bowman HF radio. And you had to make sure he didn't get anywhere near your personal electronic gear. One time when I was out on an op, he accidentally erased all 2,000 songs on my laptop.

Still tracking along the western side of the valley that lay between us and Musa Qal'ah, we were rolling across an undulating area of bare stone shale, rough sand and broken rock with no vegetation or cover for as far as the eye could see. About twenty minutes later, JC reported that he'd found what we were looking for: a good position that gave eyes onto a possible route through the Green Zone immediately to the west of Musa Qal'ah. JC told his driver, Trooper 'Glassy' Glasgow, to reverse the wagon back off the ridge, turn it round and head back to join the rest of the column. Glassy rolled the vehicle back about 10 metres.

A massive explosion blew the Spartan clean off the ground, flipping the 8-tonne lump of metal round through 180 degrees. Bits of it flew high into the air, hung as if suspended for a moment and then thumped back to earth all around us. The front decks blew clean off the vehicle, exposing its innards to view. Seeing that, I was certain Glassy Glasgow must have been killed in the blast.

For several seconds there was no sign of movement. Then JC stuck his head up out of the commander's hatch, grinned like a mad imp and gave me the thumbs-up. Glassy, who was from the Caribbean, beamed even wider. I was amazed they were alive, never mind smiling. A towering blue-brown haze of smoke and dust hung in the air, while the echo of the explosion rolled out across the surrounding hills. Nothing like keeping a low profile. Keying the radio I called, 'Contact, contact: mine strike. Wait out.'

Like the Scimitar's, the Spartan's hull is purpose-designed to deflect mine blasts outwards. It had worked: the mine might have blown the vehicle's tracks off and reduced it to scrap, but it hadn't damaged the most important thing – the people inside. In any mine strike, the key thing is to get the crew out before the vehicle catches fire or suffers a secondary explosion. That has to happen fast: the chances of the fuel or ammo stocks igniting are very strong. Quick as they could, JC and his crew: Glassy, his radio operator Lance Corporal 'Nails' Oakes and Captain Eida, who'd been hitching a ride with them, scrambled out onto the hull. They were shaken and a bit bruised, but otherwise unharmed.

I dismounted and grabbed the yellow box with the mine kit. Inside was some thick, nine-gauge wire. Other guys were there alongside me in the dirt. We got down on our hands and knees and began probing the ground up to the damaged vehicle. The approved method is: spread one hand flat on the ground in front of you, prod gently between your fingers with the wire and try not to detonate anything. Keep going slowly like that. If you find a mine, take out the paintbrush everyone carries in their back pocket and brush away the dirt until the body of the mine is uncovered: a kind of high-explosive archaeology. You then move around the device you've uncovered and probe on. As you clear a safe lane, you mark it with orange flags.

There's nothing like pressure. As we worked, we were all thinking the same thing. We were in the wrong place, at the wrong time. We should be fighting in Musa Qal'ah, not squirming through the dirt here. I kept thinking: 'We've got to get a move on. The enemy will have seen that explosion. They'll know we're coming and they'll be queuing up to attack us.'

Once we'd helped clear a lane to the Spartan, its crew could get out to safety. By the time I reached it, I'd found and marked two large Soviet-era anti-tank mines. The other lads had found several more.

In the 1979–1989 occupation, the Russian Army went mine-mad. They laid thousands of anti-tank mines, anti-personnel mines, mines that jumped up in the air and cut you in half, tiny plastic mines that could slice your foot off, you name it. Quite often, the Russians sowed them from the back of a helicopter, chucking them out all over the place. Twenty-odd years later, most of the Russian mines in Helmand were still in perfect working order. And as we'd just discovered, they could all kill and maim.

I still couldn't get over the fact that none of the Spartan's crew was hurt. Glassy was still wearing his usual big smile. But a glance said the damaged vehicle was a write-off: sections of bar armour lay all around, the rear doors were hanging off and random chunks of scrap lay strewn across the landscape. Instant junkyard. The Spartan might be wrecked, but it wasn't wrecked enough that we could just leave it there. Like all the vehicles in the column, it was packed with secret equipment. As always, we had to deny the vehicle to stop it falling into enemy hands.

I checked the GPS: we were the best part of 90 kilometres from Camp Bastion. The Spartan's shattered state meant there was no chance of slinging it under a Chinook and airlifting it out, and the minefield meant there was no way a wheeled recovery team could get in safely. I had a word with Lt Long. We agreed there was only one thing for it: we needed to blow the vehicle up.

Working quickly, we stripped the Spartan of anything valuable or secret. Its one careful previous owner, JC, then produced a phosphorous grenade. He chucked the grenade in the back and made a run for it out through the safe lane. The ammo in the wagon ought to blow up and finish it.

A thick cloud of smoke began to billow out of the Spartan's rear end. But there was no explosion and no flames. In a while, it even began to look as if the smoke was dying down. I got back into my Scimitar and selected 'fire' on the Rarden cannon. Taking careful aim, Paul Minter fired six rounds of automatic in through the Spartan's back door. This made six very loud bangs, but as far as I could tell did no serious damage. The wreckage still wasn't burning, and it still hadn't blown up. It was still staring back at us. The bugger.

Major Dick came up on the radio net: 'Don't fire any more rounds at the Spartan. I'll call in an air strike to deny it.' We stood and watched the wreckage as it cooked gently in the blinding light, adding an extra wedge of heat to the blistering day. I was looking forward to the air show – and the death of a Spartan, but any more delay and we weren't going to make it to the RV in time.

There was a low rumble from the north, followed by the roar of approaching jets. Two USAF F-16 fighter-bombers screamed into view, pulled a long, looping turn in the searing blue and rolled out, wings level. The lead aircraft was going to fire an AGM-65 Maverick anti-tank missile at the Spartan, while his wingman gave cover in case of attack from the non-existent Taliban air force.

The F-16 lined up on the Spartan and dropped its nose into a shallow dive. There was a puff of smoke from under the left wing and a tiny point of flame. The Maverick streaked towards the ground, a faint trail of propellant marking its path through the brilliant sky. We waited for the impact on the smoking hulk. Instead, the missile slammed into the ground about 80 metres to the west. There was a massive blast as the 57kg warhead exploded. Lots of bits of stone and desert flew up into the air.

My brain tried to catch up. The Spartan had struck a mine; then we'd tried to burn it; then we'd shelled it; and now, a state-of-the-art, super-accurate TV-guided missile had missed the sitting duck into the bargain. In broad daylight. Not only that, the F-16s had been returning to Kandahar air base after being on task somewhere else. They had no more missiles left to fire. And no bombs.

That bloody wagon. If we'd entered it for a battlefield survival competition, it would have won by a country mile. The Spartan had to die. But until that happened, somebody had to stay with it. Maddening. We reported the miss to SHQ. Major Dick said he'd get back on the blower to Air Tasking. The minutes ticked by. We definitely weren't going to make Musa Qal'ah by first light: it was already getting on for seven o'clock. But we couldn't all stand around for the rest of the day watching futile attempts to kill the Spartan. As it was, any watching Taliban scouts would be thinking, 'The British are blowing themselves up – let's take the day off.' The serious point was that we kept losing men and machines.

With their own vehicle blown up from under them, JC, Glassy and Nails had to stay behind with Major Alex Dick and the damaged wagon at what now became SHQ's troop position. Captain Eida, who was still badly needed to direct the 105mm guns at Musa Qal'ah, transferred onto Lt Johnson's Spartan. Under Lt Long's command, six Scimitars and the remaining Spartan formed up into a new column and got going.

A few minutes later, we reached a position 800 metres south of where JC's wagon had gone up. We pulled up just below the ridge line. I grabbed the binoculars, jumped out and walked to the crest. We were looking right over the Musa Qal'ah Green Zone.

The valley that lay before us was about 2 kilometres wide. We were now officially late, but we still needed to spend some minutes monitoring the area for any sign of enemy activity. A clipped voice came to life in my ears–Major Dick, relaying the same message Brigade had been sending for the past many hours: 'Proceed to Musa Qal'ah with all speed.'

I scanned the valley bottom through the binos. The Green Zone was thick with plantations, reed beds, drainage ditches, paddocks, walls, shrubbery and all kinds of other things that provide an enemy with perfect cover. The local fields of opium poppies had been cut to make room for new crops of maize and marijuana, whose tall stems and thick ranks made more perfect places to hide.

A village lay directly in our path, the usual run of ramshackle, interlocking compounds. Three dirt tracks bisected the settlement east – west and then led on over the opposite slope to the District Centre. Separated by blocks of vegetation and compounds, the three lanes ran roughly parallel to one another. From our present vantage point they looked like straight, pale scars cut through the huddle of buildings. There were no other crossing points for miles. We had to choose one of the tracks.

Fast.

I inspected the middle lane through the commander's sight. It was very narrow – not much wider than a Scimitar. High compound walls formed its northern side; to the south, a low stone and earth embankment supported a scraggy terrace of olive trees. At the foot of that embankment was a 1-metre-deep ditch. At 10x magnification

I could see the slim, spear-shaped leaves of the olive trees fluttering pale green and silver in the breeze. Studying the other two options, I saw they presented the same problem: whichever lane we chose, we were headed into a funnel. And a potential killing ground. We needed to get down there and take a closer look.

I had a quick conflab with the command group. Captain Eida said, 'Middle, right or left lane?'

Good question.

We decided to leave two Scimitars on the ridge as a fire support group (FSG) in case the rest of us got ambushed. We also dismounted and set up one of the 51mm mortars. Steve McWhirter, who could call in air power if needs be, was the obvious choice to take command of the FSG. Jock Ando, a rugged, ex-Black Watch infanteer, and a few of the other lads would stay with him. We mounted up again. If the crossing turned out to be as dangerous as it looked, it was better if I led from the front. And I always get a buzz out of going first.

I took the column down the barren slope. We tucked into the side of a small hill facing the village. I inspected the three lanes again. Nothing moved. Whenever you're in bandit country it's a good idea to keep thinking, 'If I were the bad guys, where would I set the ambush or lay the IED?'

The sharp roar of an engine carried suddenly on the still air. I saw a blue-grey haze of diesel exhaust: a bust-up old grey tractor was coming out of the middle lane. It rumbled towards us towing a trailer-load of straw. A local man was sitting on top of it – both he and the driver looked like your average farmer. For all I knew they might be Taliban dropping off arms and explosives, but from this distance they appeared harmless enough. The tractor hooked south and vanished in among the maze of compounds.

I stared in surprise. At first, I hadn't been able to see the tractor. That meant the wall on the north side of the middle lane was much higher than I'd thought – at least 3 metres, perhaps more. Made of mud reinforced with straw and then left to bake hard in the sun, these walls were strong enough to stop our standard high-explosive 30mm cannon shells. The only thing we'd found that punched through them was APDS. I wished I still had the Scorpion I'd had in the Falklands War: its big, fat 76mm gun would reduce the compound perimeters to instant rubble.

I watched again for signs of Taliban activity. I couldn't be certain there was none. There was plenty of cover in the deep shadow under the olive trees and in the scraggy shrubbery behind the walls.

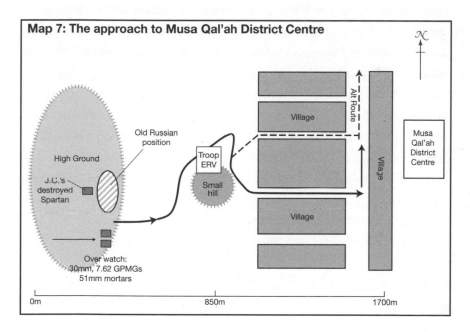

Map 7: The approach to Musa Qal'ah District Centre

Since the tractor had done its disappearing act, a deathlike stillness had fallen on the whole area. The village looked deserted and there was no movement in the olive groves beyond. There wasn't even a squeak of birdsong. The silence was setting off all my alarm bells. In a war zone, a close, brooding silence like the one we had now is a strong combat indicator. It means the locals have cleared out. Often as not, the Taliban warn them there's an ambush in the offing.

All my instincts and training told me we were taking an almighty risk. But I kept coming back to the same overriding fact: if we made it through the Green Zone, we were only twenty minutes driving time from the beleaguered garrison at Musa Qal'ah. The next available route was more than two hours' drive away, and wasn't guaranteed to be any safer. The radio crackled to life in my headset for the umpteenth time: 'Make all speed for Musa Qal'ah. Push on, push on!'

That settled it.

I gave the order to move out. Lt Ralph Johnson followed immediately behind me in the Spartan. Lt Tom Long came next with Lance corporal of Horse Lee Preston and Corporal of Horse Dave Simpson's Scimitar brought up the rear. We were well spread out, with a gap of about 50 metres between each vehicle. As soon as we started moving towards the lane I got my gunner, Paul Minter, to hit the switch that triggered the Scimitar's onboard ECM (electronic countermeasures) device. The device emits an electronic shield that jams ambient electrical signals. This makes it harder for the enemy to detonate IEDs remotely. The downside is that our own radios tend to work less well.

There was no point in delaying any longer. 'OK Leechy,' I said. 'Take us up to the entrance.'

At the mouth of the lane, I told Leechy to stop again.

CHAPTER TWENTY-EIGHT

Now we were about to enter it, I liked the look of the cutting we had chosen even less. It was decades too quiet. A tiny dust devil whipped up by a sudden gust of wind danced in front of the Scimitar for a moment, as if daring us to come on. All the hackles on the back of my neck started to rise. What I should have done was order Minty to hose down the lane, the wall and the olive groves with the co-axial machine gun to set off any mines or IEDs that had been planted and help flush out any hidden enemy. But that was a lesson I still had to learn. We moved into the lane in what we call Red Snake formation, where the vehicles in the column move forward at different times.

About 20 metres into the lane, we came on a narrow alleyway leading left and at right angles north into the village. I looked down it. The alley was about 10 metres long and ended in a high wall with two low wooden doors set in it. Both were shut fast. Staring at the doors, I started to get a bad feeling. 'Forward,' I told Leechy, 'but take it steady.'

A blinding light filled the inside of the turret like a hundred thousand flash bulbs popping at the same time. There was the sound of a massive explosion. A blast wave smashed into us, rocking the Scimitar.

I didn't know exactly what had happened, but I did know it was nothing good. A storm of small-arms fire rattled over the hull like metal raindrops. Before I could react, an RPG-7 rocket slammed into the cage armour. The Scimitar rang as if it had been struck by a wrecking ball. For a split-second, I blacked out. I opened my eyes again. The turret was filled with a blinding fog of dust and debris. I felt my legs to see if they were still attached. They were. And I had no pain. Instinctively I knew the rocket had hit us on the left side. But we'd been lucky: the warhead hadn't penetrated. If it had, then we'd all have been dead.

In that same moment a DShKa '*dushka*' heavy machine gun opened up from the far end of the lane. Fat 12.7mm slugs smacked into the turret and front armour. I heard one of the headlights smash. There was no way the thin ballistic layer fitted for Afghanistan could withstand a .50 calibre machine gun from close range. The *dushka* was ripping us to bits. For a split-second I sat numb. Then the training cut in. I smacked a palm down hard on the CPU: 'Contact, ambush, wait out!'

There was a slight dogleg in the lane ahead. Beyond and across the corner of that I could make out a ripple of orange muzzle flashes. The *dushka* was about 100 metres ahead and to the left, concealed in a dense stand of shrubbery. A second RPG crunched into our front end. The Scimitar reared back under the impact and then rocked forwards, shaking like a dog leaving water. I glanced right: Minty had a fixed, frozen look on his face but he was still breathing. What about the man in the driver's seat? 'Leechy!' I called over the i/c, 'are you OK?' The high-pitched gabble that came back told me Leechy's head was still more or less attached to his shoulders.

The enemy gun system was still pouring fire at us, knocking great chunks of metal out of the hull. I tried to fire the main armament. Nothing happened. I grabbed the trigger of the Gimpy and fired that instead. Following the tracer, I saw the rounds were missing the target by some distance. 'Machine gun and infantry. To the left of the bushes at the end of the lane!' I told Minter: 'Traverse left!' There was a growling, grinding sound but nothing moved. 'Traverse fucking left!'

'It won't fucking traverse!' Minty shouted back. The incoming fire had buckled the cage armour, jamming the turret race fast to the hull. Fuck. I was frantically pulling and pushing at the machine gun in its cradle, trying to free the weapon up enough to bring it to bear. The machine gun budged a fraction, but not enough. More *dushka* rounds smacked into the front end, the bullet strikes like blows from a club hammer. The noise rang inside my head. Then Leechy yelled, 'I can't see, I can't see!' Just what we didn't need – a blind driver. He shouted, 'I've lost my driver's sights!' That was better news: the *dushka* had smashed Leechy's sighting system, not his eyeballs.

My own eyes were everywhere, snatching looks out of all of the armoured glass episcope bricks set into the turret, trying to stay ahead of the threat. A row of black-turbaned heads popped up over the top of the wall to our left, pointed AK47 assault rifles and let rip. More bullets pinged and whanged off the Scimitar's skin. We'd get round to the wall mob, but first we had to deal with the greater threat. We might not be able to make the turret traverse, but Leech could still pull left and right sticks to make the Scimitar turn on its tracks: if need be it can turn on a sixpence.

'We'll take on the gun system!' I told him. 'Pull a bit of left stick.' Leechy pulled back on the left steering stick between his knees. The Scimitar swung round, wildly overshooting the *dushka*. 'Too much!' I told him, 'pull a bit of right stick!' Leechy eased back on the right stick: the Scimitar's battered nose swivelled, this time the exact amount. 'On!' I shouted. He stopped pulling on the stick. The sight was smack on the hammering DShKa. 'Fire!' I said. Nothing happened.

A hail of RPGs, .50 cal and AK47 coming straight at you does tend to give you pause when you're in it for the first time. The vast majority of people freeze stiff. Rabbit in the headlights syndrome. Perfectly natural. But not all that helpful when you're under enemy fire. I tried again: 'Fire!' If Minty didn't open fire with the 30mm in the next nano-second, I was going to reach over there, grab him by the throat and fucking make him fire. Trying to throttle someone Minter's size really wouldn't have been that great an idea. Especially under the circumstances. But the adrenalin was pumping, I was ready to tear limb from limb. I reached across and grabbed him by the left shoulder. 'Minter. Fire!'

His head came round. 'The fucking gun's broken. It won't fire!' I could see him squeezing the firing switch, but nothing was happening. I'd misjudged Minty – he wasn't scared, he just couldn't get the Rarden to fire. I pushed the mechanical trigger on the back of the breech. The cannon roared into life: 30mm shells smashed into the *dushka*, tearing it and its crew to shreds. I saw a body fall back. The enemy gun system stopped firing. We switched to machine gun. I grabbed the mechanical firing switch and opened up on the area around the smashed *dushka* until there was no more movement. I went to reload the Rarden. No go: the cannon had jammed; it, too, was now out of action. The hits from the *dushka* or one of the RPG rounds had disabled it.

I heard a loud whooshing sound from close by and ducked instinctively. A third RPG skimmed over the top of us. At close range, that's all you tend to hear. If the warhead hits you, your hearing days are generally over. 'Push on! Push on!' I told Leechy.

'I still can't see anything,' he shouted back.

'I'll steer you,' I said, 'I'll tell you what sticks to pull.'

As we neared the wreckage of the *dushka*, the incoming small-arms fire grew heavier still. I fired the bank of six smoke grenades positioned either side of the turret to give us cover. There was a series of loud popping sounds. The grenades flew up out of the launchers and exploded in twin arcs, six to each side; dense clouds of white phosphorus smoke and bits of burning rubber billowed out around us. The smoke bought us six seconds of perfect calm, while the Taliban worked out what we'd fired at them, how much it would hurt them and tried to see us through the curling smoke.

We rolled through the middle of the ambush. As the smokescreen cleared, a fourth RPG hit the rear caging. 'Fuck!' I thought, 'there are only so many strikes this wagon's going to take and then a rocket's going to slice through and fry us.' Every time a rocket hit the vehicle, the dust and debris it dislodged blinded me and Minty for about five seconds. With those massive, earth-shaking shocks, the overwhelming noise and the fog of dust made it difficult to tell what was real and what wasn't. I kept touching my leg to make sure I was still alive.

I poked my head up a short distance out of the commander's hatch and snatched a squint: all the front cage armour was twisted up and mangled to buggery. No wonder we couldn't make the turret traverse. But at least the last rocket had struck a bit of the rear cage armour that was still intact.

I glanced left. The wall at this point dropped away to a height of about 2 metres. Cut with rough notches, it made an irregular parapet. Then I noticed something else: a series of holes had appeared in the mud-brick below. About half a metre wide, they looked like giant mouse holes. Mouse holes? The brain throws up weird stuff when you're under extreme pressure. In a flash, I realized the Taliban had pre-cut them. They were shoving mud circles out of the wall to create superb firing ports. We'd passed three of the mouse holes and taken two RPG strikes with one near-miss. That figured. We were now moving slowly along a section of wall that lay between holes. 'Stop!' I said before we drew level with another mouse hole. We stopped.

My brain was racing but nothing useful was coming out of it. I kept thinking, 'What do we do?' You can turn into an ambush left or right, or you can push on. The chances are you'll get shot anyway. The Taliban were pouring fire in at us from the left and in front. We were cornered like a rat in a barn.

Anger flowed into me then, a cold feeling of fury and intense focus. I had the lives of all these young guys in my hands – most of them were about the same age as my sons. I'd led them into this, it was my job to lead them out. The Taliban were trying to kill us, but that wasn't going to be where the story ended. We needed to hit back, with interest.

Random thoughts fizzed through my mind at lightning speed. One stuck: I needed to stay alive to give my daughter Gabrielle away when she got married. Musa Qal'ah and its DC could wait. She might still only be twelve, but my new mission was to be there when Gabrielle walked down the aisle with her chosen man. I had to save my crew and myself; get everyone back home in one piece.

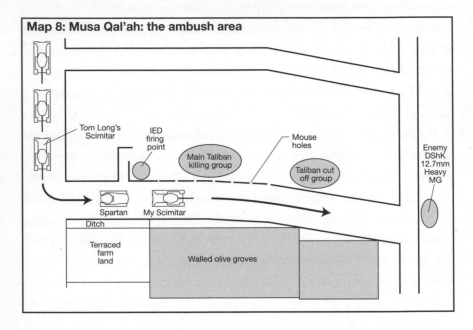

Map 8: Musa Qal'ah: the ambush area

Tom Long's Scimitar

IED firing point

Main Taliban killing group

Mouse holes

Taliban cut off group

Enemy DShK 12.7mm Heavy MG

Spartan   My Scimitar

Ditch

Terraced farm land

Walled olive groves

The Taliban were not superhuman. Like us, they were thinking soldiers. Some of them – by no means all – were more willing to go to their God than we were. But the fact that I'd made them look good made me furious. I'd fallen for the old mouse-hole trick, the same gag they'd probably played on the Russians twenty years back in this very same lane.

'Fuck it,' I said. 'We'll fight our way out of this.' I gave Leechy the heads up: 'Foot down, Leech. We're going for it. I'll guide you.' Leech put his foot to the pedal. The Cummins 5.9 litre diesel engine roared into life. We lurched towards the shot-up *dushka*. With the driver's sights smashed, I had to watch the ground ahead of us and guide Leech by voice over the i/c. The Taliban were still trying to hurt us. With any luck, we were going to hurt them.

I realized it might be a good idea to send a SITREP to let everyone know what was happening. The FSG up on the bluff might be able to put some rounds down on the enemy. Or call in some air power. I pushed the CPU. The pressel switch was already in the 'send' position. It had been stuck on send the whole time. The rest of the troop had heard every word I'd said – swearing included – and they'd relayed it back to SHQ. That very same headquarters element that was still many clicks away, trundling towards us.

'SITREP,' I said into the mike, 'am in ambush at ...' I glanced at the TNTLS – our onboard satnav/GPS system – and read out the co-ordinates: 'Am at grid 678951; taking RPG fire, heavy machine-gun fire and small-arms fire; vehicle damaged; engaging enemy.' The pressel switch was still stuck on send, still blocking everyone else's comms. Fuck. I smacked it a couple of times with the heel of my hand. It stayed stuck. Prior to the op, I'd told the radio operator in SHQ the fucking thing was fucked and they hadn't even looked at it. Reaching down, I grabbed the lower connector cable and ripped it out. But with our silence, SHQ and the rest of the troop would now think we were dead.

Tough.

Just then, the jammed pressel switch popped free again. I reconnected the cable.

The adrenalin was still pumping through me. I'd forgotten about the risk of death and injury. I had a combat high. I wanted to survive and wanted all my men to survive, and the best way to do that was to fight back. As always, I was buoyed up by the belief that we were better than the enemy: better trained, better soldiers and better looking.

It was boiling hot in the turret. The air was rank and choking, thick with cordite fumes and dust. The noise from both inside and outside was deafening. None of that mattered in the slightest. All that mattered was that we give the enemy a good kicking, bear down and win the fight. I was thinking, 'What can we do to hurt the Taliban without a working turret?' We still had our rifles. I reached down and grabbed my SA-80, stuck it over the edge of the commander's hatch and fired short bursts at the Taliban on automatic. Spray and pray. Minty saw what I was doing and followed suit. Good lad.

Anyone who has actually been in action will tell you that war movies where people stand up in full view of the enemy and blaze away are extreme fiction. If you do that, then you're going to get shot – period. Your instinct is to stay alive, which means using every scrap of available cover and exposing as little of your body as possible. The SA-80 fires about twelve rounds a second: I got through two magazines of twenty-five rounds in less than a minute, firing to the dry click and then whipping the weapon back down to reload. The SA-80's working parts stay back when it runs out of ammo. Whack on a new mag, release the working parts and you're back in business. The bullet spray had little effect, except in sending red-hot cartridge cases tumbling down and burning my neck and chest. The AK47 fire from behind and to the left was as ferocious as ever.

A T-junction came into view at the end of the lane. We reached it. 'Stop!' I told Leechy. We ground to a halt. The DShKa machine gun was smashed up opposite. It had been expertly camouflaged and brilliantly positioned: although I'd had a very careful look down the lane before we'd entered it, there was no way I could have detected the gun system. I could see one dead body in among the wreckage, a second possible.

An area of dense shrubs and trees lay opposite the intersection to either side. I had to decide: do we turn left onto the new track, turn right or go back? What would they expect me to do? 'They'll expect me to turn right or left,' I reasoned. 'They'll have secondary ambushes put in on those routes: IEDs, mines, RPG-squads, you name it. What don't they expect me to do? They don't expect me to turn around and drive back through the ambush into all of that firepower.' And I needed to find out what had happened to the rest of the troop. 'Right,' I told the lads, 'we're going back down the lane.' I'm not sure they were too overjoyed to hear this.

'Right stick,' I told Leechy-not-from-Manchester. The Scimitar began to whizz round. 'Steady!' I told him. He slowed the rate of turn.

'On!' I said. We stopped. We were now facing directly back down the lane. 'Perfect,' I said, 'let's go.'

'We can't do that,' he said, 'we're going to get killed.' Leech was streetwise and he was right: going back down the lane did entail a certain degree of risk. But no more than turning left or right onto the new track.

'Fuck it,' Minter said at exactly the right moment. 'Let's get down there.'

Check your magazines,' I said, 'the turret's still stuck.' We clipped full magazines on the rifles.

I looked down the lane. A part of me wished I hadn't. We'd just travelled 120 metres of hell. But judging by what I could now see, for some in the convoy it had been far worse. A massive plume of smoke was billowing skyward on the far side of the dogleg. The fumes were dark-grey and black – the kind you got when an armoured vehicle is on fire. I caught the acrid smell of burning diesel, and something else underneath that I couldn't identify. We were on our own at the far end of the lane. I couldn't see the Spartan that had been directly behind us with Lieutenant Johnson and Captain Eida. Why not? All I could see was that huge tower of smoke. Was that burning mass what was left of the Spartan? I took stock. The first explosion had initiated the attack. Then they'd put in the main ambush: the pop-out RPGs from the holes in the wall and the AK47 fire. The *dushka* had been there as the cut-off. Textbook stuff – but at least now we'd killed the cut-off.

In the few seconds I'd taken to catch up, the firing had died away. Now it came back with renewed force. The smoke grenades had worked for us once. Why not use them again? But we only had two grenades left for the launchers – the MoD had failed to supply enough. I stuck my head and shoulders out of the hatch and dropped a grenade into one of the left-hand launcher tubes. Minty loaded the second grenade on the right. Back in the turret, I took another look up the lane. Taliban heads appeared and disappeared along the wall to our right. The enemy were staying up and firing for slightly longer now: it was obvious they thought we were done for, they only had to finish us off. I had news for them – we weren't finished. But I wished to fuck I'd put both of the remaining smoke grenades in the right-hand launcher.

Leechy put his foot down and the Scimitar bucked forward. The second they realized we were coming back at them, the Taliban went berserk. All the fighters on the wall switched their fire onto us. A fresh hail of AK47 bullets scythed and rattled over the hull. Sticking the rifle up out of the hatch, I fired a couple of bursts back. I heard the back-blast of another incoming RPG. The rocket hammered into the wagon's right side, rattling my teeth and raising a new dust storm. We must have come level with another mouse hole. When the fog cleared I stuck my head out again and glanced down. All the shopping-trolley cage armour was wrecked and entangled in the vehicle's right-hand track. But the Scimitar refused to die. There was a lot of grinding and screeching but we were still mobile, still forging on.

As we rounded the dogleg the Spartan came into view. Slewed diagonally across the lane, it was on fire from end to end. Oily, lead-coloured smoke was pouring out of it. A long red tongue of flame suddenly licked from the heart of the towering plume. There was a large gaping hole in the Spartan's front armour: the kind you get when an RPG rocket punches through it from close range. It looked like an ugly black mouth. The rear end was devastated. The doors had been blown off, the whole back end was open to the skies. I was staring at a blazing, smoking shell.

The Spartan had been fully loaded with men and ammunition. There were live rounds exploding inside it, 7.62mm banging and flying out in every direction. The damage was so catastrophic and the timing of the explosion so precise there was only one explanation: it had been hit by a remote-controlled IED. It looked as if the Taliban had waited for my vehicle to roll over the concealed bomb and then triggered it under the Spartan. They knew the Spartans tended to carry officers and ammo. That made them a higher-value target. That doctrine has now been changed.

As we drew near the blazing hulk I saw something like an arm on the ground. A short way beyond it lay what was left of a human body. It was impossible to recognize who it was. One of the men who had been in the Spartan, blown clear and blown to pieces. Leaving three others still unaccounted for.

CHAPTER TWENTY-NINE

We were caught in a death trap. With the blazing, exploding Spartan blocking our exit. Volleys of AK47 fire were still pouring in from the compound to our right. Minty had his weapon up out of his hatch, firing back at the Taliban up on the wall. Marvellous. I was assessing what to do next. Leechy had sneaked a chancy look over his hatch rim. From the strange, random noises I could hear in my headset, I could tell he was worried that we wouldn't get out of there in one piece. Not unusual in your first firefight – especially when you're only eighteen. 'Stop babbling!' I told him. 'We're going to get through this. Pull a bit of left stick and push on! Speed up!'

Leechy could see a bit better now, peering out through a handy gash that a *dushka* round had ripped in the metal next to his smashed sight. I'd just told him to step on it, but instead he now drove us very, very slowly towards the burning Spartan. 'Speed up, Leechy!' I urged him, 'fast as you can!' It was too late: as we reached the blazing hulk he pulled too much left stick and drove us straight into the ditch. We buried in. The Scimitar stuck fast, leaning over to the left at an angle of about 20 degrees.

'I told you to fucking step on it!' I yelled. If he'd gone for it, then one of two things would have happened: we'd either have hit the ditch too fast and overturned, or the vehicle's forward momentum would have carried us through. With my usual optimism, I'd been banking on the second outcome. As it was, we had a Spartan on fire to our immediate right popping live rounds, dozens of Taliban whacking fire in on us from the same direction and we were stuck in a ditch.

That wasn't the worst of it: the Spartan's ammunition stocks were still cooking off. The wreckage was a ticking bomb. The vehicle had been carrying mortar shells and LAW anti-tank missiles, phosphorus smoke grenades, boxes of extra 7.62mm and 30mm, hand grenades, you name it. If all of that ordnance went up in one go, it would take the three of us and our wagon with it. We had to get out.

'Debus,' I said. 'Get out or we're going to get killed.'

Leech had calmed down a bit by now, his thinking functions had kicked in. 'But Corporal of Horse!' his voice sounded oddly high. 'You said if we ever had to get out of the wagon we were in the shit!'

'We *are* in the shit, Leech.' Top of the British Army's official understatement list. I glanced over to see what Minter was doing. I was about to tell him to get out, but he was already lying in the ditch to our left, firing back at the Taliban for all he was worth. Fucking good again. 'Right,' I told Leech, 'when I start firing at them, you get out and get in the ditch with Minty. Got that?'

'Yes!'

I stuck my head up just proud of the hatch. I could see the Taliban flitting around along the wall, shadowy as ever, as always hard to spot and kill. The ones I could aim at got a double top, fuck them. They were probably high as kites and one bullet wouldn't cut it. Through one of the left episcopes I saw Leechy hit the ditch: he'd made it out alive to cover. Good going. I said the mind plays tricks when it's under intense pressure: my own played another on me now. I kept thinking 'We've abandoned the wagon, so we have to destroy it.' I snatched up the radio and pressed the CPU: 'Zero, this is Whisky Three One: permission to deny the vehicle.' There was no reply. The ECM device was jamming our own radio signals along with the enemy's. For once, that was probably a good thing.

I fired at the insurgents on the wall, jumped out and took cover in the ditch. The blaze next to us was now so fierce that a section of the

Spartan's aluminium hull had caught fire. The metal was beginning to melt, dripping down in soft folds like wax from a burning candle. Even from where I was crouched I could feel the heat; it was like kneeling at the mouth of a furnace. The priority now was to account for the other three men I knew had been on that vehicle. No matter how great the fuck-fest, you have to make sure you've rescued everybody on your own side. Especially if they're still alive.

By my reckoning, I'd only seen the remains of one body. Where were the others? What if they were still in the back of the Spartan? I glanced along the ditch. Minter and Leech were lying prone, firing when they saw a target. 'Cover me!' I yelled. They started laying rounds on the Taliban. Crouching lower and moving faster than I'd ever managed in training, I ran up to the Spartan and looked in the back.

It was like staring through the gates of hell. The Spartan and everything in it was mangled and burned beyond recognition. Machine-gun rounds were still crackling and pinging off, ricocheting around the blazing interior. There was a body in there but it was on fire, a charred, smouldering mass. There was absolutely no chance the person who'd once been inside that roasting shell was still alive. I could see that carcass and what looked like bits of a body next to the Spartan's right-hand track. They included an arm or a leg. I couldn't be sure if these were the remains of one or two people. But if they were all from the same person, then there were still two men missing.

I was trying to work out whether any of the stuff I could see sticking to the inside of the Spartan was human. But we were still in a firefight: AK47 rounds spat the dust up in neat lines beside my feet, just like they do in the movies; bullets whizzed past my ears and head, slugs smashed into the Spartan and my beached Scimitar. The Taliban were still trying very, very hard to kill us.

I got back down in the ditch, rammed on a new magazine and took aim at a black-turbaned head that suddenly popped up into view opposite. The fucker was only about 10 metres away, I could hardly miss him. I squeezed off two shots. The head and the body attached to it flew backwards. I moved on to the next one. It was like shooting ducks in a funfair, except that these ducks were firing back. I shot another insurgent who showed himself next to where the last one had gone down. The Taliban stopped popping up for a few seconds: maybe they were tired of getting shot.

It gave us a fleeting chance to get away. 'We're going to extract back down lane. On three, we'll peel.' We counted three seconds in our heads and then moved. 'Smoke,' I thought, 'it might buy us a few more seconds.' I grabbed a grenade off my belt kit, pulled the pin and launched it. The metal egg flew skyward, hit the branch of an olive tree about 2 metres above my head, rebounded in a neat arc and fell straight back to earth at my feet. I'd thrown an emergency grenade: the red smoke type we used for when we were really in the shit and marking our position for friendly air. Big mistake. A red cloud enveloped us. The enemy might not be able actually to see us, now, but the swirling scarlet smoke marked our location for them nicely. Bullets whizzed and spattered close by. And we couldn't even see the fuckers to fire back. In fact, the smoke was so thick I couldn't even see Leech and Minter. Fuck, fuck and triple fuck!

But the red smoke also told the rest of the troop and the FSG up on the hill we were still alive.

I bumped into something that felt human. A leg. Minty. The smoke cleared for a second and I saw him. He was absolutely covered in crap: bits of twig and leaves, dirt, dust and gun oil, sand and grit. His hair was standing on end and there were two big saucer eyes staring out from under the thatch. Not-from-Manchester was there in the swirling smoke beside him.

Because we were moving backwards, in smoke, and at the same time observing and firing there was no way we could see what we were doing. One man kicked the next man's leg as a sign it was his turn to move: kick and move we fought our way down towards the end of the lane. As one man fell back, the other two returned fire. As the smoke began to clear I saw there was no shortage of targets: we were under fire now from three sides: the jagged-topped wall to our north, a low spur wall that ran out from the southern side of the lane to our left and, unless I was very much mistaken, there was fire coming from our own Scimitars nudging into the mouth of the lane.

Not good.

As we fought our way back down the ditch, a new group of about twenty Taliban began advancing towards us from the T-junction. Part of the cut-off group, they'd been waiting in the wooded area behind the *dushka* we'd recently erased. It felt like an age since then, at least an hour: in fact it couldn't have been more than a couple of minutes. Hugging the sides of the lane, the new enemy section shot their way towards us. We shot back. At the same time, we started coming under yet more fire from the olive plantations to our right. The Taliban had really thought this one through. They'd placed yet another group in among the olive trees to enfilade us. I put a round in a Taliban fighter advancing down the lane that punched him back clean off his feet. Kicking and moving and firing to front and sides, we kept falling back along the ditch.

We neared the end of the lane. I ran into one of our own, the gunner from Lt Tom Long's Scimitar. Andrew Radford was dismounted, advancing towards the blazing Spartan. His face was streaked with gun oil. I looked at him in amazement. 'Radders,' I said, 'what the fuck are you doing? Get back in your vehicle or you'll get killed.'

'No,' he said pointing up the lane, 'there's someone over there.'

I followed the direction of his finger. There was a figure lying on the ground about 20 metres away, in the first level of terracing between the olive groves and the Spartan. I thought it was one of the enemy. 'Well fucking engage him,' I said.

'No,' he shook his head, 'I think it's one of ours.'

I looked again – the air was so thick with gun smoke, grenade smoke and dust it was hard to tell whose side the man was on. As far as I could see he wasn't wearing any clothes. Blast often blows clothing clean off people. What if he was one of our own? Someone I'd missed? I turned to Leech and Minter. 'You two lay down covering fire. Me and Radders are going to see who that is.'

They were into the rhythm of the gunfight now, firing at any and every hostile movement. While those two kept the Taliban busy, Radders and I started moving back up the lane towards the inert shape. Shadows ghosted and slid among the olive trees – grey silhouettes armed with AK47s pouring fire at us. We fired back as we advanced, short bursts of two or three aimed shots, buddy-buddy as per.

There were still plenty of the opposition up on the wall to our north and left taking pot shots. We had to keep them under fire pressure too. Minter and Leech were laying rounds on the enemy cut-off group advancing down the lane. I switched my own point of aim onto that target, fired several aimed bursts of two rounds and saw two of the Taliban drop. As we drew near the figure in the dust, a weapon started blazing at us from the nearest mouse hole. I put a nice long burst into the gap. The firing stopped. If you're going to play cat-and-mouse, it's best to be the cat. I changed mags and carried on firing. I'd had ten full magazines when the contact kicked off; I had the nasty, sinking feeling I was running out of ammo.

CHAPTER THIRTY

We reached the man on the ground. Now we were up close I saw it was the Spartan's driver, Trooper Martyn Compton. Compo was lying perfectly still. His right leg lay broken and splayed at a horrible angle. The explosion had blasted all his clothing away except for his boots and his Matalan underpants. They were scarlet, like the rest of him. Every bit of skin on Compton's body had burned bright red. He'd lost his eyelashes, his eyebrows and part of his nose and his hair was singed to a dark, scrubby crisp. He smelled like burnt meat. His eyes were wide and staring. 'Fish eyes,' I thought. I'd seen that dead, staring look before: it almost always meant the worst. Thinking he was dead, I laid a hand on his leg, trying to straighten the limb. Compo let out a long, bloodcurdling yell. He was alive! But he was in total clip – extreme shock. He screamed again and again and he kept on screaming. I turned to Radders and shouted, 'Let's get him out of here.'

Another line of bullets smacked a neat pattern up from the dust at our feet. I fired a couple of bursts up the lane to keep the insurgents busy, reached down, grabbed hold of Compton and lifted him onto Radford's back. Compo bellowed like a stuck bull, but there was no time to be gentle. Radders was built like an ox. As soon as he had Compton in a secure grip he was off and away at a fast waddle. I started to return fire in earnest, trying to cover them, picking targets on the wall to my right and back up the lane. Radders was steaming ahead. But I was getting isolated: not the best thing that can happen in a firefight. I fired a couple more aimed shots and then ran to catch up.

As we reached the end of the lane we bumped into Lt Long's Scimitar. Its rear end was towards us, ready to extract from the lane, its turret pointing back up towards the advancing enemy. Perfect. Long had taken Radford's place in the gunner's seat. He was firing Rarden and GPMG over our heads. Through the smoke haze I saw that two more of our Scimitars had their noses in the lane. They, too, now opened up with everything they'd got. Which was fine, except that Radders, Compton and I were directly in the line of fire. There was a serious risk our own side would succeed in killing us where the Taliban had so far failed.

I waved a hand at Tom Long: 'Boss! Stop firing! Cease fire!' The Scimitar's guns fell silent. We tucked in behind the wagon. At least there we were safe from being shot by our own side.

I looked up: the Scimitar's driver, Pez, was in deep shock. He was staring at the burning Spartan and at Compton's horribly burnt body, but his gaze was only half-seeing. I shouted, 'Leechy, Minter: help me get Compo up on the vehicle!' We lifted Compo off Radford's back and laid him on the Scimitar's front deck. The metal was hot now the sun was up: Compo writhed as the heat seared his burned flesh. I snatched the morphine capsule from around my neck, flipped the cover off the syringe, held it against Compo's thigh and pushed the top with my thumb. The morphine injected automatically. Compo was still screaming.

Tom Long hopped back into the commander's seat, while Radders took over as gunner again. In the confusion, Pez's headset had come unplugged from the driver's intercom box. He couldn't hear a word Lt Long was saying. I pulled myself up and sat on the decks alongside Martyn Compton. I wanted to make sure he didn't fall off. Leechy and Minter got up on the wagon with me, we held onto it – and onto Compo – as if our lives depended on it.

They did.

I was 99 per cent certain that everyone who'd been in the Spartan except for Marty Compton was dead. What we had to do now was extract. But with all the extra people sitting on the Scimitar's front decks, Pez couldn't see to drive. And he was deaf to all commands I shouted: 'Pez! Forward! Left stick! Right stick! Steady!' and so on as loudly as I could over the continuous din of gunfire. Still in shock, Pez nearly drove us into a deep wadi.

I looked down at Martyn Compton. If anything, I was even more furious now than I'd been in the first place: Compton was only nineteen years old. He was a good soldier and look what they'd done to him. I had a strange feeling, as if I were floating or walking on air – it was probably the effect of the cordite fumes.

The Taliban were still fighting, but the two Scimitars firing in support from the end of the lane were beginning to make a difference: one Rarden/GPMG combo walked a lead storm along the top of the wall. The rounds chewed lumps out of it and any Taliban unwise enough to show themselves. The other wagon hosed a slow-moving hail of bullets and shells through the olive groves. We extracted out past the other wagons and came into clear ground. Then we stopped. Realizing what had happened, I told Pez to replug his i/c cable: I was sick to death of shouting steering commands. I needed to keep focus on the enemy, keep returning fire: I expected to get engaged from a new position at any second. There were still plenty of Taliban scurrying around. We were in a mess, and they were looking to finish the job.

Clinging fast to the Scimitar as it bounced and bucked over the rough ground, we pushed back up towards the FSG. About 20 metres further on we saw that SHQ had secured the area and set up an emergency rendezvous point that included One Four Bravo, the Samaritan ambulance with the much-needed medics aboard, and the LAD support vehicle.

It was safe to dismount. We laid Compton down next to the ambulance on a stretcher. Paul Hamnett, One Four Bravo's medic, started giving him emergency first aid. Compo was lucky: Hamnett is one of the best Army medics there is. I knew he'd be in safe hands. Paul was still working on Compo when the MERT Chinook arrived.

Dust flew up in a gigantic choking cloud, the world started to thunder and the sweet-sour tang of hot aviation fuel filled the air. The MERT had made really good time – no bad thing when every second counted. The morphine I'd pumped into him had hit Compo's system by now, and the screaming had diminished to groans. We strapped him into a stretcher and then transferred him onto the Chinook. Its huge rotors wound up and bit the air, the helicopter rose, dropped its nose and thudded off towards Camp Bastion.

I caught sight of Major Dick and the SCM, Dean Goodall. Reassuring faces in the crowd. I briefed them on what had happened. When I'd done that, I walked across to have a chat with the FSG. I was very keen to find out why the fuck they hadn't supported us. With fire. Squirty McWhirter explained that they had, I'd just been too busy to notice. 'There was another group of Taliban.' He pointed. 'They came out of the southernmost lane there, in a column of four vehicles. Right after they sprang the main ambush. Most of them had RPGs. They were going to wheel round into the lane behind you and seal the trap. Whack you with another volley of rockets.'

I studied the area below us with a fresh eye. Squirty and the lads had done a great job: they'd hit the lead Taliban 4x4 with their opening shots, stopped it dead, set it on fire and trapped the rest of the enemy convoy behind it. Then they'd shot and mortared it to pieces. I glanced at Squirty. 'Well done, mate.'

The Taliban had set up a near-perfect ambush – and they'd almost succeeded in carrying it through. If they'd closed the trap behind us and let rip with yet more RPGs, they'd almost certainly have killed us all.

CHAPTER THIRTY-ONE

The QRF landed next to us ten minutes later: four platoons of 3 Para, exactly the kind of back-up you wanted in a tight spot. 'Give me a full brief,' the Para colonel said. I looked him in the eye. As fast as I could, I detailed the enemy positions, strengths and weaknesses, and advised the best route in and out. Then I got to the really important bit. 'The real priority is the rest of the Spartan crew. I definitely identified two dead, and Compton, the driver, we know about. That makes three. There were more body parts on the other side of the Spartan, but I can't be sure if that's the fourth man.' He could tell what I was leading up to, but I said it anyway. 'We have to go back down there and make sure no one's missing.'

'You're dead right we do,' the Para RSM, John Hardy, said. 'And even if that wasn't the case, we still have to go back down there and recover the Spartan and your Scimitar.'

I turned back to Lt-Col Tootal. 'I'm the best person to lead you into the ambush position. There's a number of lanes and turnings – I know the ground.'

I watched as he tried to decide. It was a no-brainer.

'Right you are, Corporal of Horse. We're going to put in a full-scale attack and clear the whole area. And you're going to lead it.'

He ran through the plan with his staff officers, while I brushed some of the dust off myself and had a long drink of water.

The three 105mm artillery guns that were now up in support had registered onto target. There was a crump as they started putting fire on the Taliban positions. While I'd been having a chinwag with the Paras, with his FAC hat on Squirty had come up trumps: not only had he called in an air strike, he'd also managed to rustle up a pair of Apache helicopter gunships. Apaches always come in pairs, like girls at a dance.

The gunships pitched up overhead and started circling the area. If they opened up with their rockets and 30mm, the Taliban were toast. Through my binos, I could see the Taliban ransacking my Scimitar, but because they couldn't actually see the insurgents carrying any weapons, the Apache crews couldn't engage them. Under standing ISAF rules of engagement, even in a hot battlezone you can only fire at people seen to be carrying weapons with hostile intent. It's great to be decent and avoid civilian casualties. In practice, it often feels like we're fighting with one hand tied behind our backs, because the Taliban know the rules. They've got the whole system down to a T. Often, enemy fighters dump their AK47s, pick up a hoe and start weeding the second they hear the Apaches arrive.

Just when I was thinking about what I'd like to do to him, one of the looters jumped down from my Scimitar. As he leapt, his dishdasha flew up. One of the Apache gunners spotted an AK47. He put down a burst of 30mm cannon fire. It was too late: most of the Taliban had already scarpered back into the maze of compounds to the north, clutching the bags of looted gear.

I looked along the bluff. The Paras were mounted up and ready to go. 'Move now!' Hanging onto the vehicles, we rolled back down the hill towards the village. We stopped just short of the start line for the new attack. A Para FAC shouted, 'Fast air thirty seconds!' I heard the familiar throaty rumble of a jet barrelling in over the hills. A few seconds later, the unmistakable shape of a British Harrier came shooting in low and fast from the south. The Harrier had a 1,000lb laser-guided bomb (LGB) on its racks – we hoped with the Taliban's name on it. We picked up the binos and trained them on the area where the bomb was supposed to hit, in the olive groves to the south of the lane. Instead, there was a huge explosion about 500 metres away – on the opposite side of the village. Where there were no Taliban and no villagers. A hundred-odd heads swivelled from one spot to the other. It was a bit like the Wimbledon final, only a lot noisier. Unbelievable.

By now, the temperature was up to its normal oven heat. The compounds below us shimmered and danced in the roasting air. We skirmished forward in extended lines, weapons up and watching front. I found myself thinking, 'I'm forty-six years old, and I'm leading the Parachute Regiment into the attack!' That was pretty unbelievable too. To cover our advance, the guns on the hill behind us laid down a creeping barrage. The curtain of high-explosive metal chewed up the ground about 150 metres ahead of our line. It was the exact same tactic troops had employed in the First World War, only much more effective and accurate.

Unfortunately, the barrage wasn't moving forward as fast as we were: as we advanced, we were gradually walking into the shells. By the time we got to the outskirts of the village, the ordnance was landing no more than 25 metres away. Much too close for comfort. And safety. The Para FOO called up the guns and told them to stop firing. There had been enough death and injury for one day, without a blue-on-blue.

As we came up into the village we began to spot the Taliban. Most were on the eastern side of the lane, flitting and sneaking about as per usual. Still looking for it, though – and they were going to get it: with men dead on our side, no one was in the mood to fuck about. By this time, anyone left in the village had to be Taliban. We shot at anything that moved or looked as if it might be about to move.

As we reached the entrance to the lane I saw my Scimitar, lying like a drunk in the ditch. The i/c scanners picked up chatter from the wooded area at the far end of the lane: some of the enemy had re-grouped there behind the smashed *dushka*. The 'terp (interpreter) with us was right at my shoulder: 'They're saying "Open fire! Open fire! The British are advancing!"'

Even as he said that, rounds came whistling down the lane towards us. Sniper fire, well aimed. A section of Paras had deployed on the right flank: I could see them fighting their way through the olive plantation. They were putting down a murderous amount of fire, sawing through the trees and anyone still hiding among them. Three Scimitars came up in support. Taking station side by side in the mouth of the lane, they were laying down 30mm and co-ax across the Taliban positions.

The only thing that was saving the enemy from total annihilation was those bloody same mud walls they'd been building since before the time of Christ. They were pocked silver with the characteristic deep oval gouges of the 30mm shells the Apaches had fired into them, and blasted with rounds from the Scimitars. But even at close range, the shells had failed to penetrate through the decades of that ancient mud.

We came back up level with the Spartan. It was still smouldering. The heat from its dying bulk was like standing next to a radiator. Now the air was clear of smoke, I could see that the body I'd identified earlier was Lance Corporal Ross Nicholls. He was lying about 10 metres off to the right of the vehicle. Looking at him, I could see that Ross had died instantly. That body wasn't the person I'd known. Drawing a mental curtain between a man and his remains is my way of dealing with death. Shelley says I have no feelings. I say, the trouble with being a man is that if you are a man you have to get on with it and save the feelings for when you're ready to deal with it. So far in my life I've never been ready.

I looked inside the back of the stricken vehicle. With more time now I recognized the body that was lying in there. It was Captain Eida. 'Sorry pal,' I muttered. I still couldn't see any sign of the fourth man, Lt Ralph Johnson. 'Ralph,' I said out loud, 'where the hell are you?'

'Corporal of Horse, what do you think happened?' asked Lt Col

Tootal. 'Could they have grabbed him?' I replayed that bit of the firefight in my mind's eye. It was true we'd only reached the Spartan after it had been hit. But I hadn't seen any of the Taliban on or near the vehicles at any time – not until the looters had snatched all our stuff from them when we were up on the hill. 'No,' I said slowly, 'I don't think they've taken him. He's got to be here.'

I climbed further into the wreck with RSM Hardy. Everything in there was a smoking mess; I could feel the heat seeping up through the soles of my boots. I pulled at some of the smouldering debris that lay scattered around. As I moved a bit of twisted armour, I recognized another body. It was Ralph Johnson. The force of the explosion must have killed him instantly, too. RSM Hardy and the RMPs took DNA from the bodies for later identification.

By now the Paras and our Scimitars had cleared the area, either killing the Taliban or forcing them to run away. The diehards who'd made a stand in the trees at the end of the lane had done just that: died hard. To my amazement, as they swept the area for mines and booby traps, the Paras found my personal bag. It was lying where one of the looters must have dropped it in his panic to escape death by Apache gunship. I went up and gazed at it longingly from a safe distance. Inside was my wallet, along with some cash and my wedding ring. But we couldn't recover anything the looters had touched. The Taliban are expert at leaving instant booby traps. Even going near the bag presented too great a risk. I really had to get back and cancel my credit card.

We set to and stripped the secret equipment off the vehicles, starting with the ECM devices and the Bowman radios. I watched as the Royal Engineers came up and put a stack of bar mines in the back of my Scimitar, attached a length of detonator cord and ran it out to the firing box. A vehicle is just a vehicle, it has no value compared to a human life. But when you live and fight and work in the same wagon for months and years on end it becomes a part of you. You feel about it the same way you do about a well-loved car. And this vehicle had saved our lives: it had taken four close-range RPG strikes, hundreds of *dushka* and AK47 rounds, and if a certain young person who wasn't from Manchester hadn't driven it into the ditch, it would still be going strong. At the point when they were about to explode it, I looked away.

With the village secured and the wagons gone to ashes, we were ready to extract back up to the ridge. But first, we wanted to establish exactly how the Taliban had planned and executed the ambush. If there's the time and it's safe, we always try to estimate the enemy's strength, and itemize opposition tactics down to the fine detail. The Taliban had put in an exemplary ambush: as a force and an army we needed to learn from it, not least in terms of my own personal learning curve. A couple of the Paras came with me to inspect the scene of battle. We counted thirty firing ports pre-punched into the lower stretch of the northern wall. 'Mouse holes,' I muttered. 'Some fucking mice.' The Paras stared at me without speaking. On the other side of the wall beneath most of the holes lay great piles of AK47 cartridge cases, the brass gleaming butter-yellow in the brilliant light.

In the time we'd taken to regroup and launch the counterattack, the Taliban had recovered all their dead and injured. Islam demands the bodies be buried with all speed. I wanted to go to the end of the lane to inspect the *dushka* and the area behind it, but the Paras advised against that – there was a strong chance a Taliban sniper might still be hanging around, waiting to take a last scalp.

The Para QRF clearing the olive grove had found the command wire and the clacker that had initiated the IED. I gazed down at the bits of metal. The bomb had been hard-wired and one of the Taliban had triggered it. There was no way our ECM jamming signal could have stopped the damned thing detonating. How had the Taliban found out we were coming in time to set the ambush? Had the explosion that had finished off JC's Spartan alerted them? Whatever intelligence the enemy might or might not have had, like so many before us we'd failed to relieve the garrison at Musa Qal'ah DC.

CHAPTER THIRTY-TWO

Looking back on the ambush that had cost us three men dead and got Trooper Martyn Compton seriously injured, I don't believe it would have made any difference which track I'd chosen: my guess is that the Taliban had laid IEDs in all three. The enemy had known we were coming, they'd been waiting for us and they'd set up a textbook ambush.

With no vehicle left under us, Minter, Leech and I grabbed a helicopter ride back to Camp Bastion. Retasked to a new Scimitar, Brigade told me to make both it and my crew available for duty as soon as possible, then report back for a new and urgent assignment. With a determined, ruthless enemy now attacking NATO forces all over Helmand province, there was no lack of work.

Before doing anything else, I wanted to find out what had happened to Martyn Compton. I'd heard he'd survived the terrible injuries he'd sustained. Not surprisingly, I found him in the base hospital. The medics had Compo swathed from head to toe in bandages. He didn't look quite like his old self. That was the least of his worries: along with the severe burns he'd suffered over more than 70 per cent of his body, he'd taken two AK47 bullets. His heart had stopped three times in the MERT Chinook en route to Camp Bastion. Each time, the onboard medical team had fought to stop him dying. And each time, by some miracle of skill and luck, they'd succeeded.

I honestly hadn't believed Compo was going to make it, but there he was propped up inside a plastic tent, designed to help retain the moisture that remained in his scorched skin. He was in a coma – but I said a few words up close to him in case he could hear me: 'Stay with it, Compo. You're going to be home soon.' Repatriated to the UK some weeks later, Compo is still undergoing treatment. But the great thing is that he did wake up, he has pulled through, and in July 2008, he married the woman who has stood by him.

What about the garrison at Musa Qal'ah? In the end, it took a regiment of Paras, several Apache gunships, the rest of D Squadron's armour, the entire Estonian Army contingent, two Royal Irish Regiment platoons and a logistics support convoy to relieve the DC. And there were several more casualties before Operation Snakebite, as it was called, succeeded in relieving the garrison.

That's the thing about the Taliban – they don't know when to give up.

EPILOGUE

In 2008, the Army asked me if I'd go to Northern Ireland as part of a recruiting drive. I decided to visit Belfast again: there was something there I needed to do.

It's hard to believe now, but there wasn't anything like the same ceremonial attention paid to the death of a British soldier back in the 1970s as there is now. I'd seen my friends die right in front of me. But two hours after the IRA shot dead Anthony Dykes and Anthony Thornett, the Army had me back out on the streets patrolling. As far as I knew, there had never been a service for them, let alone a military funeral. I'd never really had a chance to say goodbye. And that had always bothered me.

It was hard to recognize the city I'd known so well as a young trooper. So much was new, so much had changed. Many of the buildings I'd known and needed now as landmarks had vanished. I scouted around the area, keeping an eye out for the Milltown cemetery. That still had to be there – cemeteries are hard to move. A minute later, long rows of gravestones came up on my left.

I turned towards Andersonstown. Giant, colourful murals began to appear on the walls, most of them in memory of Bobby Sands and the other hunger strikers who had died in prison. There were green, white and gold tricolours flying everywhere and plenty of anti-British graffiti. Some things hadn't changed.

As I drew near the spot where I thought the police station should be, I saw a wide open stretch of land. It looked like a public park or a garden. I slowed to a stop. There was the Andersonstown Road and there was the Falls Road – I recognized the junction. Where was the police station? It had gone. They'd knocked it flat. And yet I could remember clear as yesterday kneeling in the gateway the day of the ambush.

I got out and walked across the road. Large boulders lay here and there, as if to mark something. Perhaps two of them marked the position of the main gate? I looked down and saw a break in the kerb at my feet. The pavement stopped, and then started again on the other side of a 4 metre gap. 'That's where the gate was,' I thought to myself 'This is where Dykesy and Tony died. I'll stop here and say a few words.'

I looked around. In my memory, everything was big, but now I was there I could see that in reality it was very small. Some of the shops had changed and there was a fair bit of new housing, but the barber's shop with its red-and-white pole in the window was still there and the florist's next to it.

A little further up the street was a pub. It was late in the afternoon of a sunny summer's day, and with the smoking ban in force there was a large knot of people outside the boozer having a cigarette. I suddenly became aware that they were looking at me. Not looking – watching.

The crowd didn't seem all that friendly. It wasn't hard to understand why. I had short hair, I was smartly dressed and they'd pinged my mainland number plates. Whatever else had changed, Andytown was still very much a Republican heartland. 'This is just like the old days,' I told myself.

A new idea came into my head then, this one a lot madder: 'I know – I'll wander up and have a drink to Dykesy and Tony in the pub. They'd like that.'

It was obvious the locals wouldn't. 'No,' I thought as I walked towards them. 'That really isn't such a good plan. I know what I'll do – I'll go and buy a flower, lay it on that piece of ground over there where the gate was and say my goodbyes.'

As I walked back I had the feeling that everything was slowly becoming surreal – the surroundings, the watching people, the police station where all those things had happened. It was all somehow shrinking and floating away. 'This is all finished now,' I thought. 'It has to be finished.'

I turned into the flower shop. A woman of about sixty sat behind the counter. Right away, I could see that she knew I was British. 'What would you like?' she asked.

'A rose,' I said, 'just a single red rose, if you have one. Do you have one?' She shook her head. 'It's the end of the day. The roses have all gone.' She looked around the shop. 'I do have some lovely red carnations – you can have one of them, if you like?'

'All right,' I said. 'Thank you. How much?' There was look in her eye – she knew what was what. 'Lots of bad things have happened here,' she said.

'Yes,' I said, 'I saw one of them. A shooting.'

'What year was that?'

'It was April. April 1979.'

She nodded. 'I remember. There was two young lads killed over there. Outside the barracks. They kidnapped the old couple next door.' She meant the husband and wife I'd seen tied up in their kitchen after I'd been chasing the gunmen. 'That was the same incident,' I said. 'I was a lot younger in those days.'

She smiled sadly as she handed me the red flower. 'We were all a lot younger then.'

I offered to pay but she raised a hand: 'Please – take it.' I turned for the door but her voice stopped me. 'They were your friends, weren't they?'

I walked out into the street. The people outside the pub were still watching. I looked left and saw the bus station, where the two hijacked vehicles had been blazing that day and the machine gun in the white van had fired up the street. I crossed to the other side and looked back.

There was the barber's shop the killers had fired from. There was the alleyway I'd run down to try and kill them.

Suddenly, it all came back to me: the gunshots and the fear and the smell of cordite, the shouting and the chaos and the white faces. Tony and Dykesy lying dead outside the gate. The blood and the mess and the sorrow for young lives. I thought of them and of all the other friends who'd gone by down the years.

I walked to the gap where the main gate had been, laid the flower on the ground and stood with my head bowed. 'Yes,' I said quietly. 'They were my friends.'

Abbreviations

2 i/c Second in command

ADC Aide de camp

ANGLICO Air Naval Gunfire Liaison Company

APDS Armour-Piercing Discarding Sabot

AWOL Absent without leave

BATUS British Army Training Unit Suffield

BCR Battle casualty replacement

CAS Close Air Support

CGC Conspicuous Gallantry Cross

CIMIC Civil-Military Co-operation

CPU Chest Pressel Unit

DC District centre

DU Depleted uranium

ERV Emergency Rendezvous

FAC Forward Air Controller

FOO Forward observation Officer

FRY Former Republic of Yugoslavia

FSG Fire Support Group

GBH Grievous Bodily Harm

GPMG General purpose machine gun

GPS Global Positioning System

HE High explosive

i/c – intercom

ICTY International Criminal Tribunal for the former Yugoslavia

IED Improvised explosive device

IFOR Implementation Force

IRA Irish Republican Army

ISAF International Security Assistance Force

LAD Light Aid Detachment

LCoH Lance Corporal of Horse

LCpL Lance Corporal

LCUs Landing craft utilities

LGB Laser-guided bomb

Lt Lieutenant

MC Military Cross

MERT Medical Emergency Response Team

MREs Meals ready to eat

NAAFI Navy, Army and Air Force Institute

NCO Non-commissioned officer

NVGs Night vision goggles

OC Officer Commanding

OP Observation Post

PF Pathfinder

POW Prisoner of war

QFC Quadrant Fire Control

QRF Quick Reaction Force

RCM Regimental Corporal Major

REME Royal Electrical and Mechanical Engineers

RHA Royal Horse Artillery

RPG Rocket-Propelled grenades

RSM Regimental Sergeant Major

RUC Royal Ulster Constabulary

RV Rendezvous

SCM Squadron Corporal Major

SFOR Stabilisation Force

SHQ Squadron Headquarters

SLR Self-loading rifle

SQMC Squadron Quartermaster Corporal

TALO Tactical Air Landing Operation

TNTLS Tactical Navigation and Target Location System

WMDs Weapons of Mass Destruction